The English Renaissance

For my father, Graeme Samuel Fox,
1919–1969

The English Renaissance

Identity and Representation
in Elizabethan England

ALISTAIR FOX

The right of Alistair Fox to be identified as author of this work has been asserted in accordance with the Copyright, Designs and Patents Act 1988.

First published 1997

2 4 6 8 10 9 7 5 3 1

Blackwell Publishers Ltd
108 Cowley Road
Oxford OX4 1JF
UK

Blackwell Publishers Inc.
350 Main Street
Malden, Massachusetts 02148
USA

British Library Cataloguing in Publication Data
A CIP catalogue record for this book is available from the
British Library.

Library of Congress Cataloging-in-Publication Data
Fox, Alistair.
    The English Renaissance: identity and representation in Elizabethan England/Alistair Fox.
        p. cm.
    Includes bibliographical references and index.
    ISBN 0-631-17747-7. – 0-631-19029-5 (pbk.)
    1. English literature – Early modern, 1500–1700 – History and criticism. 2. Petrarca, Francesco, 1304–1374 – Influence. 3. English literature – Italian influences. 4. Group identity in literature. 5. Mimesis in literature. 6. Renaissance – England. I. Title.
PR129.I8F68   1997
820.9'003–dc21   97-6680
                                                                                          CIP

Typeset in 10.5pt on 12.5pt Garamond
by Brigitte Lee, redshoes cooperative, Oxon, UK

Printed and bound in Great Britain by Hartnolls Ltd, Bodmin, Cornwall

This book is printed on acid-free paper

Contents

1124 91

Acknowledgements

This book was written during a very happy sabbatical leave spent in the English Department at my alma mater, the University of Western Ontario (UWO). I chose this location partly for sentimental reasons, and partly for the superb collection of secondary sources at the University's Weldon Library, but mostly because Canada, like New Zealand, is a society of predominantly British descent that is currently in the act of formulating what its national identity might be in the post-colonial era. As such, both of these former Dominions of the British Empire are undergoing an experience not dissimilar to that of sixteenth-century England, which forms the subject of this book, with the difference that an international American culture – aided and abetted by the advancing revolution in communications technology – is assuming the role that I ascribe to the literary culture of the Italian Renaissance. I knew that in locating myself at UWO I would come in contact with the social and cultural dynamics that interested me.

In the event, I was not disappointed. The intellectual companionship I received at UWO was thoroughly vitalizing, while the hospitality was as gracious as it was humbling. My deepest thanks go to Dr Archie Young, who patiently listened and responded to my ideas as they struggled to find expression, and who made me realize that the aesthetic values of the Quattrocento and Cinquecento are as important to us now as they ever have been. I would also like to thank Dr Richard Green, who arranged for me to have the opportunity of delivering my preliminary findings to members of the Faculty of Arts. Special thanks are owing to doctoral students studying Renaissance topics in the UWO English Department – Susan MacDonald, Andrew Fieldsend, Chris Ivic – whose acumen and enthusiasm reassured me that the period of the Renaissance remains as relevant and challenging to this generation as it ever did to previous ones. There are many others in the English Department who helped me to a degree, and in ways, that they may never realize. My sincere thanks go to them also.

I realized, in the course of writing a book of this scope, that I had come to the point in my career when the range of secondary works one has read is so great that it is impossible to determine with confidence where an intellectual debt begins and ends. Accordingly, I have listed in the bibliography not only the books and articles that I have directly cited in this work, but also other works that may offer further guidance to the reader who becomes interested in the topics under discussion. My thinking has been shaped, too, by graduate students at the University of Otago who have elected in the past eight years to study the Italian influence on the likes of Spenser and Shakespeare, and found it not merely interesting but relevant to their understanding of themselves.

As always, I would like to acknowledge my gratitude to the University of Otago for the generous research grants and provisions for study leave with which it supports its scholars in the pursuit of their research. Finally, I would like to offer special thanks to Dr Janet Wilson for assisting me with the proofs.

Alistair Fox
Dunedin

'It is not the medium that is the message: the mind will find the medium for the message that it hungers after.'

Joe Schlesinger, TV broadcast of 18 May 1996

'We all write about what we need to know about most.'

John Bradshaw, TV interview of 28 June 1996

Introduction

Few would dispute the proposition that the Reformation in England was 'beyond all question a watershed of truly mountainous proportions'.[1] During the course of the sixteenth century England severed its ties with Rome, underwent a constitutional revolution as a result, witnessed a brief Catholic Counter-Reformation, and ended up an independent nation with a Protestant religion established and enforced by the state. From the 1560s onwards, this new national identity was intensified not only by prophetic preaching from many pulpits across the land, and frequent visitations of dioceses to ensure that the Act of Uniformity was implemented, but also by a foreign policy that locked England into a contest with Catholic Spain that would last for several decades. When the invading Spanish Armada was defeated in 1588, the majority of English people could not help but feel that a new order had been defined. Indeed, in the minds of many, the defeat of the Armada seemed like a providential sign of God's blessing on the new nation state – at the same time as it reminded them of how vulnerable and precarious the state itself was.

While we know a great deal about the events that brought about England's emergence as a Protestant nation – three political Reformations and a parallel evangelical Reformation[2] – we know very little about what English men and women actually thought and felt in response to this phenomenon; as one scholar has put it, 'Their sense of national identity is not something that men have been in the habit of directly recording'.[3] In the case of the English

---

[1] Patrick Collinson, *The Birthpangs of Protestant England: Religious and Cultural Change in the Sixteenth and Seventeenth Centuries* (London, 1988), p. 99.

[2] Christopher Haigh, *English Reformations: Religion, Politics, and Society under the Tudors* (Oxford, 1993), p. 14.

[3] A.J. Fletcher, 'The Origins of English Protestantism and the Growth of National Identity', in *Religion and National Identity: Papers Read at the Nineteenth Summer Meeting and the Twentieth Winter Meeting of the Ecclesiastical History Society*, ed. Stuart Mews (Oxford, 1982), pp. 309–17, esp. p. 309.

Reformation – or 'reformations' (I use Christopher Haigh's distinction) – the uncertainty is particularly acute, given that the Elizabethan regime was narrowly based and unrepresentative, while its religious system, embodied in the Thirty-nine Articles, the Book of Common Prayer and the legislation enacted by Parliament in the Settlement of 1559, were imposed from above on a population in which those actively committed to Protestantism were probably a minority. Modern historians have been divided on the extent to which the English Reformation resulted from a wave of popular religious sentiment, or was simply the product of a skilled strategy of political manoeuvring and enforcement. Haigh, referring to the two main proponents of rival viewpoints on this issue, sums up the situation thus:

> Dickens offered a Reformation without Catholics, which made it hard to understand why the Reformation was slow and difficult; Scarisbrick offered a Reformation without Protestants, which made it hard to understand why it happened at all. We need a version of religious conflict and transformation which includes both sides of the religious fence – and those who sat on the fence, those who could not find it, and those who did not see why there was such a fuss about the fence.[4]

Haigh's metaphor of the fence is apt, but I would modify it slightly. What we need is not simply a window into the minds of those who sat on the fence or were unaware of its existence, but also into the minds of those who, accepting the existence of a fence, knew that it separated them from others who were enjoying a comparatively unconstrained revelry in the sunny fields beyond, and desired to work out, in terms that gave them intellectual and emotional satisfaction, what the dimensions and construction of the fence should be, and what the implications of their separation behind it were for their own sense of identity.

A window into the minds of such people exists – in the literature of the related phenomenon known as 'the English Renaissance', and, in particular, in the very large body of writing that arose from creative imitation of Italian literary sources. Up until now, however, we have not known that a window existed in this writing, nor how to open it, largely because of false assumptions about the relationship between the English Reformation and the English Renaissance. The conventional view is stated with characteristic eloquence by one of the great historians of English Protestantism, Patrick Collinson. Appraising the contribution of Protestantism to the cultural revolution of the sixteenth century, Collinson concludes that 'English Protestantism ... produced no culture of its own but made an iconoclastic

---

[4] Haigh, *English Reformations*, p. 335. The works to which he refers are A.G. Dickens, *The English Reformation* (London, 1964; revised edn 1972), and J.J. Scarisbrick, *The Reformation and the English People* (Oxford, 1984).

holocaust of the culture which already existed'. 'The efflorescence of high culture in the age of Shakespeare ... conventionally packaged and labelled as the English (or Elizabethan) Renaissance', he continues, '[was] a secular achievement which involved a degree of emancipation from the dominance of religion and was consequently facilitated by the Protestant Reformation, but only in a negative sense.'[5] Though very widespread, the assumption that Collinson voices here is wrong, as a number of literary scholars in recent years have begun to recognize.[6] What we can now see is that writers of powerful Protestant convictions used poetry as an instrument for advancing the aspirations of the political factions to which they were affiliated. Edmund Spenser, for example, used topical allegory in *The Shepheardes Calender* to lament the fall of the reforming archbishop, Edmund Grindal, and Queen Elizabeth's dereliction in failing to protect her Protestant subjects, and thus sought to support the movement for ecclesiastical reform being urged by moderate puritans. Similarly, Sir Philip Sidney used symbolic allegory in *Arcadia* to castigate the Queen for her failure to support the aggressively pro-Protestant foreign policy being urged by his uncle, the Earl of Leicester.[7] In plays written for the theatre, too, one finds such a constant invocation of Protestant doctrinal concepts – often for the sake of questioning their justness – that the 'advanced state of separation of the secular from the sacred' that Collinson detects in the drama must be judged to be an illusion.[8]

What I want to propose in this book is that the literature which arose from creative imitation of Italian literary texts is able to supply the perspective that has been missing from our view of the Reformation and its influence on the formation of English identity during the sixteenth century. It is able to do this because the literature involved was produced as a response to a need felt by English men and women to come to terms with the awesome cultural separation from a Continental Latinate system of values – religious, moral, aesthetic and political – that was being enforced upon them by the successive political and evangelical reformations of the sixteenth century. This separation involved the replacement of a Roman Catholic ecclesiology centring upon the primacy of the Pope with a system of church government depending upon the supremacy of the English monarch. It was reinforced by the

---

[5] Collinson, *The Birthpangs of Protestant England*, p. 96.

[6] See, in particular, Alan Sinfield, *Literature in Protestant England 1560–1660* (Totawa, New Jersey, 1983), and Alan Sinfield, *Faultlines: Cultural Materialism and the Politics of Dissident Reading* (Berkeley and Los Angeles, 1992); Andrew Weiner, *Sir Philip Sidney and the Poetics of Protestantism: A Study of Contexts* (Minneapolis, 1978); Anthea Hume, *Edmund Spenser: Protestant Poet* (Cambridge, 1984); and David Norbrook, *Poetry and Politics in the English Renaissance* (London, 1984).

[7] See below, chapter 4.

[8] Collinson, *The Birthpangs of Protestant England*, p. 98. See also Jonathan Dollimore, *Radical Tragedy*, 2nd edn (Hemel Hempstead, 1984); and Alan Sinfield, 'Tragedy, God, and Writing: *Hamlet, Faustus, Tamberlaine*', in *Faultlines*, pp. 214–51.

adoption of a Calvinist-based theology – reflected in the liturgy established
by the Parliament of 1559 – that emphasized the inescapable sinfulness of
human nature since the Fall, and hence humanity's helpless dependence on
God's will for salvation – a salvation which would be attained not through
merit earned by good works, but through the merit of Christ's redemptive
sacrifice imputed to those who had faith in the truth of God's promises as
enshrined in Scripture. At a political level, the assumption that God's will was
predestinate and arbitrary was accompanied by an equally powerful belief in
the supremacy of human positive law as embodied in parliamentary statutes.
Rather than being bound by the universal laws of Christendom and divine
law as interpreted by the papacy, English men and women found themselves
obliged to conform to the will of the nation as expressed through laws pro-
mulgated by the monarch-in-Parliament. At a moral level, the new Calvinist-
based religious belief system of English Protestantism required a godly life as
the fruit of faith, based on a recognition that all forms of concupiscence are
sinful. This fundamental conviction was reiterated daily in countless forms:
by preachers, in the liturgy of the established Elizabethan Church, and in the
catechisms that were approved for use in the religious education of the
young. One example from the standard catechism of the last three decades of
Elizabeth's reign will suffice to illustrate this point. From Alexander Nowell's
A Catechisme or First Instruction and Learning of Christian Religion, which
went through forty-four editions between its publication in 1570 and 1647,
the Elizabethan youth would learn that

> Surely it is playne that all corrupt thoughtes, although our consent be not
> added to them, do procede of our corrupted nature. And it is no dout that
> sodeine desires that tempt the hartes of men, although they preuaile not so
> farre as to winne a stedfast assent of minde and allowance, are in this com-
> mandment [that is, the tenth] condemned by God as sinnes.[9]

He or she would also be instructed that

> For that, as he [God] hath created the world and all thinges, so he hath the
> same in his power, gouerneth them by his prouidence, ordereth them after his
> owne will, and commaundeth all as it pleaseth him: so as there is nothing done
> but by hys apointment or sufferance, and nothing is there which he is not
> hable to do: for I do not imagine God to haue a certayne idle power which he
> putteth not in vse.[10]

Even if the majority of the Queen's subjects remained, as Collinson surmises,
'instinctive Pelagians who found predestination an unacceptable proposition

[9] Alexander Nowell, *A Catechisme or First Instruction and Learning of Christian Religion*, trans.
Thomas Norton (Delmar, New York, 1975), fo. 117v–18r.
[10] Ibid., fo. 24v.

and many of whom were still Papists at heart',[11] they nevertheless grew up with these doctrines ringing in their ears, being under daily pressure to ensure that their life-styles conformed to the standards of probity and obedience to God's will that these convictions required. In short, they were under the influence of a ubiquitous Protestant discourse that reached into every corner of their consciousness, and which consequently found repeated expression in their literature. The scene in Shakespeare's *Othello* in which Iago manages to tempt Cassio into getting drunk may be taken to illustrate this point. Reflecting upon the unworthiness of those in positions of authority who are unwilling to pay a fair price, metaphorically speaking, in exchange for the power they wield – in Cassio's own case, this amounts to an obligation to remain sober while on duty – the Lieutenant betrays his guilty conscience at surrendering to intoxication by facetiously appealing to the Calvinist doctrine of predestination:

CASSIO … Well, God's above all; and there be souls must be saved,
and there be souls must not be saved.
IAGO It's true, good lieutenant.
CASSIO For mine own part – no offense to the general, nor any man of
quality – I hope to be saved.
IAGO And so do I too, lieutenant.
CASSIO Ay, but, by your leave, not before me. The lieutenant is to be
saved before the ancient. Let's have no more of this; let's to our
affairs. – God forgive us our sins![12]

Cassio's guilty awareness of the imperatives of Protestant doctrine, while it does not alter his actions, is sufficiently powerful to make him wonder about the validity of them, and in this, one suspects, he is characteristic of most of the Elizabethan English men and women who comprised Shakespeare's audience – the 'parish anglicans' who were not prepared to emulate the godly in the strictness and precision of their discipline, but were nonetheless not Catholics either.[13] By the 1580s, Protestant doctrine had made its presence felt in an ever-present discourse that forced all of Elizabeth's subjects to examine the quality of their belief and actions on a daily basis, and it is with this self-evaluative activity that much of the literature of the period is concerned.

Their efforts at self-examination were complicated by awareness of the attractiveness of the cultural system that godly ministers were urging them to

[11] Patrick Collinson, 'England and International Calvinism, 1558–1640', in *International Calvinism 1541–1715*, ed. Menna Prestwich (Oxford, 1985), pp. 197–223, esp. p. 202.
[12] *Othello*, II.iii.97–108, in William Shakespeare, *Complete Pelican Shakespeare*, ed. Alfred Harbage and others, 3 vols (Harmondsworth, 1969). All subsequent references to Shakespeare's plays are to this edition, and will be cited in the text.
[13] See Haigh, *English Reformations*, p. 290.

separate from. The doctrines of Protestantism did not require them merely to reject the papistical Roman Catholic Church, but also many of the values and mores that had evolved during the Italian Renaissance of the previous three centuries. Between the thirteenth and sixteenth centuries Italy had undergone its own crisis in human self-perception, leading in turn to a separation from the value systems of the previous medieval order. The biggest change came with the discovery of the human self as 'creative self-consciousness, no longer the Other or shadow of divine totality'.[14] In Renaissance Italian culture, this liberation of the self had been reflected in the exploration and expression of subjective emotions in poetry, painting and the other arts, together with an emphasis on humane subject matter and the felicities that were attainable through human self-agency. Liberated energies had also resulted in a new impulse to explore the world, both literally and metaphorically, with consequent geographical and scientific discoveries, and a revolution in educational and epistemological methods. Finally, a new ideology had arisen – voiced by such humanists as Pico della Mirandola – that stressed human dignity and infinite human possibility, a doctrine which was paralleled in the commercial world by the rise of a new economic system: capitalism. Altogether, then, the Italian Renaissance had opened the way for an experience of the world which freed men and women from many of the restrictions imposed by the more theocentric systems of dominance that had propped up the medieval order. In the eyes of many envious northern Europeans, the achievements of the Italian Renaissance constituted those of a 'progressive' era, and the attempts of Tudor courtiers to ape the fashions of their Italian counterparts show just how deeply they were drawn to the idea of sharing in this new way of experiencing the world. On the other hand, the values of this Renaissance Italian culture – especially as expressed in the racy literature that flooded into England from the 1560s onwards – merely seemed to the godly to epitomize the amorality, atheism and sinful decadence of the papistical order their country had rejected.

Faced with two rival value systems – the religious system of English state Protestantism and the aesthetic, epistemological and intellectual systems of Renaissance Italian culture – many English people felt an urgent need to find a way of locating themselves in relation to both that would allow them to obey the imperatives of their religion while still participating in the humane outlook of the Italian Renaissance. Their instinctive impulse was not unlike that which had produced the ambiguities of the Book of Common Prayer in the Settlement of 1559: 'a liturgical compromise which allowed priests to perform the Church of England communion in Catholic regalia, standing in the Catholic position, and using words capable of Catholic interpretation'.[15]

---

[14] Albert Russell Ascoli, *Ariosto's Bitter Harmony: Crisis and Evasion in the Italian Renaissance* (Princeton, 1987), p. 43.

[15] Haigh, *English Reformations*, p. 241.

Metaphorically speaking, that is precisely what English writers who turned to Italianate literary imitation were seeking to do: to find a way of celebrating their faith without needing to relinquish the aesthetic or humane appeal of the Latinate culture of the Italian Renaissance. In short, Italianate literary imitation constituted one of the main sites in which reflective minds sought to work out imaginatively how – or, indeed, whether – the conflicts and disparities between the two rival systems that affected them could, or should, be resolved, and this is why a study of it can add a great deal to our understanding of what English men and women thought about their emergent identity.

It is time now to consider why Italianate imitation was able to serve this function. In the first instance, the inherent clash of values between the two cultures presented English writers with an invitation to select and modify the material they wished to imitate according to the extent to which they recognized, and were troubled by, the clash. The nature of this selection provides us with a means of identifying the concerns of the writers and their audiences, while the nature of their modifications of Italian source material allows us to infer what they were thinking about these issues.

For example, when the Elizabethan poets began to read Petrarch's *Rime sparse* they encountered an egotism which, viewed through the filter of Calvinist doctrine, seemed to embody a sinful desire that was the product of pride. In translating and imitating him, therefore, they faced the necessity of either concurring with his indulgence of this desire, or else of turning the imitation into a vehicle for affirming the illegitimacy of doing so. Almost invariably, the major sonneteers of the 1580s and 1590s choose, in different ways, to correct those aspects of Petrarch that would create a problem for anyone who believed in the teachings of the catechisms through which they had received their religious instruction. Similarly, in reading the *novelle* of Italian authors like Boccaccio, Ser Giovanni Fiorentino, Matteo Bandello or Giambattista Giraldi Cinthio, English writers looking for narrative material were struck by the comparative amorality, not to say sexual impropriety, of their Italian sources. This is reflected in their constant attempts to convert the original effect of the story into a more acceptable one by interpolating a corrective moral commentary. George Turbervile, translating the story of Lisabetta, Lorenzo and the pot of basil from Boccaccio's *Decameron* (Novella 5, Day 4) in his *Tragicall Tales* (1587), adds an envoy that replaces Boccaccio's emphasis on the pathos of the story (which in the original is 'much appreciated' by the ladies to whom the tale is addressed) with a sternly Protestant castigation of the sinfulness of illicit love:

Loe here the lotte of wicked loue,
Behold the wretched end

Of wilfull wightes, that wholy doe
On Cupides lawes depend.[16]

Geoffrey Fenton's translation of tales by Bandello, based on the massively expanded and moralized versions of the French Huguenot writer, Belleforest, does even greater violence to the effect of the originals. In his account of the story of Livio and Camilla, two star-crossed lovers who die tragically as a result of events that ensue when Camilla's brother, Claudio, refuses to allow them to marry, Fenton deliberately intervenes to destroy any sympathy that might have been generated for the lovers in the original. At the moment when Livio and Camilla are consummating their love, he intervenes to warn the reader of the misfortune suffered by Attila the Hun on his wedding night. Soon after, he denounces the lovers as a pair in whom one can see 'a derogation of the honour and integrity of the mind, with a manifest prejudice and hazard to the health of the soul', and this because they obeyed 'the summons of a beastly and unbridled lust of the flesh'.[17] The same sort of tendentious Protestantization can be seen in Arthur Brooke's versified version of another of Bandello's tales, *The Tragicall Historye of Romeus and Juliet* (1562). Brooke tells the reader that he has written 'this tragicall matter'

> to describe unto thee a coople of unfortunate lovers, thralling themselves to unhonest desire, neglecting the authoritie and advise of parents and frendes, conferring their principall counsels with dronken gossyppes, and superstitious friers (the naturally fitte instrumentes of unchastitie) attemptyng all adventures of peryll, for thattaynyng of their wished lust, usyng auriculer confession (the kay of whoredome, and treason) for furtheraunce of theyr purpose, abusyng the honorable name of lawefull mariage, the cloke the shame of stolne contractes, finallye, by all meanes of unhonest lyfe, hastyng to most unhappye deathe.[18]

The efforts of these translators are very crude compared with the creative imitations of the great literary artists of the period – and one only needs to compare Brooke's perception of the meaning of the Romeo and Juliet story with Shakespeare's more profoundly tragic sense – but they do graphically illustrate the need felt by Elizabethan writers to bring their Italian sources into conformity with the moral schemes of their Protestant Church.

[16] George Turbervile, *Tragicall Tales Translated by Turbervile in Time of His Troubles out of Sundrie Italians, with the Argument and Lenuoye to Eche Tale* (London, 1587), fo. 100, sig. N3.
[17] Geoffrey Fenton, *Bandello: Tragical Tales. The Complete Novels Translated by Geoffrey Fenton* (Anno 1567), ed. Robert Langton Douglas (London, [n.d.]), p. 154. The original tale may be found in Matteo Bandello, *Tutte le opere di Matteo Bandello*, ed. Francesco Flora, vol. 1 (Verona, 1966), Prima Parte, Novella 49.
[18] Geoffrey Bullough, ed., *Narrative and Dramatic Sources of Shakespeare*, 8 vols (London and New York, 1957–75), vol. 2, pp. 284–5.

When creative imitation rather than mere translation was involved both the procedure and the results were more complex – and more illuminating for our purpose. For some writers with a fully formed Protestant conviction, like Edmund Spenser, creative imitation meant adapting the archetypes, motifs, aesthetic strategies and conventions of an Italian source to show that they carried latent within them a signification – not yet fully revealed in the original – that was consistent with, and corroborated, the truths of Protestant doctrine as revealed in Scripture. When imitating Petrarch in the *Amoretti* (1595), for instance, Spenser developed a system of symbolic imagery – comprising what Northrop Frye would categorize as 'apocalyptic' images contrasted against 'demonic' images[19] – that are reiterated from poem to poem to build up a progressive correction of the experience depicted in the original. In *The Shepheardes Calender* (1579), he exploited the generic conventions of Italianate pastoral for the purpose of constructing an allegory that allowed him to present a religious polemic in support of the moderate puritan reformist faction, but at a displaced remove. In *The Faerie Queene* (1590, 1596), he imitated the subject matter and methods of the Italian romantic epics to present, through the use of symbolic allegory, his vision of the virtues by which the governors of Protestant England should govern the affairs of the new state, and themselves. For Spenser, therefore, Italianate imitation meant the accommodation of Italian sources through creative correction and differentiation.

For other writers of a fervent, though less settled, Protestant persuasion – like Sir Philip Sidney – Italianate imitation meant wrestling with the temptations provided by the seductive values inherent in the originals to which he was drawn, in order to forge, through writing, an instrument of corrective self-admonition and guidance. Like Spenser in the *Amoretti*, Sidney, in *Astrophil and Stella* (1582), imitated the Petrarchan pose for the sake of evolving an understanding of why it must be rejected. In his persona, Astrophil, he depicted as much wilfulness, self-deception and illicit determination to satisfy a self-regarding, sinful desire as any puritan divine might allege in a castigatory sermon. Nonetheless, Sidney accords himself the benefit of a sincere self-pity and compassion, which reflects the extent to which conformity with the spiritual expectations he held for himself was, for him, no simple or easy matter. In his imitation of Sannazzaran pastoral, *Arcadia* (1581), and especially in the revised *New Arcadia* (left unfinished at his death in 1586), the problematical nature of Sidney's faith was even more marked. Sidney's great need was to reconcile the frustration of his desires, both erotic and political, with the temptation to gain satisfaction through adopting illicit means – even, as the fiction of the *New Arcadia* implies, through rebellion against his monarch. To do this, he systematically elaborated the conventions

[19] Northrop Frye, *Anatomy of Criticism: Four Essays* (New York, 1966), pp. 141–50.

of Italian pastoral romance in order to show the discrepancy between wish-fulfilment and reality as understood through the insights imparted by Calvinist doctrine. The fact that Sidney left the work unfinished half-way through, in the middle of a sentence, may indicate the difficulty he experienced in coming to terms with the frustrating reality of what God's arbitrary will seemed to have predetermined for him. For Sidney, unlike Spenser, Italianate imitation served, therefore, as an exploratory instrument, rather than one for affirmation and assertion.

There were still other writers, like Shakespeare, who were nowhere near as committed to the Protestant Reformation as Spenser and Sidney were, but who nevertheless felt a powerful need to come to terms with its pressures and effects. Whereas Spenser and Sidney were closely associated with the big players in the Protestant court elite – or at least aspired to be – Shakespeare and the members of his mass audience of theatregoers probably typified the vast majority of the population living in Elizabethan England, in that they were not zealously committed to any identifiable or determinate single position. Christopher Haigh offers a good description of the situation in which the members of this group found themselves:

> The combination of successful political Reformations and less successful Protestant Reformation had established an anomaly: the Church of England was Protestant – not as Protestant as many wished, yet Protestant; but its people – most of its people – were not. They were accused of 'popery and atheism' by godly ministers, but unfairly. Though they retained a works religion, they were certainly not Catholics; they were beyond the reach of Catholic priests, outside and opposed to the institutional Church of Rome. And nor were they atheists, by which the godly meant that they were mere conformists ... The majority were conformists, but not mere conformists. They conformed to what suited them. ... The churchgoers were de-catholicized but un-protestantized. What they were not is a good deal clearer than what they were.[20]

For writers such as Shakespeare who represented and wrote for this category of English men and women, Italianate imitation served still another purpose: it was a means of interrogating and evaluating the assumptions of those on both sides of the fence, especially concerning issues which impinged upon the conduct of their daily lives.

Again, we can infer what Shakespeare and his mass audience of playgoers were concerned about by examining the nature of the Italianate material he selected for imitation, together with the nature of the modifications he made to it. Many of Shakespeare's Italianate plays focus on the progress of inter-personal relationships and the conduct of marriage, and it is not difficult to see why. In the numerous conduct books of the day outlining the Protestant

[20] Haigh, *English Reformations*, p. 290.

view of marriage – works such as Henry Smith's *A Preparative for Marriage* (1591) or Robert Cleaver's *A Godly Form of Household Government* (1598) – the members of Shakespeare's audience would have found themselves exhorted to accept an extreme patriarchal system of marriage in which the husband was the woman's head by nature and God's direction, and in which a wife's duty was to submit obediently to her husband's authority, 'to be directed and advised by him for her self, her attire, her behaviour, her carriage, her company, the marshalling and managing of domestical affairs'.[21] In a play like *The Taming of the Shrew* (1593–4), Shakespeare puts this kind of assumption to the test by combining a 'taming' plot that exemplifies the Protestant prescription for marital relationships with an Italianate plot based on Ariosto's *I suppositi* (1509) that exhibits a much more liberal attitude towards the behaviour upon which a marriage is likely to be founded. By allowing the two actions to interrogate each other, Shakespeare invites his audience to appraise the relative merits of the two attitudes, with perplexing and indeterminate results over which interpreters continue to argue. Most of Shakespeare's other romantic comedies display a similar concern with the nature of the obligations and responsibilities that bind relationships together, whether at the individual or social level.

Another recurrent pattern one can discern in Shakespeare's Italianate plays is a preoccupation with sin, evil and the corruptibility of human nature. When an Italian source lacks a character who exemplifies sinful corruption, Shakespeare makes sure that he invents one. In *Much Ado About Nothing* (1598–1600), for example, he substitutes the malcontent, Don John, for the pining rival lover of the Italian source as the instigator of Claudio's deception, so that malice rather than 'a frenzy of desire' becomes the motive force of the action. Similarly, in *Cymbeline* (1609–10) the machinations of the duplicitous Iachimo (based on a character from one of the sources, a tale in Boccaccio's *Decameron*) pale by comparison with the evil intent of the Queen Shakespeare invents, along with her debased son, Cloten. Shakespeare's purpose in introducing these sinister characters into his source material is for the sake of activating evil, destructive forces in the situations that the other characters confront, in order to explore the extent to which, and the ways in which, human nature is liable to be subverted by the encounter, or, conversely, to resist its potentially corrupting effects. As usual, it is Calvinist teaching about the inescapability of natural human depravity that Shakespeare is testing in these plays, and, as usual, the conclusions he reaches are mostly indeterminate and indecisive.

---

21 Thomas Gataker, *Marriage Duties Briefly Couched Together out of Colossians 3: 18 & 19* (London, 1620), pp. 14–16, quoted in Anthony Fletcher, 'The Protestant Idea of Marriage in Early Modern England', in *Religion, Culture and Society in Early Modern Britain: Essays in Honour of Patrick Collinson*, ed. Anthony Fletcher and Peter Roberts (Cambridge, 1994), pp. 161–81, esp. p. 170.

Perhaps Shakespeare's most persistent concern, visible not just in the plays but in the *Sonnets* as well, was to explore the truth of Calvinist views on the sinfulness of desire, especially sexual desire. Changes he makes to the Petrarchan archetype in the *Sonnets* show Shakespeare both acknowledging the baseness of carnal sexual desire while also trying to promulgate a corrective 'Platonic' alternative in a homoerotic relationship with a young man. This relationship, however, turns out to be potentially just as flawed as that which it seeks to correct, in that it turns out to be equally mutable, and involves a jealousy and possessiveness that attest to a concupiscence of emotion that is just as powerful as the carnal concupiscence of the poet's relationship with his mistress. In the *Sonnets*, at least, Shakespeare seems, reluctantly, to affirm the justness of the Calvinist view.

In the plays, especially in *Measure for Measure* (1604–5) – based on a story from Cinthio's *Gli ecatommiti* (1565) that reached Shakespeare in several versions – Shakespeare propounded a similar view of the corrupting power of sexual desire. He used Italianate imitation, however, as a means of exploring the humane contexts in which desire operates, in order to contemplate the extent to which awareness of human fallibility should, through charitable compassion, mitigate the severity of the coercive human systems – such as the regulatory moral codes being urged by the godly – which were designed to restrain it. The changes Shakespeare made to his source show that he, and undoubtedly many in his audience, felt that the issues were more problematical than the definitive pronouncements of Protestant doctrine would make them appear, even though they lent their assent to the fundamental truth of the doctrine itself. Finding a way of translating abstract doctrine into a practicable mode of living was what mattered, and, on the evidence of Shakespeare's plays, one suspects that the vast majority of 'parish anglicans' were finding that task to be no easy matter.

What, then, is the bigger picture that emerges when one looks at English society in the light of the evidence provided by the Italianate literature of the English Renaissance? Clearly, the English Reformation(s) and the English Renaissance as expressed in its great literature were integrally connected, not separated by a gulf between sacred and secular as earlier commentators have for the most part supposed. Equally clearly, a thorough-going process of self-definition was taking place, in which the values of English Protestantism were being triangulated with the values of foreign cultural systems – notably that of Renaissance Italy – in order to allow English people to work out where they stood in relation to each, and the nature of the national identity that they wished English to assume. It was, however, a time when different conceptions of the values, practices and policies that should determine the character of the nation were in a contest with one another. At one extreme were the minority of zealously committed Protestants, eventually to be known as 'Puritans', who wanted a strict application of the precepts of Protestantism to the governance of the Church, and to the manner in which individual men and women were to be permitted to conduct their daily life. At the other extreme were the Papists, largely driven underground by the late 1580s but nevertheless fortified in their convictions by the activities of a constant stream of Catholic missionaries from the Continent, and hopeful that sooner or later a Catholic regime would replace Elizabeth's Protestant one, just as Mary I's reign had reversed the religious policies of that of Edward VI. In between were the mass of the people representing every conceivable shade of opinion and predisposition. All of the writers who engaged in Italianate literary imitation can be ranged across the spectrum of this middle group, from Spenser at one end to Shakespeare at the other. On the evidence of their writings, all of them were committed to the new Protestant order, but all of them were suspicious of the extreme implications of Protestant doctrine, which is reflected in the lengths to which they went to question these implications, and test themselves and their audiences in the light of them. Italianate literary imitation, in fact, represented an attempt to find a middle ground as one writer after another sought to legitimize the appropriation of a 'papist' literature that was human-centred in its subject matter and whose aesthetic strategies were designed to gratify the imagination, mind and emotions through an appeal to the senses. Aesthetically, this literary enterprise was the equivalent of the compromise that is evident in the religious Settlement of 1559 – which was more Catholic than Protestants wanted, and more Protestant than religious conservatives wanted – and of the principles according to which Elizabeth I's administration governed the country itself; for example, by conducting a foreign policy that stopped just short of outright support for the Protestant princes on the Continent while nurturing hopes in the Catholic regimes of France and Spain for as long as possible that England might yet be reclaimed to its former faith. As such, this literature indicates a state in which the final form of English identity was far from resolved, and, as it were, up for grabs – at least in the minds of the vast majority of the populace, including men like Sir Philip Sidney, whom one might have thought, given his political alignment with the Protestant faction of his uncle, Robert Dudley, the Earl of Leicester, to have been more resolutely determined in his vision of what should constitute the new order. What all of these writers agree on implicitly in their literary practice is that the values of Continental Latinate culture should not be entirely discarded in the adoption of the new Protestant ones, even though, in certain respects, they needed to be corrected in the light of the verities of the reformed religion.

The model of cultural identity-formation suggested by the phenomenon of Italianate literary imitation differs somewhat from that proposed by other commentators who have addressed the issue. Following in the footsteps of Stephen Greenblatt, whose *Renaissance Self-Fashioning: From More to Shakespeare* invoked a binary oppositional model of identity-formation that has dominated new-historicist studies ever since,[22] Richard Helgerson has proposed that England under Elizabeth constituted itself as a nation-state according to a model that depends upon an assumption that self-definition comes from corrective cancellation of the not-self, the alien 'Other'.[23] In the case of England, Helgerson argues, under the influence of the humanist revival of classical antiquity, writers experienced a form of self-alienation, with a recognition of the self as the despised 'Other' (that is, medieval, and therefore 'barbaric'), followed by a move to repair the damaged self-image by aligning themselves with (neo-classical) standards of order and civility that transcended national boundaries but enforced boundaries of social class.

My investigation of the material under discussion in this book has found the oppositional model underlying Helgerson's theory to be inadequate as far as offering an explanation of English identity-formation in the reign of Elizabeth is concerned. A binary polarity in which classical and medieval were pitted against one another as contrary values is evident in the work of some writers, but it plays far less of a role in the determination of the formative values most writers assert than the interreferential relationship between English Protestant and Renaissance Italian values that this book will describe. When one examines the dynamics of Italianate imitation, it becomes apparent that self-definition through a series of triangulations is involved rather than definition through opposition, and that the process was a two-way one of constructive selection, correction and assimilation rather than oppositional cancellation of the 'Other' that is deemed to be alien.[24] Equally, even though most of the writers I discuss, apart from Shakespeare, are connected to the court, or else associated with the patronage of the Sidney family, the effort to formulate English identity through creative imitation of Italian literature was not circumscribed by social class. The very fact that the Italianate plays of Shakespeare were designed for a mass audience confirms that the need to reconcile the values of Protestant religious culture with the secular Latinate

[22] Stephen Greenblatt, *Renaissance Self-Fashioning: From More to Shakespeare* (Chicago, 1980).
[23] Richard Helgerson, *Forms of Nationhood: The Elizabethan Writing of England* (Chicago, 1992), esp. chap. 1.
[24] Thomas Greene comes much closer to the truth in his study of imitation in Renaissance poetry in his assumption that: 'The imitative poem sketches ... its own etiological derivation: it acts out its own coming into being. And since its subtext is by definition drawn from an alien culture, the imitative poem creates a bridge from one *mundus significans* to another' (Thomas M. Greene, *The Light in Troy: Imitation and Discovery in Renaissance Poetry* (New Haven and London, 1982), p. 41).

values of the Continental Renaissance extended across any barriers of class that there might have been – otherwise, why would a mass audience have flocked to see these plays, and why would Shakespeare have been concerned to cater to their interests?

Finally, before embarking into a detailed analysis of the evidence, I wish to speculate on the extraordinary failure among scholars to recognize the importance of Italianate literary imitation as a phenomenon in Elizabethan England. Between the mid-1560s and the early 1660s over 400 separate titles were translated from the Italian, representing over 200 authors,[25] and this does not even begin to take into account the hundreds of original compositions that were based on direct or indirect imitation of Italian sources. Yet for all its manifest importance, there have been, in fact, only three book-length studies devoted to the phenomenon as a whole: J. Ross Murray's *The Influence of Italian upon English Literature during the Sixteenth and Seventeenth Centuries* (1886), Lewis Einstein's *The Italian Renaissance in England* (1902), and, more recently, Robin Kirkpatrick's *English and Italian Literature from Dante to Shakespeare* (1995).[26] Even among these, Murray's essay is barely seventy pages long, while Einstein devotes a mere fifty-six pages to the Italian literary influence in a book of more than 400 pages. Given the insatiable appetite for Italianate literature in late sixteenth-century England, and the constant efforts of English writers to imitate it, this paucity of scholarly studies is striking, and the reasons for it are worthy of speculation.

25 J.R. Hale, *England and the Italian Renaissance* (London, 1954), p. 18.
26 Other studies which give partial accounts of the influence of Italian literature on specific authors, texts or genres include: H.H. Blanchard, 'Imitations of Tasso in the *Faerie Queene*', *Studies in Philology*, 22 (1925): 208–9; C.P. Brand, *Tasso: A Study of the Poet and His Contribution to English Literature* (Cambridge, 1965); C.P. Brand, 'Tasso, Spenser, and the *Orlando furioso*,' in *Petrarch to Pirandello: Studies in Italian Literature in Honour of Beatrice Corrigan*, ed. Julius A. Molinaro (Toronto, 1973), pp. 95–110; Louise George Clubb, *Italian Drama in Shakespeare's Time* (New Haven, 1989); Helen Cooper, *Pastoral: Mediaeval into Renaissance* (Ipswich, 1977); Reed Way Dasenbrock, *Imitating the Italians: Wyatt, Spenser, Synge, Pound, Joyce* (Baltimore and London, 1991); Graham Hough, *A Preface to the Faerie Queene* (London, 1962); Veselin Kostić, *Spenser's Sources in Italian Poetry: A Study in Comparative Literature* (Belgrade, 1969); David Orr, *Italian Renaissance Drama in England before 1625: The Influence of Erudita Tragedy, Comedy, and Pastoral on Elizabethan and Jacobean Drama* (Chapel Hill, 1970); Mario Praz, *The Flaming Heart: Essays on Crashaw, Machiavelli, and Other Studies in the Relations between Italian and English Literature from Chaucer to T.S. Eliot* (New York, 1958); Thomas P. Roche, *Petrarch and the English Sonnet Sequences* (New York, 1989); Sergio Rossi, ed., *Italy and the English Renaissance* (Milan, 1989); A. Lytton Sells, *The Italian Influence in English Poetry from Chaucer to Southwell* (Bloomington, Indiana, 1955); and V.K. Whitaker, 'Shakespeare's Use of His Sources', *Philological Quarterly*, 20 (1941): 377–88.

The older commentators, one suspects, were limited in their perception by prejudices arising from a nineteenth-century Anglo-American sense of cultural superiority. Here is Murray's conclusion:

> The 'Italianate' polish which sometimes obscured our authors' native worth was only superficial; when that was rubbed off the discovery was made how much better the plain British oak was without such varnish. So the absurd and objectionable fashions copied 'apishly' from Italy passed away, and there was left behind the glorious workmanship of all the noble thoughts and musical strains that we associate with the names of Shakspere, Spenser and Milton.[27]

Similarly, Einstein limited the Italian influence simply to formal models and external decoration: 'Shakespeare's individual genius was far too great to be deeply touched by outward influences. His spirit, like Spenser's remained English, unaffected by foreign imitation'.[28] At this point in history, we can see these earlier judgements as the product of a cultural self-privileging induced by an imperial and economic hegemony that is in the process of passing.

More recently, Robin Kirkpatrick has tried to rectify the balance in an important book, *English and Italian Literature from Dante to Shakespeare* (1995).[29] This study identifies with informed care the direct and indirect lines of Italian influence and their crucially formative effect on English Renaissance literature. Kirkpatrick's approach, however, is generalized and loosely, but not specifically, comparative, and the connection between Italianate literary imitation and Protestant concerns is missed altogether. As valuable as this study is for supplying basic information concerning the Italian influence, it does not explain why this influence should have occurred when it did, nor what the sociological function and effects were. Like earlier studies, it neglects to contextualize the Italianate phenomenon in convincing terms, and hence has no means of gaining access to the dialogical activity that one can detect in Elizabethan Italianate imitation which turned it into such a powerful instrument for self-constitution and for the promotion of a unique variety of Protestant consciousness.

It is very timely at this moment in history to examine the dynamics of the Italianate cultural influence on the formation of English identity, because the Western world is standing on the brink of another watershed as mountainous as that which was formed by the Reformation itself. I am referring to the

[27] J. Ross Murray, *The Influence of Italian upon English Literature during the Sixteenth and Seventeenth Centuries* (Cambridge, New York, 1971, 1886), p. 63.
[28] Lewis Einstein, *The Italian Renaissance in England*, Burt Franklin Research and Source Works Series No. 26 (New York, 1902), p. 371.
[29] Robin Kirkpatrick, *English and Italian Literature from Dante to Shakespeare: A Study of Sources, Analogy, and Divergence* (London, 1995).

major shift in consciousness that has been coming for at least three decades and which has accelerated under the influence of the contemporary revolution in technology wrought by the discovery of the microchip. This epochal change has been accompanied by a differential relativism that has called into question all forms of social and political domination, together with the institutions and value systems that have customarily been used to enforce them. We are faced, in fact, with the prospect of a shift in mindset that is likely to be as momentous in its consequences as the English Reformation and Renaissance itself. Given that the values that supported Britain's emergence as a world imperial power in the centuries following the reign of the Tudors were mostly formulated during the period under investigation in this book, it is as well that we understand the cultural process that led to their formulation. In this way, we can learn how we have come to be the way we are, before we launch into the equally difficult task of trying to determine what we shall be once the new watershed that confronts us has been traversed in the years ahead.

1

The Reception of Italian Literary Culture: Motives and Dynamics

The convergence of the English literary Renaissance with the entrenchment of the Protestant Reformation was no accident. To understand why this was so one needs to establish, first, why Italianate imitation was such a dominant feature of the literature produced in this period and, second, why Italianate literary imitation was able to serve the sociological function that called it into being. Before either question can be addressed, it is important to assess the characteristics of Italian literature that made it so attractive to English people, and then to appraise the significance of the pattern revealed in the stages by which it was received into England. I shall begin, therefore, by briefly retracing the spectacular development of Italian vernacular literature between the late thirteenth century and the end of the sixteenth century, focusing especially on those Italian writers whom the English chose most often to imitate.

With the emergence of the Tuscan dialect as the dominant literary language for the whole of Italy, a growing confidence in the value of the vernacular as a vehicle for expression developed in the course of the thirteenth and fourteenth centuries. Its effects are seen in the naturalization in writing of various traditional forms of oral poetry, such as the *strambotto*, *ballata* and Provençal romance, and the invention of new forms of poetry such as the *canzone* and the *sonnetto*. In prose, a new type of fiction emerged in the latter half of the thirteenth century with the appearance of collections of *novelle*. A whole new literature of very high artistic attainment rapidly appeared, including such masterworks as the *Vita nova* and *Commedia* of Dante Alighieri (1265–1321), the lyric poems of Francesco Petrarca (1304–74) that he named *Le rime sparse*, and the *Decameron* of Giovanni Boccaccio (1312–75)

– works whose influence would quickly be felt in every vernacular literature in Western Europe.[1]

The creative impulse which inspired these writers, and which their own example helped to reinforce, persisted throughout the fifteenth and sixteenth centuries. It led to a fusion of the Carolingian and Arthurian traditions of the Middle Ages into a new type of romantic epic with the *Orlando innamorato* of Matteo Maria Boiardo (1434–94), its sequel, the *Orlando furioso* of Ludovico Ariosto (1474–1533), and the *Gerusalemme liberata* of Torquato Tasso (1544–95). Meanwhile, a new type of pastoral romance was brought into being with the *Arcadia* of Jacopo Sannazzaro (1456–1530), which, in the world of drama, would soon spawn a new form of pastoral tragi-comedy, with the *Aminta* of Tasso and *Il pastor fido* by Giambattista Guarini (1538–1612). Continuing with the tradition of Boccaccio, writers of prose continued to produce further collections of colourful tales, with works such as the *Novelle* of Matteo Bandello (1480–1561) and *Gli ecatommiti* of Giambattista Giraldi Cinthio (1504–73). In the course of the sixteenth century, dramatists would rediscover the theatrical potential of Plautine new comedy, with plays like Ariosto's *I suppositi* (1509), and of Senecan tragedy, with works like Cinthio's *Orbecche* (1541). All of these writings would have a profound influence on the culture of early modern England.

At the same time as this remarkable creative outpouring of imaginative literature in the vernacular was occurring in Italy, another movement began to take shape which would become known as 'humanism'. The relationship between humanism and the burst of creativity in the Italian vernacular is complex. They both sought to find inspiration in the classical cultures of Greece and Rome, and they both shared a delight in, and a concern to attain, eloquence of linguistic expression and artistic effect. Beyond that, however, their aims, methods and preoccupations were very different, and frequently in competition or conflict with one another.

Renaissance Italian humanism arose in the second half of the fourteenth century and was characterized by an enthusiastic study of the classics, an attempt to recover the texts of ancient writers through careful editorial labours, and the advocacy of classical Latin as the preferable instrument for effective expression and persuasion.[2] The name used to describe the movement (coined in the nineteenth century) comes from the term 'humanist', which itself derives from '*umanista*', a fifteenth-century slang term used by students in the Italian universities to refer to proponents of the new type of educational curriculum then being advocated.[3] Instead of concentrating on

---

[1] For an account of the rise of Italian vernacular literature, see Ernest Hatch Wilkins, *A History of Italian Literature*, revised by Thomas G. Bergin (Cambridge, Massachusetts, 1974).

[2] See Wilkins, *A History of Italian Literature*, chap. 14.

[3] See Alistair Fox and John Guy, *Reassessing the Henrician Age: Humanism, Politics and Reform 1500–1550* (Oxford, 1986), chap. 1, esp. pp. 31–3.

logic and metaphysics as the former medieval scholastic system of learning had done, the new 'humanist' system focused on the liberal arts, or *litterae humaniores*, and prioritized the study of rhetoric, and natural, moral and political philosophy. Its aim was to provide the individual with a moral and civic education that equipped him – there were no women in the universities at this time – for acting effectively in the world as the means of promoting the public good.

With its belief that the key to reform lay in the more effective communication of rational wisdom through the persuasive eloquence of a purified Latin, humanism stood in opposition to, and tended to have a repressive effect on, the use of the vernacular. Moreover, the didactic preoccupations of humanists led them to favour a literary discourse that did not readily lend itself to the kind of imaginative 'feigning' and story-telling pursued by writers in the vernacular. Hence, when they assumed the mantle of humanist discourse, writers tended to adopt expositional forms such as the dialogue, the oration, the treatise and the verse epigram.

In Italy, the two modes of cultural engagement, humanist and vernacular, evolved alongside one another, with writers frequently switching between the two. Petrarch, for example, while remembered chiefly for his lyric poetry in the vernacular, wrote Latin works in all the major humanist forms: dialogues (the *Secretum, De remediis utriusque fortunae*), treatises (*Rerum memorandarum libri, De vita solitaria* and *De otio religioso*), several collections of letters (*Familiarum rerum liber* and *Epistolae sine nomine*), a collection of biographies (*De viris illustribus*), and an imitation Virgilian epic (*Africa*). Similarly, Boccaccio spent the last twenty years of his life engaged in comparable humanist endeavours, including collections of exemplary biographies (*De casibus virorum illustrium, De claris mulieribus*), a genealogical dictionary of the classical gods (*Genealogia deorum*), and an elaborate geographical dictionary. The distinction between the two modes is important to bear in mind when appraising the English response to Renaissance Italy, for they would be received in turn diachronically, not synchronically, and the reasons for this will turn out to be of crucial significance to an understanding of the early modern era in England as a whole.

The first writer in England to respond to the influence of the Italian Renaissance was the man whom later generations would regard as 'the father of English poetry', Geoffrey Chaucer.[4] After a visit to Italy in the late 1370s, Chaucer began to imitate the works of the three great Italian writers of his century, Dante, Petrarch and Boccaccio. He was the first to respond to

---

[4] For Chaucer's response to Italian literature, see Piero Boitano, *Chaucer and the Italian Trecento* (Cambridge, 1983), and Robin Kirkpatrick, *English and Italian Literature from Dante to Shakespeare: A Study of Sources, Analogy, and Divergence* (London, 1995), chap. 1.

Petrarch's representation of erotic psychology, by translating Petrarch's sonnet, 'S' amor non è, che dunque è quel ch' io sento?' into the words uttered by the love-sick Troilus: 'If no love is, O God, what fele I so?'[5] From Dante he derived his conception of 'gentillesse', and much of the thematic content and narrative strategy for *The House of Fame*. His greatest Italian source of inspiration, however, was Boccaccio, whose *Teseida* provided the foundations for *The Knight's Tale*, whose *Filostrato* furnished the substance of *Troilus and Criseyde*, and whose *Filocolo* yielded thematic elements that would find their way into several of his other works. Chaucer's response to Italian sources was marked not by servile imitation but by a thorough-going creative assimilation and transformation, and in this, as in so many other things, he showed the way forward for writers in generations to come. However, for the time being, he was alone: there would be no further creative reworking of imaginative Italian writing in England for over 200 years.

The next significant response in England to the Italian literary Renaissance was that of Sir Thomas Wyatt, who began to translate certain of Petrarch's sonnets and *canzoni* soon after his return from a journey to Italy in 1527. Emulating Wyatt, the Earl of Surrey, his younger contemporary at the court of Henry VIII, soon followed suit. Altogether, Wyatt translated or imitated over thirty of Petrarch's poems, and Surrey six. Some of these translations, together with the efforts of several other anonymous English poets, found their way into Tottel's *Miscellany*, whence they became known to subsequent generations in the next few decades.[6] In addition to Petrarch, Wyatt also translated or imitated lyric poems by later Italian poets such as Serafino d'Aquila, Dragonetto Bonifacio, Giusto de' Conti, Marcello Filosseno and Jacopo Sannazzaro, and introduced the epistolary satire into England by imitating the Provençal satires of his contemporary, Luigi Alamanni. Later in his career he turned to the prose paraphrase of Pietro Aretino's *I sette salmi de la penitentia di David* for the fictive framework of his own rendering of the Penitential Psalms. The extent of Wyatt's borrowings attests to an awareness of the expressive art and representational usefulness of Italian poetry that had not been present in England since the 1380s.

In spite of the fact that Wyatt and Surrey had again brought Italian literature to the attention of the English, there would be yet another gap of forty years before any further creative engagement with the imaginative writing of

---

5 *Rime sparse*, no. 133, in Francesco Petrarca, *Petrarch's Lyric Poems: The Rime sparse and Other Lyrics*, trans. and ed. Robert M. Durling (Cambridge, Massachusetts, and London, 1976); *Troilus and Criseyde*, Book 1, ll. 400–20, in Geoffrey Chaucer, *The Riverside Chaucer*, gen. ed. Larry D. Benson, 3rd edn (Oxford, 1987). All subsequent references to Petrarch's *Rime sparse*, hereafter cited as *Rime*, will be to Durling's edition.
6 Wyatt imitates *Rime sparse* nos 1, 19, 21, 25, 37, 49, 57, 82, 84, 102, 103, 121, 124, 129, 134, 135, 140, 145, 153, 169, 173, 189, 190, 199, 206, 224, 234, 248, 258, 269 and 360; Surrey imitates nos 11, 22, 140, 145, 164, 310.

the Italian Renaissance revealed itself. Protestant reformers in the reign of Edward VI knew of Petrarch, but they valued him chiefly as a proto-Protestant whose authority could be invoked in the attack on Roman Catholicism. Hence, John Harington of Stepney in about 1550 would translate two of the apocalyptic sonnets in which Petrarch denounces the Avignon papal court as the whore of Babylon (*Rime*, no. 136, 'Fiamma dal Ciel su le tue treccie piova', and no. 138, 'Fontana di dolore, albergo d'ira'). Similarly, an anonymous poet in the Hill Manuscript (*c.*1553–62) would, among a scattering of erotic verses, translate another apocalyptic poem by Petrarch (*Rime*, no. 114) and several moral and penitential ones (nos 102, 103 and 365).[7] But Petrarch was appreciated more for his edifying matter in these sonnets than for his manner, and although the Edwardians produced a voluminous literature of satire, polemic and complaint during this period of radical religious reform, it was to the earlier English 'ploughman' tradition that they turned, not to Italian modes of representation.[8]

Then, suddenly, there was an explosion of interest in Italian literature in the 1560s and 1570s that quickly developed into a major era of Italianate literary imitation during the 1580s and 1590s. The onset of a dramatic change of attitude was signalled by a sudden upsurge in the number of Italian books being imported, printed and translated in England, at a rate that was sufficiently remarkable to cause alarm among many Elizabethans with puritan leanings, such as Roger Ascham and Stephen Gosson.[9] In his treatise, *The Scholemaster*, written between 1564 and 1568, Ascham lamented that 'there be moe of these vngratious bookes set out in Printe within these fewe monethes, than haue bene sene in England many score yeare before', and he noted that 'fonde bookes, of late translated out of *Italian* into English, [are] sold in euery shop in London, commended by honest titles the soner to corrupt honest maners'.[10] The phenomenon to which he refers began in the mid-1560s and lasted through into the 1600s, during which time over 400 separate titles were translated from the Italian, representing over 200 authors.[11] Picking up where Wyatt and Surrey had left off, other poets turned to Italian poetry. Further renderings of Petrarch's sonnets appeared in George Turbervile's *Epitaphes, Epigrams, Songs and Sonets* (1567), Thomas Howell's *The Arbor of Amitie* (1568), George Gascoigne's *A Hundreth Sundrie Flowers*

---

[7] See Kenneth Muir, 'Sonnets in the Hill Manuscript', *Proceedings of the Leeds Philosophical Society*, 6 (1944–52): 464–71.

[8] See David Norbrook, *Poetry and Politics in the English Renaissance* (London, 1984), pp. 45–7.

[9] See Stephen Gosson, *Plays Confuted in Five Actions* [1582], ed. Arthur Freeman (New York and London, 1972); also Lewis Einstein, *The Italian Renaissance in England*, Burt Franklin Research and Source Works Series No. 26 (New York, 1902), p. 167.

[10] Roger Ascham, *English Works: Toxophilus, Report of the Affaires and State of Germany, The Scholemaster*, ed. William Aldis Wright (Cambridge, 1904), pp. 229, 231.

[11] See J.R. Hale, *England and the Italian Renaissance* (London, 1954), p. 18.

(1573) and Thomas Watson's *Ekatompathia, or Passionate Centurie of Love* (1582). The appetite for Italian *novelle* was just as great, and was fed with tales from the *Decameron* appearing in William Painter's *The Palace of Pleasure* (1566–7), George Pettie's *A Petite Pallace of Pettie his Pleasures* (1576), George Whetstone's *The Rocke of Regard* (1576), Barnabe Rich's *Riche His Farewell to Militarie Profession* (1581), and George Turbervile's *Tragicall Tales Translated by Turbervile in Time of His Troubles out of Sundrie Italians* (1587). Other *novelle* writers to be translated at this time included Matteo Bandello, some of whose tales appeared in Geoffrey Fenton's *Certaine Tragicall Discourses* (1567) and Painter's *The Palace of Pleasure*, and Giambattista Giraldi Cinthio, from whose collection *Gli ecatommiti* (1565) Whetstone drew stories for *An Heptameron of Ciuill Discourses* (1582). In drama, *novelle* stories began to be dramatized for stage presentation, such as *Gismond of Salerne* (1567–8), based on Boccaccio's tale of Tancred and Gismonda,[12] or the Romeo and Juliet play (not extant) that Arthur Brooke refers to in the preface to his own *Tragicall Historye of Romeus and Juliet written first in Italian by Bandell, and nowe in Englishe …* (1562).[13] About this time, George Gascoigne introduced two new types of Italian neo-classical drama into England by translating Lodovico Dolce's *Giocasta* and Ariosto's *I suppositi*, both in 1566. At least one-third of all the extant plays written between the 1560s and the closing of the theatres in 1642 would be based on Italian sources.[14]

By the 1580s the new Italian influence had moved well beyond translation into freer forms of creative imitation. Sir Philip Sidney combined Italian pastoralism in both its Arcadian and tragi-comic versions into a major pastoral epic, *The Countess of Pembroke's Arcadia*. English Petrarchism also spread its wings with the unauthorized publication in 1591 of Sidney's *Astrophil and Stella* (written in 1582), prompting a craze for sonnet sequences that would include Samuel Daniel's *Delia* (1592), Henry Constable's *Diana* (1592), Michael Drayton's *Idea* (1594), Thomas Lodge's *Phillis* (1593), Giles Fletcher's *Licia* (1593), Edmund Spenser's *Amoretti* (1595) and William Shakespeare's *Sonnets* (published in 1609, but written largely in the preceding decade). These decades saw the great Italian romantic epics advance into the forefront of English awareness, not merely in the form of translations of Ariosto's *Orlando furioso* by Sir John Harington the younger in 1591, and of Tasso's *Gerusalemme liberata*, first by Richard Carew in 1594 and then by Sir

---

[12] Giovanni Boccaccio, *Decameron; Filocolo; Ameto; Fiammetta*, ed. Carlo Salinari, Enrico Bianchi and Natalino Sapegno, vol. 8, La Letteratura Italiana: Storia e Testi (Milan and Naples, 1952), Giorn. iv, Nov. 1; for an English translation see Giovanni Boccaccio, *The Decameron*, trans. and ed. G.H. William (London, 1972).

[13] See Geoffrey Bullough, ed., *Narrative and Dramatic Sources of Shakespeare*, 8 vols (London and New York, 1957–75), vol. 2, pp. 284–5.

[14] See Hale, *England and the Italian Renaissance*, p. 18.

Edward Fairfax in 1600, but more importantly in a transfigured guise in Spenser's summative epic of the Protestant nation, *The Faerie Queene* (1590, 1595–6). Finally, the 1590s also witnessed the astonishing transformation of Italian literary material by William Shakespeare into some of the most arresting works of art the world has ever seen, with no fewer than ten of his plays being directly or indirectly based on Italian sources – a pattern that would be repeated by other late-Elizabethan and Jacobean dramatists, such as John Marston, Robert Greene and John Webster.[15]

Almost as quickly as it had come, this remarkable phase of intensive Italianate imitation began to wane, especially once James I had ascended the throne. It lingered on in varieties of court entertainment, notably in the masks contrived by Ben Jonson and Inigo Jones, and in imitations of Italian pastoral tragi-comedy by Samuel Daniel, in *The Queenes Arcadia* (1605), and by John Fletcher, in *The Faithful Shepherdess* (1608–9) – even though the latter was a disastrous flop in the popular theatre. It persisted, too, in the evocation of a sinister Italianate world of perversion, decadence and corruption as the backdrop for much of the Jacobean tragedy written at this time. Essentially, though, its power as a stimulus to profound imaginative creativity had gone, and when John Milton returned to the imitation of the Italian romantic epics in constructing his own great epic at the conclusion of the civil war period, he was writing idiosyncratically and anachronistically, and in this, like so many other things, he was alone.

The patterns visible in this process of reception raise very important questions. Why, after Chaucer's brilliant early response, was there a gap of nearly 200 years before the English responded again to the imaginative possibilities inherent in Italian fictive writing? Why, when Wyatt and Surrey again brought the Italian poets to notice in the reign of Henry VIII, was there another gap of around forty years before anyone else would follow their example? Why, when it did come, was the impulse to imitate the Italians so powerful and pervasive, and why, when it began to wane, did the beginnings of its demise appear to coincide with the death of Elizabeth I? The answers to these questions are crucial to an understanding both of the social dynamics operating in what was one of the most formative periods in the evolution of English national identity, and of the very distinctive body of literature that it produced.

---

[15] Plays derived from Italian sources by these dramatists include Marston's *Parasitaster, or the Fawne* (1606), based on Boccaccio's *Decameron*; *The Insatiate Countesse* (1613), based on Bandello's story of the Contessa di Celant; Greene's *Perimedes the Blacksmith* (1588), based on the *Decameron*; *Orlando furioso* (1594), based on Ariosto's epic of that name; *The Scottish History of James IV* (1594), based on Cinthio's *Gli ecatommiti*; and Webster's *Duchess of Malfi* (1612), based on Bandello. For a detailed treatment of Shakespeare's Italianate drama, see below, chapter 6.

If the condition of England during the fifteenth century is borne in mind, it becomes clear that the gap between Chaucer and the revival of Italianate literary imitation nearly two centuries later occurred because English political and social circumstances required something else, and that something was humanism. By the early years of the fifteenth century, late-medieval institutions in England were showing signs of debility, manifest in usurpation and regicide, the growth of heresy, a century of civil warfare, and a general fraying of the fabric of intellectual and spiritual life. In such circumstances, the prime imperative was to find some means of modifying intellectual conditions as a precondition for social reconstruction, and humanism, with its new system of learning based on belief in the superior ethical and political wisdom of a recoverable classical culture, seemed providentially to offer itself as the way forward.

In England, therefore, the years between the death of Chaucer and the Elizabethan literary reawakening witnessed recurrent attempts to harness the capacities of humanism to a renovation of society and the restoration of a stable political order.[16] The prime mover of this endeavour was Humfrey, Duke of Gloucester, the younger brother of Henry V, who established the pattern of a type of patronage that would influence subsequent literary and intellectual activity well into the sixteenth century. Duke Humfrey's interests in humanism focused on two concerns: to import into England the fruits of humanist learning, and to employ the rhetorical skill of humanists to the enhancement of the contemporary political regime. In pursuit of the first goal, he imported a number of humanist scholars from Italy, including Antonio Beccaria of Verona and Tito Livio Frulovisi of Ferrara, and assembled a collection of humanist works.[17] In pursuit of the second aim, he commissioned Frulovisi to write a *Vita Henrici Quinti* to magnify the achievements of the Lancastrian dynasty and make it accessible to a Continental audience.

A survey of books owned by Duke Humfrey and the scholars attached to him shows where the main interests of this circle lay. Most numerous are works of classical ethical philosophy (Aristotle's *Ethics*, translated into Latin by Leonardo Bruni, and the letters, orations, Tusculan disputations and *De officiis* of Cicero), and works of classical political philosophy and history (Plato's *Republic*, translated into Latin by Piercandido Decembrio, Plutarch's *Lives*, Suetonius' *De duodecim Caesaribus*, and historical writings by Livy and Tacitus). Writings by Italian humanists comprise the second largest category, but there are no works of imaginative fiction in the vernacular among them;

[16] See Roberto Weiss, *Humanism in England During the Fifteenth Century*, 2nd edn (Oxford, 1957).

[17] For Duke Humfrey's gifts of humanist books to the Universities of Oxford and Cambridge, see Anon, *Duke Humfrey and English Humanism in the Fifteenth Century: Catalogue of an Exhibition Held in the Bodleian Library Oxford* (Oxford, n.d.).

rather, they are one of a kind with the works of the classical authors in dealing with issues of philosophy, education or history. Petrarch is represented by his *De remediis utriusque fortunae* and his Latin translation of Boccaccio's *Vita Griseldis*, Boccaccio by Latin translations of his bitter misogynistic invective, the *Corbaccio*, and his *Tancredi*, while the collection also contains Guido de Columna's *Historia destructionis Troiae*, and various works by Coluccio Salutati, Guarino, Vergerio and Poggio. The only significant fictive works in the collection are the tragedies of Seneca, plays by Terence, Homer's *Odyssey* (in a Latin translation) and Virgil's *Aeneid*, which, one suspects, were included more for their exemplary matter and eloquence than for their imaginative appeal *per se*.

A similar situation reveals itself in the later fifteenth and early sixteenth centuries. The educated elite preoccupied themselves almost exclusively with acquiring knowledge of classical learning, often by travelling to study at Italian universities, and with learning how to master the classical languages for purposes of study and persuasion. At home, a second generation of scholars, including Thomas Linacre, William Grocyn, John Colet and Thomas Latimer, worked hard to disseminate humanism more widely, with the establishment of humanist education in the universities and the introduction of a new type of humanist grammar-school curriculum that aimed to blend the method of Vergerio and Guarino with Erasmian piety.[18] At the political level, Henry Tudor continued to follow the example set by the Lancastrians by commissioning Polydore Vergil to write a history of England in the new humanist manner, the *Anglica historia*, to provide the trappings of respectability for his newly planted dynasty.[19] By the time of Henry VIII, many had come to believe that humanist learning was the key to advancement, with the result that the prime literary energies of many were devoted to the composition of humanist treatises that would blazon their credentials. Among those who expended their energies in this way were Richard Pace, who dedicated his treatise on the benefits of a liberal education, *De fructu qui ex doctrina percipitur*, to Cardinal Wolsey, and Sir Thomas Elyot, whose prescription for the preparation of administrators, *The Governour*, was designed to secure him a place in the royal service. This trend continued through the ascendancy of Thomas Cromwell, with a number of younger humanist scholars from the circle of Reginald Pole in Padua proffering themselves as a kind of 'think-tank' for the formation of policy, with works such as Thomas Starkey's *Dialogue between Thomas Lupset and Reginald Pole*, or Richard Moryson's *A Remedy for Sedition*.[20]

[18] See Kalyan K. Chatterjee, *In Praise of Learning: John Colet and Literary Humanism in Education* (New Delhi, 1974); and J.B. Trapp, 'From Guarino of Verona to John Colet', in *Italy and the English Renaissance*, ed. Sergio Rossi (Milan, 1989), pp. 45–53.

[19] See Alistair Fox, *Politics and Literature in the Reigns of Henry VII and Henry VIII* (Oxford, 1989), pp. 15–19, 110–13.

[20] For further comment on these works, see W. Gordon Zeeveld, *Foundations of Tudor Policy*

What these preoccupations show is that for well over a century the exigencies of the time prompted the literate class to devote most of their energies to the acquisition and display of the wisdom that they believed the new learning could supply; hence, when they turned to Italy, they opted for Italian humanism rather than the Italian vernacular literary tradition to which, in Italy, the former was allied. Fictive writing did continue in England through this period, but at court it was manifest either in aureate didactic dream allegories in the Gallic tradition of *Le roman de la rose*, or in late-medieval forms of lyric, complaint and satire that were closely related to the popular forms of oral culture. Writers like Stephen Hawes and John Skelton knew about Petrarch and Boccaccio, but showed interest only in their didactic works in Latin.[21] In brief, the thirst of the times for sources of ethical and political enlightenment had distracted potential authors from attempting the kind of creative engagement with the Italian vernacular writers that Chaucer had so triumphantly inaugurated.

If one turns to the related question of why there was a sudden outburst of interest in Italian literature in the reign of Elizabeth I, the answer is even more complex. There is a simple answer, and a more profound one.

The simple answer is that fashion changed. Soon after the accession of Henry VIII in 1509 a cultural transformation began in the Tudor court that, in the course of the sixteenth century, would see the international French culture that had dominated court life through the Middle Ages progressively replaced by an Italianate one.[22] It became fashionable during this period for members of the court circle and gentry to travel to Italy, prompted by a desire to see the antiquities of the ancient world, together with the new culture that had resulted from the Italian Renaissance.[23] By the 1530s, English travellers had witnessed for themselves the refined elegance and splendour of the courts of Urbino, Mantua and Ferrara, and Baldassare Castiglione had published his compelling image of Italian courtiership to the world in 1528 with *Il libro del cortegiano* (translated by Sir Thomas Hoby into English in 1561). It was an image that the English monarchs and those surrounding them quickly felt impelled to emulate.[24] Henry VIII learnt Italian, as did many of his courtiers, including Lord Rochford, Lord Morley, the Earl of Surrey, and Sir Thomas

---

(Cambridge, Massachusetts, 1948), and Arthur B. Ferguson, *The Articulate Citizen and the English Renaissance* (Durham, North Carolina, 1965).

[21] See *The Garland of Laurel*, ll. 365–79, in John Skelton, *John Skelton: The Complete English Poems*, ed. John Scattergood (Harmondsworth and New Haven, 1983). I concur with Scattergood's view that Skelton seems to have had in mind Boccaccio's encyclopaedic works, *Genealogia deorum*, *De casibus virorum illustrium* and *De claris mulieribus* (ibid., p. 500, note to l. 365), and Petrarch's didactic writings such as *De remediis utriusque fortunae*.

[22] See Einstein, *The Italian Renaissance in England*, pp. 58–114, and esp. pp. 109–10.

[23] Ibid., chap. 3.

[24] Ibid., pp. 97–9.

Wyatt, and the king also retained many Italians to propagate the new culture: 'Il Re medesimo ha molti Italiani ... al suo servitio, di ogni professione' (the King himself has many Italians ... of all professions in his service).[25] Elizabeth I, like her sister Mary, was taught Italian as a child, and Italian visitors to Queen Elizabeth's court were impressed by her proficiency in the language. Many of her courtiers shared her facility, to the extent that a Venetian envoy was able to report that at a dinner for him hosted by Cecil, attended by the entire Privy Council, the conversation was conducted mostly in Italian, 'almost all of them speaking our Italian tongue, or at least all understanding it'.[26] The adoption of Italianate manners was facilitated during her reign by the translation of several influential manuals of polite conversation, including Giovanni Della Casa's Il Galateo (translated by Robert Peterson in 1576) and Stefano Guazzo's La civil conversatione (translated by George Pettie in 1581). Castiglione's great work was itself translated into English by Sir Thomas Hoby in 1561.

The craze to emulate the Italians extended into almost every domain of court life, and in the second half of the sixteenth century began to be more widely diffused among the English gentry. Italian-style clothing had made its appearance as early as the 1520s, when Henry VIII and his retinue attended the festivities of the grand peace treaty between England, France and the Habsburg empire in 1520 dressed, as the Mantuan ambassador reports, 'in long gowns in the Milanese fashion, checkered with hoods of gold tissue and gold brocade'.[27] Several decades later, the dandyism of Elizabethan courtiers would owe much to the imitation of Italian costumes, as Gabriel Harvey observed in a letter to Edmund Spenser in which he gives a satiric sketch of an Englishman infected with 'Tuscanism':

> His cringing side necke, Eyes glauncing, Fisnamie smirking,
> With forefinger kisse, and braue embrace to the footewarde.
> Largebellied Kodpeasd Dublet, vnkodpeased halfe hose,
> Straite to the dock, like a shirte, and close to the britch, like a diueling.
> A little Apish Hatte, cowched fast to the pate, like an Oyster,
> Eueryone A per se A, his termes, and braueries in Print,
> Delicate in speach, queynte in araye: conceited in all poyntes.[28]

---

[25] Calendar of State Papers, Venetian, ed. R. Brown and others (London, 1864–98), IV, 287. Ubaldini, Add. MSS. BL 10169, f. 116 b. Quoted by Einstein, The Italian Renaissance in England, p. 97.

[26] Calendar of State Papers, Venetian, VII, 524 et seq.; quoted by Einstein, The Italian Renaissance in England, p. 99.

[27] Calendar of State Papers, Venetian, III, 72; quoted by Einstein, The Italian Renaissance in England, p. 80.

[28] Edmund Spenser, The Works of Edmund Spenser: A Variorum Edition, ed. Charles Grosvenor Osgood, Edwin Greenlaw, Frederick Morgan Padelford and Ray Heffner, 11 vols (Baltimore, 1932–57), vol. 9: Spenser's Prose Works, ed. Rudolf Gottfried, p. 467.

The Italian influence was seen equally in the mounting of the spectacles, pageants and tourneys by which successive Tudor regimes sought to define their magnificence. Italian masks began to be a regular part of court life soon after Henry VIII's accession, with Edward Hall noting in his chronicle entry for 1512–13 that 'On the Day of Epiphany, at night, the King with eleven others were disguised after the manner of Italy, called a Mask, a thing not seen before in England'.[29] As late as the reign of James I, artificers like Inigo Jones were still going to Italy to discover the mechanisms and scenic devices that were necessary for the mounting of these elaborate spectacles. Chivalric tourneys – an anachronism by the sixteenth century – were revived by Henry VIII in emulation of Italian practice, and later became a key part of the strategy by which the Earl of Essex sought to claim and blazon his status in the 1590s.[30]

The transition from a French to an Italianate court culture was especially marked in music and poetry. As John Stevens puts it, 'the mid-sixteenth century gets its character from the appearance of such "newfangilnes" as the consort of viols, the pavane and galliard, the metrical psalm, the art-song for voice and lute, the new polyphonic style', replacing such French forms as the *basse-danse*, the *rondeau*, the *virelai* and the carol.[31] Later, the Italian influence on English music would culminate in the Elizabethan madrigal. A similar kind of sea change can be observed in poetry. As George Puttenham acknowledged in 1589, a significant transformation of English poetry had commenced with the efforts of Sir Thomas Wyatt and Henry Howard, Earl of Surrey, to write English verse of an Italianate quality: 'hauing trauailed into Italie, and there tasted the sweete and stately measures and stile of the Italian Poesie as nouices newly crept out of the schooles of *Dante, Arioste*, and *Petrarch*, they greatly pollished our rude & homely maner of vulgar Poesie, from that it had bene before, and for that cause may iustly be sayd the first reformers of our English meetre and stile'.[32] This polishing of the 'rude & homely maner' of English poetry involved the adoption of new poetic forms, the forging of a new poetical language and the discovery of more effective rhythms. Thus, whereas in the earlier decades of the sixteenth century poets wrote dream allegories and didactic complaints, or else lyrics of a late-medieval type, by the 1580s they were writing sonnets, *strambotti, sestine, canzoni* and madrigals. Likewise, the pausing line, rhyme royale stanzas, poulter's measure and fourteeners favoured by earlier generations had given way to an iambic pentameter line that sought to emulate the fluidity found

[29] Quoted in Einstein, *The Italian Renaissance in England*, p. 76.
[30] Ibid.; also Richard C. McCoy, *The Rites of Knighthood: The Literature and Politics of Elizabethan Chivalry* (Berkeley, 1989).
[31] John Stevens, *Music and Poetry in the Early Tudor Court* (London, 1961), p. 109.
[32] George Puttenham, *The Arte of English Poesie*, ed. Gladys Doidge Willcock and Alice Walker (Cambridge, 1936), p. 60.

in the Italian hendecasyllabic line, together with new metrical forms such as *terza rima, ottava rima* and '*versi sciolti*' (blank verse).[33] Above all, by the 1590s English poets had learnt from Petrarch, Sannazzaro, Serafino Aquilano and Ariosto how to evoke more powerful complexes of thought and feeling and a more intense effect of beauty, through combining a wider range of metaphoric reference with more skilfully contrived patterns of sound and melody.

In the face of such a general swing towards Italian culture in the English court, it is not surprising that interest in the writers of Italy should have revived along with it. Barnabe Rich admits as much in apologizing for publishing the Boccaccesque tales in his *Riche His Farewell to Militarie Profession*: 'in the writyng of them, I haue used the same maner, that many of our yong Gentlemenne vseth now adaies, in the wearyng of their apparell, whiche is rather to followe a fashion that is newe (be it neuer so foolishe) then to bee tied to a more decent custome, that is cleane out of vse'.[34] Undoubtedly, many other writers were drawn to the Italians for similar reasons, in response to what had become a fashionable craze.

Fashion alone, however, does not fully account for the extraordinary intensity of the revival of interest in Italian literature that was evident from the late 1560s, nor for its timing. If it were a self-sufficient cause, there is no reason why the period of sustained literary influence should not have occurred earlier, given that Italian culture was dominant in the Henrician court by the 1520s, and certainly no reason why the brief foray of Wyatt and Surrey should have been followed by a hiatus of forty years before English poets would again engage in Italianate literary imitation.

The more compelling and profound explanation is that the revived interest in Italian literary culture was called into being just as surely by the social and political circumstances of the mid- and later parts of Elizabeth I's reign as the preoccupation with humanism in the fifteenth century had been elicited by the differing circumstances of that era. It remains, then, to find an explanation as to why Italian literature, and especially Italianate creative imitation, was able to answer to the psychological, social and political needs of a significant number of Elizabethans, as it manifestly did.

At the heart of the matter, the deeper causes of the Italian phenomenon arose from factors relating to the Protestant Reformation itself. In April and May of 1559 the Queen and her Parliament had enacted a settlement, through the

---

[33] On Wyatt's attempts to unloosen the restraints of the pausing line, see F.T. Prince, *The Italian Elements in Milton's Verse* (Oxford, 1954), pp. 12–16.

[34] Barnabe Rich, *Riche His Farewell to Militarie Profession: Conteinyng Verie Pleasaunt Discourses Fit for a Peaceable Tyme* ... (London, 1581), sig. Ddii^v.

Act of Supremacy and the Act of Uniformity, that would determine the nature of doctrinal orientation and governance in the re-established Church of England. It was a compromise between the Queen and her Protestant subjects designed to steer a middle way between the excesses of Protestant radicalism experienced in the reign of Edward VI, and the excesses of reactionary Catholicism in the reign of Mary I. As such, it was sufficiently Calvinist in doctrine to satisfy all but the most austere Protestants, and sufficiently traditional in organization to allow the inclusion of all but the most extreme Catholics. Initially, most people found that they could tolerate this moderate system, but it was only a matter of time before 'puritans', who regarded the religious settlement as only an interim measure, demanded that further, more radical reforms be enacted to 'purify' the Church of its Romish remnants.[35]

As the 1560s advanced, the resurgence of religious feeling let loose by the Settlement led puritans to become increasingly vociferous in demanding a more zealous implementation of measures to enforce the observance of God's word. In December of 1566, for example, the puritan opposition in Parliament introduced no fewer than six bills aimed at forcing the clergy to observe more strictly the Genevan rule.[36] In the Parliament of 1571, seven bills for religion and the regulation of Church affairs were introduced, including one demanding that a new confession of faith should be made, 'as was among other professors of religion in foreign parts, as those of Strasburge and Frankford'.[37] Simultaneously, in pulpits across England, zealous preachers castigated the moral and personal sins of the 'reprobate' and 'carnal' multitude, exhorting the whole population to repentance.[38] The puritans may have been a vocal minority, but no one in England could avoid hearing the clarity and insistence of their voice.

Was the coincidence of this aggressive puritan radicalism and the extraordinary growth of interest in Italian literature merely accidental? To the contrary, it is conceivable that the appetite for Italianate fiction was experienced most strongly by those who felt disinclined to be bound to the austerity that puritanism was urging upon them, and, in many cases, the appetite itself may actually have been provoked by such a disinclination.

Hints to this effect can be gleaned from Roger Ascham's denunciation of the fascination that many English men and women were displaying for Italian culture in general, and Italian books in particular. The reasons for his

---

35 See G.R. Elton, *England Under the Tudors*, 3rd edn (London and New York, 1991), pp. 269–76.

36 Ibid., p. 290.

37 John Strype, *Annals of the Reformation and Establishment of Religion and of the Various Occurrences in the Church of England during Queen Elizabeth's Happy Reign*, 4 vols, vol. 2, part 1, Burt Franklin Research and Source Works Series, no. 122 (New York, 1824), pp. 96–7.

38 See Patrick Collinson, *The Birthpangs of Protestant England: Religious and Cultural Change in the Sixteenth and Seventeenth Centuries* (London, 1988), esp. pp. 18–22.

hostility show clearly in his condemnation of the habit of travelling to Italy: 'I am affraide, that ouer many of our trauelers into Italie, do not exchewe the way to *Circes* Court: but go, and ryde, and runne, and flie thether, they make great hast to cum to her'.[39] As the metaphoric allusion to Circe's court reveals, Italy, for Ascham, had become the symbolic embodiment of all the spiritual vices that 'licentious vanitie' can breed out of 'vayne pleasure'.[40] It had, in other words, come to represent the depraved cultural 'Other' that stood in diametric opposition to the Protestant Reformation.

Just as dangerous as actual travel, for Ascham, was the proliferation of the Italian books that he noted were being sold in every shop in London. It had been bad enough in former times, he declares, when few books were read except works of chivalry like the *Morte d'Arthur*, 'the whole pleasure of which booke standeth in two speciall poyntes, in open mans slaughter, and bold bawdrye', but 'ten *Morte Arthures* do not the tenth part so much harme, as one of these bookes, made in *Italie*, and translated in England'. These Italian works are especially pernicious, Ascham thinks, because of their power to allure wits to wantonness through their arousal of pleasure. Once that happens, such books, 'carying the will to vanitie, and marryng good maners, shall easily corrupt the mynde with ill opinions, and false iudgement in doctrine', so that 'Mo Papistes be made, by your mery bookes of *Italie*, than by your earnest bookes of *Louain*'. In fact, Ascham surmises, the proliferation of Italian books in England was a plot by papists at home to speed up the turning of English men and women from the true religion.[41]

Reading between the lines of Ascham's diatribe, one can infer what had happened. The extremity of puritan moral castigation, and the self-righteous insistence of puritans on a pleasure-denying austerity of 'godly' living, had provoked a reaction. This can be inferred from Ascham's concession that those reading the 'bawdie bookes' translated out of Italian 'do now boldly contemne all seuere bookes that sounde to honestie and godlines'.[42] Symptomatically, 'they haue in more reuerence, the triumphes of Petrarche: than the Genesis of Moses: They make more accounte of *Tullies* offices, than *S. Paules* epistles: of a tale in *Bocace*, than a storie of the Bible'.[43] Ascham viewed such reading as promoting epicureanism on one hand, and atheism on the other: 'They mocke the Pope: They raile on *Luther*: They allow neyther side: They like none, but onelie themselues: The marke they shote at, the ende they looke for, the heauen they desire, is onelie, their owne present pleasure, and priuate proffit'.[44] Behind the polemical colorations of Ascham's rhetoric, one can discern a situation in which a very large body of English men and women were rejecting the world-renouncing strictures of

39 See Ascham, *English Works*, p. 228.
40 Ibid., p. 226.
41 Ibid., pp. 230–1.
42 Ibid., p. 230.
43 Ibid., p. 232.
44 Ibid., p. 233.

puritanism in favour of the very different discursive configurations to be found in Italian fiction. Quite simply, these people did not want to be deprived of all things ornamental, nor did they wish to be denied the possibility of a vicarious engagement with the most basic realities of human experience through the sensuous imagination. For men and women of this inclination, Italian literature provided a source of the very type of pleasure that Calvinist doctrine was denouncing as the 'inchantementes of sinne'. More than that, this literature was configured in ways that suggested an alternative, very different vision of life to that which Protestantism in its extreme tendency was trying to enforce. Ascham was indeed right to fear 'the Siren songes of Italie', because they had the power to divert wayfaring Christians from their journey to Geneva. The only way to resist these songs, in his view, was for a man to imitate Ulysses in stopping his ears with wax, binding himself to the mast of his ship, and feeding daily upon the sweet moly of truth that is given and taught by God alone – yet this was what many English men and women were obdurately refusing to do.[45]

Unsurprisingly, this desire to experience the Italianate fictive world as an alternative to the austerities of Calvinism manifested itself first in a phase of reception and reading – the one noted by Ascham – which began in the mid-1560s and lasted until the late 1570s. Then, a prolonged period of creative imitation and transformation began in about 1580 that would last through to the early years of the seventeenth century. In part, this second phase evolved naturally out of the earlier interest in reading and translation, but there were also particular causes for it that related directly to the changing political circumstances of Elizabeth I's reign.

In case after case, the nature of the transformations wrought by those who imitated Italian literary works suggests that, whether consciously or unconsciously, Italianate imitation was a response to the very real threat of national disintegration, and that its purpose was to construct, variously and individually, a sense of identity that could enable people to feel that their individual impulses could be reconciled with the imperatives of the state as it sought, through coercive measures, to impose the religion by which, according to the Settlement of 1559, it had decided its nature should be defined. Above all, the vast majority of English people wanted their nation to retain the distinctive national identity that had been tossed to them by Henry VIII's decision to break from Rome in pursuit of his 'great matter'.

By the late 1570s, the Elizabethan regime and the social order it sustained faced a multitude of dangers, largely as a consequence of events precipitated by Pope Pius V's excommunication of the Queen in February 1570.[46] By

45 Ibid., pp. 226–7.
46 See Elton, *England Under the Tudors*, pp. 295–314.

declaring Elizabeth excommunicate and deposed, the Pope terminated any likelihood that the Anglican Church could remain comprehensive. On one hand, the obligations of conscience forced English Catholics to choose between their country and their religion, while on the other, fear that England would revert to Catholicism and foreign domination moved Protestants towards an intensifying extremism. Lurking in everyone's minds was the prospect that the imprisoned Mary Stuart might be made queen in the event that the Pope's decree could be enacted, and thereafter she became the focus of ceaseless plots aimed at destroying Elizabeth's rule.

An equally sinister danger surfaced in 1579 with the renewed suit of Francis, Duke of Alençon, the younger brother of the French king, for marriage with Elizabeth. To her subjects, the Queen looked as if she was seriously contemplating a French match, and the country took fright. The massacre of Huguenots on St Bartholomew's Eve, 1572, had given English Protestants a horrific image of what they might expect should English government fall under the influence of a French consort from a family notorious for its fanatical Catholicism.

Furnishing the backdrop to these internal tensions was a further source of anxiety: the prospect of a war with Spain. Such a war grew increasingly likely with the gradual crumbling of the traditional alliance between England and Spain after the accession of Elizabeth, and the development of commercial rivalry and religious hostility between the two nations. From the moment Pius V excommunicated Elizabeth, the onset of war was delayed only by the skill of the Queen in disguising her intentions, and the difficulty experienced by France and Spain in discovering the grounds of an alliance that would make a successful war against England possible. But throughout the 1570s and early 1580s the threat of war was constantly hovering in the air, and when it came in 1585, it would last through the remaining eighteen years of Elizabeth's reign.

In the circumstances, the prospect of the disintegration of the Elizabethan Protestant state made it all the more necessary for those who wished to pre-serve it to find a way of sustaining a sense of national unity and identity, par-ticularly given that the Queen – upon whom that unity depended – professed a deep-rooted abhorrence towards the puritan vision of a reformed Church and state that was the likely alternative to compromise embodied in the Settlement of 1559.[47] In its own way, Italianate imitation made possible an imaginative image of the only kind of unity that could hold the country together – by creating a discourse in which the signifying world of Catholicism could be reconciled with the most essential tenets of Protestant belief in order to give expression to a distinctive sense of English Protestant identity commensurate with that which the Elizabethan state had sought to secure.[48]

---

[47] Strype, *Annals*, vol. 2, part 1, p. 94.

[48] I here invoke the concept of a *mundus significans* proffered by Thomas M. Greene: 'the

The task that writers like Sidney, Spenser and Shakespeare set themselves was to seize upon the attributes of Italian writing that they and their compatriots were finding attractive, and to imitate them in such a way as to construct an illuminated understanding of the right relation between worldly and spiritual goods as viewed from a Protestant perspective. To do so, they sought to appropriate the signifying capacities, thematic preoccupations and expressive devices of Italian literature – its symbolic vocabulary, verbal polyphony, plot configurations, character types, generic forms and, above all, its preoccupation with the most basic experiential realities of human life. Thus, in Petrarch's lyric poems they found the representation of a struggle between erotic and religious desire that made the attainment of a stable location for self well-nigh impossible. The more reflective among English sonneteers were quick to exploit the potential of Petrarchism to serve as a vehicle for the investigation of their own comparable struggles, made all the more acute by the contest taking place in the English Church between opposed religious tendencies. In Boccaccio and the other *novellieri*, English writers found tales dealing with almost every imaginable aspect of ordinary human life – of sexual intrigue, youthful love, hypocritical deceit and clever resourcefulness capable of turning vicissitudes to advantage – narrated with a sense of irony that underscored the comedy, folly, pathos and tragedy inherent in human situations, and the multitudinous variety of different human types, from princes to artisans, bishops to friars, merchants to money-lenders, lechers to lovers, and a host of virtuous virgins, deceitful wives, and noble men and women of the most egregious folly or criminal depravity. In the epic romances of Ariosto and Tasso they found heroic actions performed against powerful enemies by noble characters who were humanized through the experience of love, and governed by the chivalric gallantry of contemporary Italian culture. And in the Italian pastorals of Sannazzaro, Tasso and Guarini, they discovered how effectively the actuality of worldly troubles could be counterpoised against the haunting imaginative possibility of a golden world of idealized simplicity, tranquillity, harmony and absence from care, as a means both of recuperating the mind and sensibility, and also of intimating the hypothetic regenerative possibilities inherent in the created world.

The aim of imitation was to intercept the secondary codes inherent in these expressive forms so as to modify any epistemological assumptions in them that were not consistent with a Protestant sense of human nature and humans' spiritual responsibilities. In this way, the signifying world of the original could be transformed and extended, either by seeking a synthesis between the codes of the two cultures, or by placing them in an interrogatory

---

meaning of each verbal work of art has to be sought within its unique semiotic matrix, what might be called a mundus significans, a signifying universe, which is to say a rhetorical and symbolic vocabulary, a storehouse of signifying capacities potentially available to each member of a given culture' (*The Light in Troy: Imitation and Discovery in Renaissance Poetry* (New Haven and London, 1982), p. 20).

relationship with one another. In both cases, the result was the creation of a new cultural complex serving the needs of the discursive communities who pursued or responded to this activity: the royal court, the aristocratic patronage network that centred on the Earl of Leicester, and the circle surrounding Sidney known as the 'Areopagus'.[49]

One can see this transformative engagement with Italian literature in action throughout the 1580s and 1590s and, to a decreasing extent, in the first decade of the seventeenth century. It is apparent in Spenser's metamorphosis of Petrarch's introverted 'desio' into a reciprocal charity attained by the lovers of the *Amoretti*, which in turn makes possible a fulfilment of desire in the 'spotlesse pleasure' legitimized by marriage unknown to Petrarch. It is also apparent in Spenser's conversion of the representational configurations found in *Orlando furioso* and *Gerusalemme liberata* into a symbolic allegory of psychological processes encountered by the individual in a regenerative experience of the world, and also of England's experience of those processes in the larger arena of English history. If one turns to the world of pastoral, it is apparent in the way that Sidney introduces sin into Sannazzaro's golden world of tranquillity, peacefulness, simplicity and harmony, so as to turn Arcadia into a mirror of the forces at work in political situations, capable of furnishing an educative insight into how subjects – like himself – should conduct themselves.

A comparable impulse is visible in English imitations of the pastoral plays of Tasso and Guarini, which a poet like Daniel will turn into a vehicle for the representation of vices afflicting England in *The Queenes Arcadia* (1605), and which a dramatist like John Fletcher will use to show, in *The Faithful Shepherdess* (1608), the symbolic cleansing of the commonwealth through the healing power of chastity allied with an unmoveable constancy.

Above all, it is pre-eminently manifest in Shakespeare's handling of his Italian sources. One observes how he exposes the presence of darker forces at work in human nature, as when, for example, he changes the instigator of the deception in *Much Ado about Nothing* from a young knight driven by 'a frenzy of amorous desire' into a bastard malcontent who is motivated by malice and envy, or when in *Twelfth Night* he replaces the farcical *senex amans* of *Gl' ingannati* with the more morally sinister Malvolio. One also notes how he replaces the indulgent morality of his Italian sources with a sterner value system, as when he symbolically forces Falstaff to hide in 'stinking clothes that fretted in their own grease', rather than the 'fresh washing' of the source,[50] or when he replaces the amoral copulations of Fabrizio and Isabella, and Flammineo and Lelia, with the chaster 'betrothals' of Viola and Orsino,

---

[49] See Richard Helgerson, *Forms of Nationhood: The Elizabethan Writing of England* (Chicago, 1992), pp. 14–15.
[50] *The Merry Wives of Windsor*, III.v.100–1.

and Olivia and Sebastian. On a larger scale, one watches Shakespeare interrogate both Italian codes and English Protestant ones by putting them into problematical relationship with one another, as when in *Measure for Measure* he transforms Cinthio's Epitia, who easily surrenders her chastity to save her brother, into the puritanical Isabella, who chooses her chastity over her brother's life, thus turning a focus on right versus might into an issue of charity and how far it might extend in a world where sinful impulses are a fact of human nature. Shifting to the world of tragedy, one watches him, in *Othello*, take the lurid and comparatively mundane tale of an Italianate love triangle from *Gli ecatommiti* and discover in it the very well-springs of the capacity for evil in human nature.

Altogether, then, Italianate literary imitation came to serve a far more important purpose than the mere observance of fashion in the later Elizabethan period. It allowed people to engage imaginatively with a cultural 'Other' from which tendencies within their own ethos were threatening to bar them; it allowed Protestant assumptions and values to be illuminated before what Sidney would describe as 'the imaginative and judging power' because of the more powerfully affective representations it enabled; and it allowed the codes of both cultures to be imaginatively scrutinized and evaluated through the interreferential processes that imitation entailed. In its effects, creative imitation had the potential to inform and affirm opinion so as to influence political outcomes, especially through the creation of a persuasive new discourse in whose mode and manner could be felt the inclusive principles underlying the Elizabethan state itself. The rest of this book will be concerned with a more particular demonstration of the ways in which these functions of Italianate imitation realized themselves in the works of some of the greatest writers of the age.

2

Wyatt, Surrey and the Onset of
English Petrarchism

The earliest and most obvious manifestation of Italian literary influence in
England was Petrarchism, which – apart from Chaucer's brief translation of
Petrarch's 'S' amor non è, che dunque è quel ch' io sento' in *Troilus and
Criseyde* – was introduced by Sir Thomas Wyatt when he began to imitate
certain of Petrarch's *Rime sparse* in English from the late 1520s onwards, and
by his younger contemporary, Henry Howard, Earl of Surrey. It is extremely
instructive to compare these Petrarchan poets who wrote in the reign of
Henry VIII with those who wrote in the reign of Elizabeth I, for the
comparison underlines the decisive effect that the Protestant Reformation
had on the work of most of the later writers.

When Wyatt and Surrey composed their Petrarchan poems, although the
political Reformation was well and truly under way, the religious
Reformation had hardly begun; indeed, early steps taken in that direction
were largely reversed in the later years of Henry VIII's reign. Surrey, moreover,
was a staunch Catholic. Their respective personal situations are reflected in
the tenor of their respective Petrarchan imitations. Wyatt, because of his deep
personal entanglement in the troubles of the Henrician political
Reformation, wrote many of his Petrarchan imitations as a response to the
traumatic effects of those troubles on his psychic being.[1] Surrey, one suspects,
imitated Petrarch simply in response to the taste for Italian fashions that was
invading Henry's court through this period. In both cases, the nature of their
circumstances and motives ensures that the Protestant inflections and
thematic preoccupations to be found in the Petrarchan poems of Sidney,
Spenser and Shakespeare are completely absent. Protestant overtones do enter

---

[1] See Alistair Fox, *Politics and Literature in the Reigns of Henry VII and Henry VIII* (Oxford,
1989), chap. 14.

the works of Wyatt in his *Penitential Psalms* (1541), based on Pietro Aretino's *I setti salmi*,[2] but these were written towards the end of his career, long after he had composed the erotic poems that he derived from imitation of Petrarch. Surrey's erotic Petrarchan imitations were written well before his own encounter with the political manoeuvrings that were to lead to his own untimely beheading in 1547. Before one can appreciate the subtle effects of these differences, however, it is necessary to identify the basic characteristics of Petrarch's own poetry that turned it into such a useful vehicle for personal expression once evolving historical circumstances in the sixteenth century gave English poets an incentive, through creative imitation, to turn it to their own purposes.

The enormous impact of Francesco Petracco (or Petrarca) on Western Europe during the Renaissance is too well known to need much rehearsing. Born in Arezzo on 20 July 1304, Petrarch was instrumental in fostering the revival of classical learning and composed a large number of poems in the Italian vernacular that form one of the most striking bodies of lyric poetry the world has seen. Through the patronage of ecclesiastical and secular potentates like Cardinal Giovanni Colonna in Rome and the Visconti in Milan, and through his network of learned and princely correspondents across Europe, Petrarch, because of his unique talent, achieved both fame and influence. It is with the response of English poets to his vernacular lyric poetry, and especially his erotic poems that Petrarch named *Rime sparse*, that this chapter will be primarily concerned.

Europe's fascination with Petrarch's poetry resulted from his unique poetic persona and the distinctive devices he used to express a very complex emotional experience. Throughout his life, Petrarch was torn between rival impulses: on one hand, a powerful desire to gratify worldly desires, and, on the other, a yearning to abandon the 'false fleeting sweetness which the treacherous world gives' ('quel falso dolce fuggitivo / ch 'l mondo traditor può dar') in search of heaven.[3] The struggle was unequal, as Petrarch constantly tells us in his poetry:

> vo ripensando ov' io lassai 'l viaggio
> da la man destra ch' a buon porto aggiunge:
> et da l'un lato punge
> vergogna et duol che 'ndietro mi rivolve,
> dall'altro non m'assolve
> un piacer per usanza in me sì forte
> ch' a pattegiar n'ardisce co la Morte.

2 See H.A. Mason, *Sir Thomas Wyatt: A Literary Portrait* (Bristol, 1986), pp. 160–3.
3 *Rime*, no. 264, ll. 28–9, in Francesco Petrarca, *Petrarch's Lyric Poems: The Rime sparse and Other Lyrics*, trans. and ed. Robert M. Durling (Cambridge, Massachusetts, and London, 1976). All references to Petrarch's *Rime* are to this edition.

(I go thinking back where I left the journey to the right, which reaches a good port: and on one side I am pierced by shame and sorrow, which turn me back; on the other I am not freed from a pleasure so strong in me by habit that it dares to bargain with Death).[4]

As Petrarch confesses in the *Secretum* (an imagined dialogue between himself and his spiritual mentor, St Augustine of Hippo), two great impediments blocked him from fulfilling his spiritual quest: love for a woman named Laura, which lasted from the time he first saw her on 6 April 1327 until her death twenty years later, and his immoderate desire for glory.[5] At times, Petrarch toyed with a belief that he could sublimate the erotic impulse by viewing it as the means whereby he might attain the fulfilment of his spiritual desire – as when he sees in his lady's eyes 'un dolce lume / che mi mostra la via ch' al ciel conduce' (a sweet light that shows me the way that leads to Heaven).[6] More often than not, however, he simply seeks release from a fierce and uncontrollable erotic desire ('quel fero desio ch' al cor s'accese') that seems like a 'pitiless yoke'.[7] Even when Laura was dead, Petrarch found that his love for her, and his thirst for the poetic fame that eulogizing her had procured him – so aptly conflated in his use of the laurel image to pun on her name 'Laura' ('laurel') while suggesting the laureate poet's triumphal wreath. – still had the power to lead him astray: 'veggio 'l meglio et al peggior m' appiglio' (I see the better but I lay hold on the worse).[8]

The presence of this deeper conflict between rival earthly and spiritual impulses, along with the admixture of guilt, shame and anxiety that it produced, invested Petrarch's poetry with a peculiar force, even when he was using motifs that were conventional in earlier medieval or classical traditions. Characteristically, he presented himself as being caught in the grips of an infinitely protracted, unresolvable and indefinable tension:

Amor, avegna mi sia tardi accorto,
vol che tra duo contrari mi distempre.

(Love, though I have been tardy in seeing it,
wishes me to be untuned between two contraries).[9]

---

[4] *Rime*, no. 264, ll. 120–6.
[5] Francesco Petrarca, *Petrarch's Secret, or the Soul's Conflict with Passion: Three Dialogues between Himself and S. Augustine*, trans. W.H. Draper (London, 1911). The original Latin text may be found, with an Italian translation, in Francesco Petrarca, *Prose*, ed. G. Martellotti and others, La Letteratura Italiana: Storia e Testi, vol. 7 (Milan and Naples, 1955), pp. 22–215.
[6] *Rime*, no. 72, ll. 2–3.
[7] *Rime*, no. 62, ll. 3, 10.
[8] *Rime*, no. 264, l. 136.
[9] *Rime*, no. 55, ll. 13–14.

To convey a sense of this suspended, decentred state, Petrarch often creates images of dispersion, fragmentation, turbulence or aimlessness that are often developed in the form of evocative comparisons, or 'conceits':

> Fra sì contrari venti in frale barca
> mi trovo in alto mar senza governo,
>
> sì lieve di saver, d'error sì carca
> ch' i' medesmo non so quel ch' io mi voglio,
> e tremo a mezza state, ardendo il verno.

(Amid such contrary winds I find myself at sea in a frail bark, without a tiller, so light of wisdom, so laden with error, that I myself do not know what I want; and I shiver in midsummer, burn in winter.)[10]

Perhaps his favourite device was the rhetorical figure of oxymoron, the paradoxical antitheses of which Petrarch similarly used to evoke the experience of simultaneously undergoing contradictory processes for which there is no resolution:

> Pace non trovo et non ò da far guerra,
> e temo et spero, et ardo et son un ghiaccio,
> et volo sopra 'l cielo et giaccio in terra,
> et nulla stringo et tutto 'l mondo abbraccio.

(Peace I do not find, and I have no wish to make war; and I fear and hope, and burn and am of ice; and I fly above the heavens and lie on the ground; and I grasp nothing and embrace all the world.)[11]

The distinctive state of feeling that Renaissance Europe found so fascinating in Petrarch's poetry was generated largely by this pervasive oxymoronism, the effects of which have been excellently described:

> [t]his collapse and this division in the oxymoron constitute a powerful *modus significandi*, a brilliant expressive device which, in the radicality of its use by Petrarch, ceases to be a cliché of the rhetoric of love and becomes an original, disturbing vehicle for statement. The language is forever falling back into a consciousness so mercurial as to seem ineffable. The succession of each mood, feeling, image, analysis seems to contaminate its predecessor, to pile up paradoxical simultaneities; the language seems always to be straining to represent an inner state more mobile, more divided and elusive, than itself so that even its reflexive reference to the consciousness that grounds it is finally frustrated. The division of meaning is meaningful; it corresponds to the shifts, velleities,

---

10 *Rime*, no. 132, ll. 10–14.
11 *Rime*, no. 134, ll. 1–4.

reflexivities, antagonisms, and ruptures of a psyche torn by moral conflict, ill at ease within a body, and suspicious of its own good faith.[12]

Petrarch's poetry appealed to his contemporaries and successors because the state of consciousness it evoked could serve as an imaginative correlative for the divided impulses that many men and women were experiencing during their encounter with the shifting circumstances of the Renaissance world itself.

The first to respond to Petrarch's influence were contemporaries such as Boccaccio, Antonio da Ferrara and Geri Gianfigliazzi, whose example would be followed by countless others among succeeding generations of Italian poets, including Sannazzaro, Serafino Aquilano (1466–1550), Agnolo Fiorenzuolo, Ariosto, Michelangelo Buonarroti (1475–1564) and Torquato Tasso. Elsewhere in Europe, Petrarch's poems were soon being imitated in France and Spain, and when English poets belatedly responded to Petrarch in the sixteenth century, it was often by way of French authors such as Joachim Du Bellay (1522–60), Philippe Desportes and Pierre de Ronsard (1524–60), who in turn had based their work on imitations of Petrarch by a host of his later Italian successors (many of them comparatively minor), such as Angelo di Costanzo, Antonio Tebaldeo (1463–1537), Luigi Tansillo, Pamfilo Sasso and Gesualdo.[13] These subsequent poets were quick to appropriate the new poetic mode for their own purposes. From the *Rime* they learnt how to sustain 'invention' through the use of conceits; to achieve emotive and thematic effects through figurative devices such as oxymoron, antithesis and the repetition or variation of key words; to create a quality of music new to verse through phonological and rhythmic patterning; and to enrich poetic representation through the allusive evocation of the great classical poets, especially Ovid, Virgil and Horace. They also found Petrarch's erotic psychology useful for constructing their own erotic personae as part of the 'game of love' that remained fashionable in Renaissance courts. During the next two centuries, in fact, there was a mania across Europe to copy 'poore *Petrarch's* long deceased woes / With new-borne sighes and denisend wit'.[14]

Petrarchism, as with other types of Italianate literary imitation, was very late in arriving in England, and, as I have suggested, its first appearance was due to Sir Thomas Wyatt's discovery that Petrarchan imitation could be actively

---

[12] Thomas M. Greene, *The Light in Troy: Imitation and Discovery in Renaissance Poetry* (New Haven and London, 1982), p. 118.

[13] On the French influence on English Petrarchists, see Anne Lake Prescott, *French Poets and the English Renaissance: Studies in Fame and Transformation* (New Haven, 1978).

[14] Philip Sidney, *Astrophil and Stella*, no. 15, l. 7. All quotations from Sidney's sonnet sequence are from Philip Sidney, *The Poems of Sir Philip Sidney*, ed. William A. Ringler, Jr (Oxford, 1962).

instrumental to a complex form of psychological, social and political self-management.

The reasons for Wyatt's absorption in Petrarch are not difficult to discern. Initially, his interest may have been stimulated, as with Surrey, by the affectation among Henry VIII and his courtiers of Italianate fashions at court soon after the new king's accession in 1509. It undoubtedly grew when Wyatt himself spent some time in Italy in 1527. During this time he was captured and imprisoned by imperial troops for several months, which may have given him the opportunity and leisure to read the poetry of Petrarch and the other Italian writers whom he imitates in his own poetry, such as Serafino and Sannazzaro. A deeper prompting, however, sprang from his own temperament and psychology. Wyatt led a very troubled love life that is likely to have rendered him very responsive to the psychological condition he found represented in Petrarch.[15] On one hand he was married to a woman for whom he had an acute aversion. On the other, having been involved in a love affair with Anne Boleyn, who deserted him to marry Henry VIII, Wyatt found himself besotted by desire for someone he could never obtain. The defection of his mistress, which Wyatt viewed as a treacherous betrayal that he ascribed to venality, dealt a severe shock to his psychic being. It left him feeling helplessly vulnerable at an emotional level because of the unguarded extent to which he had committed his fidelity to her, and because it removed the foundations of his sense of personal identity:

> Alas! I tred an endles maze
> That seketh to accorde two contraries;
> And hope still, and nothing hase,
> Imprisoned in libertes,
> As oon unhard and still that cries;
> Alwaies thursty and yet nothing I tast:
> For dred to fall I stond not fast.[16]

When, as a result of his close relationships with Anne Boleyn and Thomas Cromwell, Wyatt became entangled in the dangerous political fallout attending their downfalls in 1536 and 1541 respectively, this existential anxiety and insecurity of identity merely intensified.

For a man with Wyatt's psychological complexes and emotional uncertainties Petrarch's representation of a self caught in the processes of an infinitely protracted warfare between unresolvable conflicts and desires held irresistible appeal. While the two men were a world apart in terms of sensibility and worldly circumstances, in the crucial matter of psychological

---

[15] See Fox, *Politics and Literature*, pp. 260–7.
[16] Thomas Wyatt, *Collected Poems of Sir Thomas Wyatt*, ed. Kenneth Muir and Patricia Thomson, Liverpool English Texts and Studies (Liverpool, 1969), no. 21, ll. 8–14.

construction they were remarkably similar. Both were prisoners of an erotic attraction from which they could not break free; both experienced an unresolvable instability of self as a result of it; and both would express a powerful urge towards penitence and a desire for spiritualized transcendence as the final remedy for their struggles – Petrarch in the concluding poems of the *Rime*, and Wyatt in the *Penitential Psalms* written in 1541 near the end of his life. It is not surprising, therefore, that Wyatt should have been instinctively drawn to Petrarch: the experience represented poetically by the Italian poet could provide the imaginative form through which the essence of his own experience could be expressively actualized and projected.

The primary function of Petrarchan imitation for Wyatt was to serve as a vehicle for displaced self-expression. Having been severely damaged at an emotional level by the Boleyn affair, Wyatt needed to find an outlet for his feelings, and he discovered that the state of mind and emotions represented by Petrarch could, with minor modifications, be used for the vicarious representation of his own. Even when Wyatt translates a Petrarchan poem so closely as to suggest that his main motive is simply to copy its form and substance, subtle transformations take place that imply a deeper purpose than imitation alone.

This can be illustrated from Wyatt's translation of Petrarch's sonnet, 'Son animali al mondo'. Petrarch's original reads:

Son animali al mondo de sì altera
vista che 'ncontra 'l sol pur si difende;
altri, però che 'l gran lume gli offende,
non escon fuor se non verso la sera;

et altri, col desio folle che spera
gioir forse nel foco, perché splende,
provan l'altra vertù, quella ch' ncende,
lasso, e 'l mio loco è 'n questa ultima schera.

Ch' i' non son forte ad aspettar la luce
di questa donna, et non so fare schermi
di luoghi tenebrosi o d'ore tarde;

però con gli occhi lagrimosi e 'nfermi
mio destino a vederla mi conduce,
et so ben ch' i' vo dietro a quel che m'arde.[17]

(There are animals in the world of sight so audacious that it withstands even the sun; others, because the great light harms them, do not come out except toward evening;

---

[17] *Rime*, no. 19.

and others, with their mad desire that hopes perhaps to enjoy the fire because it shines, experience the other power, the one that burns; alas, and my place is in this last band.

For I am not strong enough to look on the light of this lady, and I do not know how to make a shield of shadowy places and late hours;

therefore my destiny leads me, with tearful and weak eyes, to see her: and I know well I am pursuing what burns me.)

Wyatt's translation follows the original very closely:

> Som fowles there be that have so perfaict sight,
>   Agayn the Sonne their Iyes for to defend,
>   And some, because the light doeth theim offend,
>   Do never pere but in the darke or nyght.
> Other reioyse that se the fyer bright
>   And wene to play in it as they do pretend,
>   And fynd the contrary of it that they intend.
> Alas, of that sort I may be by right,
> For to withstond her loke I ame not able;
>   And yet can I not hide me in no darke place,
>   Remembraunce so foloweth me of that face,
> So that with tery yen swolne and vnstable,
>   My destyne to behold her doeth me lede;
>   Yet do I knowe I runne into the glede.[18]

It is a testimony to Wyatt's skill that his version seems even closer to the original than the literal translation, despite the fact that a number of words are not rendered so precisely. This is because Wyatt seeks to reproduce the form of Petrarch's poem as well as its meaning. He goes as far as to copy several of Petrarch's rhymes ('difende', 'offende' / 'defend', 'offend'), and also his syntax (for example, in lines 12–13). Indeed, it is hard to imagine that anyone could come closer to achieving a more exact translation of the poem as a whole than this.

Nevertheless, in spite of the closeness of the translation, the words chosen introduce a new set of connotations that betray its personal signifying function for Wyatt. He specifies Petrarch's 'animali' more narrowly as 'fowles', and reduces 'altera vista' (proud sight) to 'perfaict sight'. Both alterations have the effect of diminishing the stature of the beasts by suppressing the sense of their pride and audacity. These beasts nonetheless have a power of seeing that is further reinforced by the reference to 'peering' in the darkness, an idea not present in the source at all. Altogether these changes in the first stanza

---

[18] Wyatt, *Collected Poems*, no. 24, pp. 19–20.

introduce a new set of metaphoric overtones that intimate a more restrained sense of what would constitute prudent action, and that sense in turn implies Wyatt's own awareness of what it would take to negotiate one's way successfully in the world of the Tudor court.

Wyatt's more highly developed sense of Tudor political realities, in fact, lies behind most of the changes he makes to the source in this poem. It leads him to tone down the suggestion, in the second quatrain, of a reckless surrender to libido in Petrarch's reference to 'altri, col desio folle che spera gioir forse nel foco' (others, with their mad desire that hopes perhaps to enjoy the fire), which Wyatt changes to the more innocuous 'Other reioyse that se the fyer bright / And wene to play in it as they do pretend'. Indeed, every detail in the poem that suggests the perception of life in romanticized terms is converted to a bleaker, more constrained alternative so as to accord with Wyatt's sense of the different context in which he had to operate. Petrarch's 'luoghi tenebrosi' (shadowy places), with their sensuous evocation of a romantic setting and an alleviating shade, is replaced by an emotionally blacker 'darke place' that foreshadows the 'dark Cave / Within the grownd' into which Wyatt would later have King David withdraw to enact his penitence, 'Fleing the lyght, as in pryson or grave'.[19] He also substitutes the man for the lady as the object of the gaze in line 9, by rephrasing Petrarch's 'non son forte ad aspettar la luce / di questa donna' as 'to withstond her loke I ame not able', which deprives the lover of any remaining vestiges of self-agency. The additional line that Wyatt adds immediately following may contain a hint of the root cause of both his erotic and political pessimism. When Wyatt confesses that he is unable to find a place to hide because 'Remembraunce so foloweth me of that face' (l. 11), he is probably alluding to the face of 'Her that did set our country in a rore' (Anne Boleyn) whom he had been forced to 'refrayne'.[20] At a later date, when Wyatt had found a new mistress, that face would be replaced by 'Th' unfayned chere of Phillis',[21] but for the time being, the daily necessity of seeing, and serving, the woman of whom he had been deprived invested Wyatt's translation of the final two lines of Petrarch's sonnet with an extra depth of meaning:

> My destyne to behold her doeth me lede;
> Yet do I knowe I runne into the glede.

> (mio destino a vederla mi conduce,
> et so ben ch' i' vo dietro a quel che m'arde.)

Most of Wyatt's Petrarchan translations function in this way. The changes are slight, but they all serve to turn the poem into a vehicle for Wyatt's own self-

---

19 Wyatt, 'Penitential Psalms', *Collected Poems*, p. 100/60–2.
20 Wyatt, *Collected Poems*, no. 97, p. 78, variant reading.
21 Ibid.

expression.[22] Apart from substituting words with different connotations, he frequently suppresses Petrarch's rhythmic and melodic effects when to replicate them would create a contrary emotional impression to that which he is seeking. For instance, whereas Petrarch, in likening himself to a ship passing through a stormy sea ('Passa la nave mia'), describes how

la vela rompe un vento umido eterno
di sospir, di speranze et di desio

(a wet, changeless wind of sighs, hopes and desires breaks the sail),

Wyatt's version reads:

An endles wynd doeth tere the sayll a pase
Of forced sightes and trusty ferefulnes.[23]

Here, in the process of translation, Wyatt has flattened the rhythm of the original through replacing its carefully arranged pattern of consonants, syllables and words with a more prosaic and regular arrangement, the monotony of which serves to evoke a bleaker, more depressed emotional condition.

Similarly, Wyatt almost invariably suppresses the more decorative and sensuously evocative of Petrarch's visual images. For example, when he translates Petrarch's charming madrigal, 'Or vedi, Amor', Wyatt replaces the picture of the young woman 'in treccie e 'n gonna / si siede et scalza in mezzo i fiori et l'erba' (in a mere robe with loose hair ... sitting barefoot amid the flowers and the grass) with the comparatively bland reference to a mistress who 'vnarmed sitteth'.[24] In translating the sonnet 'O bella man che mi destringi 'l core', he eliminates most of the detail with which Petrarch describes his lady's hand: Petrarch's 'cinque perle oriental colore, ... diti schietti soavi ... ignudi' (neat soft fingers ... naked ... the colour of five oriental pearls) becomes simply 'fyngers slight ... So long, so small, so rownd', while the reference to her 'Candido leggiadretto et caro guanto / che copria netto avorio et fresche rose' (White, light, and dear glove, that covered clear ivory and fresh roses) is replaced with a far less voluptuous and more conventional reference to the

---

22 For example, Wyatt, *Collected Poems*, no. 32 ('How oft have I, my dere and cruell foo'), translating *Rime*, no. 21 ('Mille fiate, o dolce mia guerrera'); no. 98 ('So feble is the threde'), translating *Rime*, no. 37 ('Sì debile il filo'); no. 25 ('Bicause I have the still kept fro lyes and blame'), translating *Rime*, no. 49 ('Perch' io t'abbia guardata di menzogna'); no. 9 ('Was I never, yet, of your love greved'), translating *Rime*, no. 82 ('Io non fu' d'amar voi lassato unquanco'); and no. 26 ('I fynde no peace and all my warr is done'), translating *Rime*, no. 134 ('Pace non trovo et non ò da far guerra').

23 Wyatt, *Collected Poems*, no. 28 ('My galy charged with forgetfulnes'), translating *Rime*, no. 189 ('Passa la nave mia colma d'oblio').

24 *Rime*, no. 121, ll 4–5; Wyatt, *Collected Poems*, no. 1, l. 6.

lady's hand as having the colour of 'Lilis whight / And Roses bright'.[25] The reason for the suppression of these sensuously evocative details is that their inclusion would intimate an emotional attitude towards the beloved that was very different from the one that Wyatt actually wished to represent.

As well as facilitating the expression of private emotion, Petrarchan imitation had a secondary function in assisting Wyatt to conduct himself publicly in the world of the Tudor court. It did this by allowing him to construct a socially convenient persona – that of the Petrarchan lover. Ritual flirtation, affected in accordance with the conventional codes of courtly love, was a fashionable aspect of contemporary courtiership, and one of the ways it was conducted was through the exchange of poems that circulated round the court in manuscript miscellanies. Indeed, most of Wyatt's own poems first appeared in miscellanies of this sort, such as the Devonshire MS, which was owned by Mary Shelton, one of the ladies in the circle of Anne Boleyn. The persona created by Petrarch ideally lent itself to this courtly 'game of love', and by imitating it, Wyatt could disguise the depth of his true feelings by masquerading them publicly as convention, at the same time as he gave free expression of them. Such a strategy had the double advantage of allowing Wyatt to acknowledge his situation publicly, but in a way that emptied it of social humiliation because of the pretence that it was conventional.

Something of this social function is suggested in the final lines of Wyatt's translation of Petrarch's sonnet, 'Cesare, poi che 'l traditor d'Egitto'. Having likened himself to Caesar and Hannibal, in feeling a need to disguise his true feelings, Petrarch concludes:

> ... s' alcuna volta io rido o canto,
> facciol perch' i' non ò se non quest'una
> via da celare il mio angoscioso pianto.
> (ll. 12–14)

(... if at any time I laugh or sing, I do it because I have no way except this one to hide my anguished weeping.)

In Wyatt's version, the changes, as always, are subtle but revealing:

> ... if I laugh at eny tyme or season
>   It is by cause I have none other way
>   To cloke my care but vnder spoort and play.[26]

Wyatt's substitution of 'care' for Petrarch's more demonstrative 'angoscioso

---

[25] *Rime*, no. 199; Wyatt, *Collected Poems*, no. 86.
[26] Wyatt, *Collected Poems*, no. 3, ll. 12–14. I have adopted the reading of the Devonshire MS for these lines in preference to the one given by Muir and Thomson.

pianto', and his reinterpretation of the idea of laughing and singing as 'spoort and play' indicates a grief that has to be concealed decorously in a far more public context than that imagined by the Italian poet. In fact, it is a social performance that Wyatt is intimating, not the act of private introspection out of which Petrarch's poem arises.

A third function of Petrarchan imitation for Wyatt was that of disguised political comment and complaint. Its presence becomes apparent on occasions when Wyatt's substitutions wrench the Petrarchan original so far away from any erotic point of reference as to suggest that indignation or grief have intensified beyond self-pity. In Wyatt's translation of Petrarch's 'Passa la nave mia colma d'oblio', for example, the image of subjugation under the erotic power of Cupid in the original is made to suggest a helpless domination under the political power of the King by the transmutation of every detail that has an erotic referent. The sail on Wyatt's ship is torn not by 'un vento umido eterno / di sospir, di speranze et di desio' (a wet, changeless wind of sighs, hopes and desires), but by 'An endles wynd … Of forced sigh(t)es and trusty ferefulnes', which contains no suggestion of either hope or desire. Petrarch's reference to Laura's eyes, 'Celansi i duo mei dolci usati segni' (My two usual sweet stars are hidden), is rephrased as 'The starres be hid that led me to this pain', which allows for the idea of an evil fortune to be substituted for the erotic referent. Perhaps the most daring substitution is the translation of 'sightes' for Petrarch's 'sospir' in the version of the poem that appears in Wyatt's own personal manuscript, the Egerton MS, as against the literal 'sighes' that occurs in later editions such as the Arundel MS or Tottel's *Songes and Sonettes* (1557). The reading of 'sightes' may be the correct one, as it verbally echoes Wyatt's description of the occasion in June 1536 on which he watched the execution of Anne Boleyn from his cell in the Tower:

> The bell towre showed me suche syght
> That in my hed stekys day and nyght;
> Ther dyd I lerne out of a grate,
> Ffor all vauore, glory or myght,
> That yet *circa Regna tonat*.[27]

Through the addition of one consonant, Wyatt has audaciously shifted the referent from the erotic to the political in accordance with the general drift of the whole poem. These changes, combined with a stripping away of all decorativeness in the source (for example, the allusion to Scylla and Charybdis) create an emotional tonality that permits the poem to be read as a protest against despotism, for which the poet cannot be held to account should any reader be inclined to follow the hints.

---

[27] Wyatt, *Collected Poems*, no. 176, ll. 16–20. I have added the emphasis on 'syght'.

A further strategy Wyatt uses to turn Petrarch's poems into vehicles of political protest is to replace idealized images with debased alternatives. The most striking instance of this occurs in Wyatt's transmogrification of Petrarch's 'Una candida cerva' into 'Who so list to hounte'.[28] The extraordinary changes Wyatt effects in this poem have been frequently analysed, so they need be only briefly noted here.[29] Whereas Petrarch alludes to his mistress as a 'white doe on the green grass' who appears to him 'with two golden horns, between two rivers, in the shade of a laurel, when the sun was rising in the unripe season', for Wyatt the woman is simply a 'hynde' whom many men are pursuing in a 'hounte'. Wyatt has thus replaced images of chastity, beauty and vernal regenerative freshness with sordid antitheses, as 'hynde' and 'hounte' in the English tradition both have obscene sexual connotations. Similarly, whereas Petrarch describes the message around her 'lovely neck' ('al bel collo d'intorno') as being 'written with diamonds and topazes' ('scritto avea di diamanti et di topazi'), Wyatt eliminates the reference to topazes and substitutes 'graven' for 'written', thus transmuting what had been emblems of steadfastness and chastity in Petrarch into an emblem of cupidity. The message inscribed on the deer's collar is also altered. Petrarch alludes to the inscription which, in legend, was found on the collars of white deer that had belonged to Julius Caesar: 'Nessun mi tocchi ... Libera farmi al mio Cesare parve' (Let no one touch me ... It has pleased my Caesar to make me free). In doing so, he suggests that Laura, because of her chastity, belongs to a higher power, God. Wyatt reverts the wording of this inscription to that of the Scriptural text that it echoes: 'Noli me tangere for Cesars I ame'. Through this simple stroke, he evokes the warning of the resurrected Christ to Mary Magdalene that she should not touch him because he had not yet ascended to the Father, and thus activates a parodic comparison between the holiness of Christ and the polluted condition of his former mistress, who has ascended not into the possession of God but into that of a more literal Caesar, the King. The effect of these stunningly audacious transpositions is to deliver a vindicative protest at the treatment Wyatt feels he has received, which he would hardly dare to do in a more explicit way.

A final example of Wyatt's use of Petrarch for political comment can be found in 'The piller pearisht is whearto I Lent', a poem that expresses Wyatt's dismay at the fall and execution of his mentor and protector, Thomas Cromwell, in 1541. For this purpose he chose as his model a sonnet written by Petrarch on the death of his own patron, Cardinal Giovanni Colonna, on 3 July 1348: 'Rotta è l'alta colonna e' l verde lauro'.[30] Wyatt subjects this source to exactly the same kind of treatment that is evident in his conversion

[28] *Rime*, no. 190; Wyatt, *Collected Poems*, no. 7.
[29] See Greene, *The Light in Troy*, pp. 245–56; and Fox, *Politics and Literature*, pp. 262–4.
[30] Wyatt, *Collected Poems*, no. 236; *Rime*, no. 269.

of Petrarch's erotic poems. All decorative detail is removed: the allusion to the 'green laurel' (Laura), to exotic geographical locations ('dal mar indo al mauro'), and to orient gems and the power of gold ('né gemma oriental né forza d'auro'). In addition, any possibility of histrionic self-romanticization is stripped away. Wyatt achieves this by removing Petrarch's direct address to Death – 'Tolto m'ài, Morte, il mio doppio tesauro' (You have taken from me, O Death, my double treasure) – and replacing it with a reference to a depersonalized ill fortune that is responsible for his troubles:

> ... happe away hath rent
> Of all my ioye the vearye bark and rynde;
> And I (alas) by chaunce am thus assynde
> Dearlye to moorne till death do it relent.

He also eliminates the sententious moralizing comment with which Petrarch ends his poem:

> O nostra vita ch' è sì bella in vista,
> com' perde agevolmente in un matino
> quel ch 'n molti anni a gran pena s'acquista.

(Oh our life that is so beautiful to see, how easily it loses in one morning what has been acquired with great difficulty over many years!)

Wyatt replaces this by expanding and intensifying the rhetorical question in which Petrarch states his personal feelings:

> che posso io più se no aver l'alma trista,
> umidi gli occhi sempre, e 'l viso chino?

(what can I do except have my soul sad, my eyes always wet, and my face bent down?)

This becomes:

> What can I more but have a wofull hart,
> My penne in playnt, my voyce in wofull crye,
> My mynde in woe, my bodye full of smart,
> And I my self my self alwayes to hate
> Till dreadfull death do ease my dolefull state?

At moments such as these, one sees that imitation of Petrarch was anything but a distancing technique for Wyatt, even when it was designed to provide a protective shield. The cues are there in Petrarch, but Wyatt's 'mynde in woe' differs somewhat from Petrarch's 'alma trista', and the replacement of his reference to 'umidi occhi' (moist eyes) by Wyatt's admission of bodily pain and self-loathing suggests a far more troubled state of mind, reflective of the more dangerous circumstances Wyatt was confronting, than anything suggested in the Italian original.

One can conclude, on the basis of the use Wyatt made of Petrarch, that he was drawn to imitate him because of a compelling need to relieve the psychological pressures generated by his own troubled erotic and political experiences. Because the two were linked – in that his political difficulties were largely the product of his amorous entanglement with a woman whose doings, as he put it, 'did set our country in a rore' – he could adapt the pose and attitude he found represented in Petrarch's *Rime* to make them function as a displaced correlative for the expression of emotions relating to his own circumstances. Moreover, the Petrarchan pose allowed him simultaneously to construct a public mask that made it possible for him to negotiate his way through the world in which he had to move with decorum and some shreds of dignity. This complex blend of deeply personal and public motivations in Wyatt makes his response to, and use of, Petrarch absolutely unique and idiosyncratic. No one else was likely to experience anything resembling his dilemma, and, lacking his motives and distinctive temperamental makeup, no other English poet tried to make Petrarchan imitation function as Wyatt had done. As far as the general thesis of this book is concerned, the important point is that the changes Wyatt makes to his Petrarchan sources in the process of creative imitation are for the sake of existential self-definition, rather than for self-castigatory, self-corrective moral definition of the sort that one finds in the sonnets of Sidney, Spenser and Shakespeare.

None of the handful of Petrarchan imitations by Henry Howard, Earl of Surrey, have the signifying complexity of the poems by Wyatt just discussed. Several of his imitations, like 'The soote season, that bud and blome furth bringes', which imitates Petrarch's 'Zefiro torna e 'l bel tempo rimena',[31] are very loosely based on the original, with Surrey simply domesticating the Petrarchan sentiment by dressing it in Chaucerian diction and substituting particular details from the English natural setting for Petrarch's more aureate classical references to Zephyrus, Procne and Philomena. In other poems, like 'Set me wheras the sonne dothe perche the grene' (imitating 'Ponmi ove 'l sole occide i fiori et l'erba'), 'Love that doth raine and live within my thought' (imitating 'Amor, che nel penser mio vive et regna') and 'I never saw youe, madam, laye aparte' (imitating 'Lassare il velo per sole o per ombra'), Surrey's translation is extremely close, with what slight alterations of meaning there

---

[31] Henry Howard, Earl of Surrey, *Poems*, ed. Emrys Jones (Oxford, 1964), no. 2; *Rime*, no. 310.

are reflecting a difference of sensibility rather than a different signifying intention.[32] His most ambitious attempt at Petrarchan imitation is 'The sonne hath twyse brought forthe the tender grene', which is a pseudo-sestina imitating Petrarch's 'A qualunque animale alberga in terra', except that Surrey gives up altogether on attempting the Italian poet's intricately revolving rhyme scheme and substitutes a much simpler stanzaic form.[33] The poem consists of a tessellation of phrases, lines and motifs from a range of poems by Petrarch, which shows Surrey trying to appropriate the Petrarchan pose without any significant critical or affective modifications, other than those wrought by a slightly more prosaic, less demonstratively passionate sensibility. Surrey's ambition was to display his facility in fabricating newly imported poetic wares in English cloth, just as in his own manner of dress – on the evidence of the portrait by William Scrots – he affected the style of the Italian potentates whose equal, in his pride, he believed he was.

The brief excursion into Petrarchan imitation by Wyatt and Surrey came to an end with Surrey's execution for high treason as an overmighty subject who Henry VIII feared was aiming to usurp the throne. Following his death, apart from a desultory scattering of translations among the poems of Tottel's *Miscellany*, no further significant imitation would take place in England for another forty years – that is, until poets again felt a sufficiently powerful incentive – and when it did return, the motivations for Petrarchan imitation would be vastly different.

Signs of renewed interest began to appear in the late 1560s with the tentative efforts of George Turbervile, in *Epitaphes, Epigrams, Songs and Sonets* (1567), and of Thomas Howell, in *The Arbor of Amitie* (1568), both of which contained a small number of Petrarchan translations. The young Edmund Spenser also tried his hand at Petrarchan imitation by transforming Petrarch's *canzone* 'Standomi un giorno solo a la fenestra' into a series of epigrams for the Protestant polemical compilation, *A Theatre wherein be Represented as wel the Miseries & Calamities that Follow the Voluptuous Worldlings, as also the Greate Ioyes and Plesures which the Faithfull do Enioy*, printed in London by Henry Bynneman in 1569.[34] The onset of the real Petrarchan revival, however, was marked by the composition of Sir Philip Sidney's *Certain Sonnets* (1581) and *Astrophil and Stella* (1582). It was not until even later, when the posthumous publication of *Astrophil and Stella* in 1591 made Sidney's sequence available to a wider readership, that the major period of Petrarchan imitation got under way, with most English poets of the time trying their hand at the new mode under Sidney's influence.

---

[32] The poems are, respectively, Surrey, *Poems*, no. 3 / *Rime*, no. 145; Surrey, *Poems*, no. 4 / *Rime*, no. 140; Surrey, *Poems*, no. 6 / *Rime*, no. 11.

[33] Surrey, *Poems*, no. 11 / *Rime*, no. 22.

[34] *Rime*, no. 323.

Poetic responses to the explosion of interest in Petrarchism in the 1580s and 1590s tend to divide into two types. One group of poets seem to have been motivated primarily by an interest in the forms, themes and techniques of Petrarchism for much the same reasons as Surrey. Among the members of this group, one can number most of the sonneteers customarily viewed as minor: writers like Thomas Watson, Henry Constable, Barnabe Barnes or Richard Barnfield. A second type of response is to be found among those who, like Sidney, Edmund Spenser and Shakespeare, felt moved by the injunctions of contemporary Protestantism to use Petrarchan imitation as an instrument for the exploration of problematical issues inherent in erotic experience itself, and for self-constitution. Before dealing with the class of Petrarchists who engage in imitation as a response to Protestantism – which requires a chapter to itself – I shall deal in the rest of this present chapter with some of those writers who imitated Petrarch primarily as a response to fashion.

The Petrarchan imitators who comprise this group have one especial thing in common: their imitations show no signs of any dynamic activity of self-reference comparable to that displayed earlier by Wyatt, or later by the three great poets in the second group whose compositions are conditioned by an awareness of Protestant doctrine. Instead, these lesser poets tend simply to marshal Petrarchan techniques for their respective purposes, which variously include virtuoso display, homoeroticism, libertine counter-reaction and burlesque. In many cases, they write as if they are chiefly concerned to play with a new toy to see how it works, and also to impress the reader with the clever things they can do with it.

This is especially true of Thomas Watson, who, in his *Hecatompathia*, includes rubrics that explain how his effects are being achieved. For example, in a poem in which he likens his lady to a 'second sun', rather than allowing the Petrarchan conceit to speak for itself, Watson (or his rubricator) laboriously expounds the grounds of the trope in a prefatory gloss: 'throughout the whole Sonnet hee fayneth his Mistres to bee a *Second Sunne*: and by expressinge his priuate infelicitie, in either always meltinge away with *Loue*, or growinge stiffe throughe Death approachinge neere him by reason of dayly cares, hee maketh allusion vnto the diuerse effectes of the Sunne, which maketh the clay much harder, and the wax softer, then it was before'.[35]

Henry Constable is another poet whose primary aim seems to be to reproduce Petrarchan externalities for the effects they can produce, rather than for constructing the meaning of a genuine erotic relationship. In his *Diana* (published 1592), he dutifully puns on his lady's name ('Grace full of grace') just as Petrarch had.[36] He also adopts a pose of Petrarchan adoration, alluding to

[35] Thomas Watson, *Poems*, ed. Edward Arber (London, 1870), no. 44, p. 80.
[36] Henry Constable, *The Poems of Henry Constable*, ed. Joan Grundy (Liverpool, 1960), p. 113.

the fire from her eyes, the sweetness of her white hand, rose lips, lily breast and so forth. But his interest soon strays from his erotic subject matter, and in the second part of the sequence he digresses into the praise of particular notable persons, including the King of Scotland as well as a host of aristocratic women. In spite of the shift of subject, Constable continues to replicate the commonplaces of the Petrarchan style even when they are of dubious appropriateness, as when he offers consolation to the Princess of Orange upon the occasion of the murder of her father and husband:

> So in thyne eyes at once, we fire and water see,
> Fire doth of beautie spring, water of griefe ensue.
> Whoe fire and water yet together euer knew,
> And neyther water dry'd nor fire quencht to be?
>
> But wonder it is not thy water and thy fyre
> Vnlike to others be, thy water fire hath bred,
> And thy fire water makes, for thyne eyes fire hath shed
> Teares from a thousand hearts, melted with loues desire:
> And griefe to see such eyes bathed in teares of woes,
> A fire of revenge inflames against thy foes.[37]

In this application of Petrarchan commonplaces to subject matter outside its usual range of reference, one can detect a foreshadowing of the baroque sensibility of late sixteenth-century Catholicism to which Constable, in real life, was in the process of converting.[38] When, in the Third Part, he renounces love, acknowledging that 'myne owne follie did procure my payne',[39] there is no suggestion that his being has been affected by the experience he has purportedly undergone in any essential way.

Indeed, in all of these performances, one is struck by an indifference on the part of the author to any of the dialogical possibilities inherent in intertextual engagement. Richard Barnfield, in his *Cynthia* (1595), treating of his homoerotic attraction for a beautiful youth, Ganymede (identified as Charles Blount),[40] potentially had the subject matter for just such a dialogical exploration. Unlike Shakespeare, who fully seized upon the dialogical possibilities of this topic in his *Sonnets*, Barnfield is content simply to switch the referents for the Petrarchan commonplaces he uses from female to male. The twin stars of Laura's eyes in Petrarch become those of Ganymede:

> Two stars there are in one faire firmament,
> (Of some intitled Ganymedes sweet face),

---

[37] Ibid., 2.iii.1, p. 152.   [38] Ibid., p. 33.   [39] Ibid., 3.iii.1, p. 171, l. 10.
[40] Richard Barnfield, *Richard Barnfield: The Complete Poems*, ed. George Klawitter (Selinsgrove; London and Toronto, 1990), pp. 30–1.

> Which other stars in brightnes doe disgrace,
> As much as Po in clearnes passeth Trent.[41]

So, too, does her hair, in the sonnet in which Barnfield asks an echo how he may call his love:

> How tearm'st his golden tresses wav'd with aire?   *Haire.*[42]

The bathos of the echo's response in this line illustrates the dangers risked by English poets who fell into the trap of imitating the externalities of Petrarch's style without engaging fully with the deeper purpose of its signifying activity.

A similar limitation of understanding is apparent in Barnabe Barnes' imitation of Petrarch's use of oxymoron, in *Parthenophil and Parthenophe* (1593):

> I burne yet am I cold, I am a could yet burne
> In pleasing discontent, in discontentment pleased
> Diseas'd I am in health, and health-full am diseased
> In turning backe proceede, proceeding I returne
>
> ...
>
> Vnmou'd I vexe my selfe, vnuext yet am I moued
> Belou'd she loues me not, yet is she my beloued.[43]

The problem with these lines is that the relationship between Barnes' oxymora is too disparate for them to be able to serve convincingly as signifiers for the emotional state they claim to describe. This indicates that Barnes has not understood the infinite deferral of determinate volition in Petrarch revealed through his use of oxymoron, so that the poem creates the dissatisfying impression that the rhetorical figure is being used merely for the sake of cleverness. Perhaps unwittingly, Barnes sums up the limitation of his approach in the penultimate line of the sonnet: remaining 'unmou'd', his pretence at 'vexing' himself fails to convince, and because he is 'vnuext' his efforts to persuade the reader that he is 'moued' likewise fail to carry conviction. The whole purpose of the sequence is to portray Parthenophe's lust – with considerable lubricity – and show the progressive movement towards its gratification in the literal act of coition. Barnes, in fact, develops a libertine counter-discourse that is fundamentally at odds with the Petrarchan mode he is using, causing him to supplement it with a far more voluptuous Ovidianism. Far from having his lover sublimate desire in the service of a

---

[41] Ibid., Sonnet 4, p. 124.
[42] Ibid., Sonnet 13, p. 128.
[43] Barnabe Barnes, *Parthenophil and Parthenophe*, ed. Victor A. Doyno (Carbondale and Edwardsville; London and Amsterdam, 1971), Sonnet 31, p. 20, ll. 1–4, 13–14.

higher spiritual good when its fulfilment is frustrated by the lady's denial, Barnes depicts its bodily consummation in the final sestine of *Parthenophil and Parthenophe*.[44] Here, Parthenophil's invocation of the assistance of Hecate and the furies to help him procure Parthenophe, and the sexual explicitness with which the climactic *liebestod* is enacted, are about as far from the ethos of the Petrarchan archetype as can be.

Other counter-discourses created by poets in the 1590s moved still further away from the actively self-constituting engagement with the Petrarchan archetype that Wyatt had displayed.[45] Michael Drayton, in *Idea* (published in 1594), explicitly defined himself *against* Petrarchism from the outset:

> *To the Reader of these Sonnets*
> Into these Loves who but for Passion looks,
> At this first sight here let him lay them by
> And seek elsewhere, in turning other books,
> Which better may his labour satisfy.
> No far-fetched sigh shall ever wound my breast,
> Love from mine eye a tear shall never wring,
> Nor in Ah me's my whining sonnets drest,
> A libertine, fantasticly I sing.
> My verse is the true image of my mind,
> Ever in motion, still desiring change;
> And as thus to variety inclined,
> So in all humours sportively I range;
>   My Muse is rightly of the English strain,
>   That cannot long one fashion entertain.[46]

Drayton was being somewhat disingenuous here, as he goes to considerable lengths in his sonnet sequence to evoke the basic Petrarchan *topoi* and experiential pattern, in order to subvert their susceptibility to sentimentalization. His gruesome elaboration of the conceit in Sonnet 50, in which he likens his mistress to surgeons who are allowed to conduct experiments on the body of a condemned prisoner,

> Which on the living work without remorse,
> First make incision on each mastering vein,
> Then staunch the bleeding, then transpierce the corse,
> And with their balms recure the wounds again,
> Then poison, and with physic him restore,[47]

---

[44] Ibid., Sestine 5, pp. 127–30.
[45] See Heather Dubrow, *Echoes of Desire: English Petrarchism and its Counterdiscourses* (Ithaca and London, 1995).
[46] Samuel Daniel, *Daniel's Delia and Drayton's Idea*, ed. Arundell Esdaile (London, 1908), p. 67.
[47] Ibid., p. 117.

functions as a spoof of the Petrarchan conceit through its evocation of what real pain is actually like. Throughout *Idea*, Drayton works hard to de-romanticize all that had been idealized in Petrarch, even if he is finally unwilling to abandon the mode itself completely. Others, like Sir John Davies in his *Gullinge Sonnets* (written some time between 1594 and 1595), would not be so reticent, and would push the anti-Petrarchan counter-discourse to the extreme point of outright burlesque.[48]

It was inevitable that the comparatively superficial response to Petrarchism by poets of this group would have little staying power, as the ability of the mode to provide lasting satisfaction in the absence of more substantial matter was very limited. At the same time as these poets were exercising their talents in playing with their new toy, however, a much more profound response was being imaginatively articulated by other poets of a vastly different order, and it is to the consequences of that response that this investigation will turn in the following chapter.

[48] See John Davies, *The Poems of Sir John Davies*, ed. Robert Krueger (Oxford, 1975), esp. no. 3, which burlesques the device of *gradatio* (p. 165); no. 4, which burlesques Petrarchan conceits (p. 165); and no. 5, which burlesques correlative verse (pp. 165–6).

3

Elizabethan Petrarchism and the Protestant Location of Self

The years intervening between the early forays into Petrarchan imitation by Wyatt and Surrey and the great proliferation of imitations in the 1580s and 1590s witnessed one of the most radical transformations of national consciousness in English history. It occurred when a spiritualized Calvinist divinity became entrenched among both the laity and the clergy as a normative, and possibly the most powerfully normative, discourse of the time.[1] While many of the poets who embraced the Petrarchan mode, such as Constable or Barnfield, show only light traces of the new Protestant discourse, the major Petrarchan imitators – Sir Philip Sidney, Edmund Spenser and William Shakespeare – were deeply affected by it. It is worth while, therefore, to sketch in the outlines of the new ideology that conditioned the ways in which they, and others like them, developed their own versions of Petrarchism.

Elizabethan Protestantism assumed its basic character almost as soon as Elizabeth I ascended to the throne on 17 November 1558. In her father's reign, reformation had been far more political than doctrinal, and even though an attempt had been made to introduce more far-reaching reforms of religious beliefs and practices in the brief reign of her brother, Edward VI, it had been countermanded and reversed by the efforts of Mary I to return England to allegiance to Rome. Raised a Protestant in the household of Catherine Parr, Elizabeth had become the centre of Protestant hopes even

---

[1] On the entrenchment of Calvinism in Elizabethan Protestantism see, in particular, Patrick Collinson, *The Birthpangs of Protestant England: Religious and Cultural Change in the Sixteenth and Seventeenth Centuries* (London, 1988); Patrick Collinson, *The Religion of Protestants* (Oxford, 1982); Peter Lake, *Moderate Puritans and the Elizabethan Church* (Cambridge, 1982); and Peter Lake, *Anglicans and Puritans? Presbyterianism and English Conformist Thought from Whitgift to Hooker* (London, 1988).

before the death of her Catholic sister, and when Mary died a new religious order was quickly established by the strongly Protestant Parliament of 1559 through the enactment of a new Act of Supremacy to restore royal control over Church government, and an Act of Uniformity to restore a Protestant liturgy and regulate religious observance through the use of a slightly modified version of the second prayer book from the reign of Edward VI.[2] Even though the Settlement of 1559 contained elements of compromise – designed to retain the loyalty of as many of the realm's Catholic subjects as possible – it was Calvinist at the core of its doctrine, especially in the wording to the participant at the offering of the bread at the Communion: 'take and eate this in remembraunce that Christ died for thee, feede on him in thine heart by faith, with thankesgeuynge', with its acceptance of the figurative nature of the sacrament, its emphasis on the prime agency of faith, and its denial of literal transubstantiation.[3]

The statutes enacted in the Parliament of 1559 were only the cornerstones of the new religious order that would be erected in the years ahead. Its doctrinal foundations were extended by the publication in 1560 of a new Protestant English translation of the Scriptures, the Geneva Bible, containing a Calvinist commentary, to which two Calvinist catechisms were added in 1568 and 1570. In the following year, the classical statement of Protestant theology, Calvin's *Institutes*, was published in an English translation by Thomas Norton, *The Institution of Christian Religion, Wrytten in Latine by Maister Jhon Calvin, and Translated into Englysh According to the Authors Last Edition. Seen and Allowed According to the Order Appointed in the Quenes Maiesties Instructions* (1561). Both works were to prove enormously influential. For the first time, the English people had a Bible in the vernacular designed for use by the laity, and in the *Institutes* they had access to a brilliantly lucid and persuasive exposition of the main tenets of the reformed religion. In spite of the fact that first the Great Bible (in its revised edition of 1540) and then the Bishops' Bible (1568) were designated for official use, the Geneva Bible quickly became the most popular Bible in England, being supported by the clergy and providing the basis for most sermons. Not surprisingly, writers used it. The Geneva Bible was the version most frequently used by Spenser, Thomas Dekker preferred it, and Shakespeare is known to have shifted from using the Bishops' Bible to the Geneva Bible after 1596.[4] By the mid- and later years of Elizabeth's reign, Calvinist beliefs dominated the Elizabethan Church of England. They were also enforced in the universities. In 1579, a new statute at Oxford ordered that all students be instructed from

[2] See Norman L. Jones, *Faith by Statute: Parliament and the Settlement of Religion, 1559*, Royal Historical Society Studies in History Series, no. 32 (London and New Jersey, 1982).
[3] *The Prayer-Book of Queen Elizabeth, 1559*, ed. Edward Benham (Edinburgh, 1909), p. 103.
[4] See *The Geneva Bible: A Facsimile of the 1560 Edition*, ed. Lloyd E. Berry (Madison, 1969), pp. 19–20; Richmond Noble, *Shakespeare's Biblical Knowledge* (London, 1935), pp. 75–6.

the catechisms of Calvin, Nowell and the Heidelberg theologians, and then from Bullinger, Jewel, Calvin's *Institutes* and the Thirty-nine Articles. Most importantly, Calvinist beliefs were espoused by many of the most powerful figures in the lay and clerical establishments, including the Queen's favourite, Robert Dudley, Earl of Leicester and his circle (Philip Sidney among them), her Secretary, Sir Francis Walsingham, and her chief minister, William Cecil, Lord Burghley.

What, then, were the distinguishing features of this new Protestant belief system and the discourse that accompanied it? At the heart of Elizabethan Protestantism lay a deepened sense of human sinfulness. The very first words an Elizabethan English man or woman would hear in the order for morning prayer to be used daily throughout the year would be drawn from a number of scriptural readings affirming the wickedness of sinners and their need for forgiveness and mercy:

> At what tyme soeuer a synner doth repent him of his sin
> from the bottome of hys harte; I wil put al his wickednes out
> of my remembraunce sayeth the Lord.   Eze. xviii
> I do know mine awne wickednes, and my syne is alwaies
> against me.   Psalm li.
> Turne thy face awaye from our sinnes (O lorde) and blotte
> out all our offences.   Psalm li.
> A sorowful spirite is a sacrifice to God: despise not (O Lorde)
> humble and contrite hartes.   Psalm li.
>   ... 5

This deep sense of sinfulness sprang from the Calvinist conviction that human nature was inherently depraved:

> Original sin ... may be defined [as] a hereditary corruption and depravity of our nature, extending to all the parts of the soul, which first makes us obnoxious to the wrath of God, and then produces in us works which in Scripture are termed works of the flesh. ... Hence, those who have defined original sin as the want of the original righteousness which we ought to have had, though they substantially comprehend the whole case, do not significantly enough express its power and energy. For our nature is not only utterly devoid of goodness, but so prolific in all kinds of evil, that it can never be idle. Those who term it concupiscence use a word not very inappropriate, provided it were added ... that everything which is in man, from the intellect to the will, from the soul even to the flesh, is defiled and pervaded with this concupiscence; or, to express it more briefly, that the whole man is in himself nothing else than concupiscence.[6]

5 *The Prayer-Book of Queen Elizabeth, 1559*, p. 41.
6 Jean Calvin, *Institutes of the Christian Religion*, trans. Henry Beveridge, 3 vols (Edinburgh, 1845), II.1.8, vol. 1., pp. 292–3.

One consequence of this natural sinfulness is that 'all our faculties are so vitiated and corrupted, that a perpetual disorder and excess is apparent in all our actions', which means that men and women are constantly propelled towards an intemperance which contends against God's control: 'all human desires are evil, and we charge them with sin not in as far as they are natural, but because they are inordinate, and inordinate because nothing pure and upright can proceed from a corrupt and polluted nature'.[7]

Several corollaries follow from this basic assumption. First, human depravity, in the Calvinist view, removes the freedom of will with which humanity was endowed at its creation. Second, the bondage of the will to sinfulness makes humanity entirely dependent on Christ for redemption through faith, resting upon God's word in Scripture, rather than any personal merit. Faith therefore becomes correspondingly elevated in importance and is tied more closely to God's promises in Scripture. It is 'a knowledge of God's will toward us, perceived from his Word', which is revealed in our hearts by the Holy Spirit,[8] and because this activity takes place within the heart of the individual, there is an emphasis on interior illumination and 'the indwelling of the Spirit', rather than on any external ceremonies. Regeneration is born of faith and issues in the fruits of repentance, which consist of piety towards God, charity towards others, holiness and purity in the whole of life. Above all, it leads to the denial of ourselves through devotion to God, along with a shedding of the impulses that spring from self-love, such as ambition, a craving for glory, lasciviousness or any other desires of a self-regarding sort.[9] Finally, this Protestant view assumed a constant spiritual warfare against evil, both within the individual and in the larger domain of world history, as is expressed in the dedicatory epistle to Queen Elizabeth that prefaced the Geneva Bible:

> euen aboue strength you must shewe your selfe strong and bolde in Gods matters: and thogh Satan lay all his power and craft together to hurt and hinder the Lordes building: yet be you assured that God wil fight from heauen against this great dragon, the ancient serpent, which is called the deuil and Satan, til he haue accomplished the whole worke and made his Churche glorious to him selfe, without spot or wrincle.[10]

In pursuit of this warfare, Elizabethan Protestants, moved by varying degrees of zeal – especially those of a more radical 'puritan' tendency[11] – were tireless

---

[7] Ibid., III.3.12, vol. 2, p. 163.

[8] Ibid., III.2, vol. 2, pp. 92–148.

[9] Ibid., esp. III.3.14–15, vol. 2, pp. 165–9; and III.7.3–4, vol. 2, pp. 262–5.

[10] *The Geneva Bible*, iii^v.

[11] The term 'puritan' covers a wide range of religious opinions and refers to an intensity of zeal rather than any particular ideological or political position. On the necessity for a broad-based definition of puritanism, see Lake, *Moderate Puritans and the Elizabethan Church*.

in their efforts to secure further reformation, whether through purging the English Church of its popish remnants, exhorting individual men and women to 'godly' living, or urging Elizabeth and her advisers to commit England to a European Protestant alliance against the great enemy, Spain.

By the late 1560s, the discourse generated by this fervent Calvinistic Protestantism had become unquestionably the most powerful and dominant normative discourse in Elizabethan England. Inevitably, by the time that Petrarchan imitation had resurfaced as a major poetic activity in the 1580s and 1590s, few English poets were likely to ignore its insistent and ubiquitous presence. In particular, Protestant injunctions tended to sharpen poets' awareness of a basic problem deeply embedded in Petrarchism itself: its indulgence of a sinful desire that was the product of an even more sinful egotism and pride.

Petrarch himself had been aware of this problem; indeed, he makes his anxiety concerning it one of the main thematic preoccupations of the *Rime sparse*. By his own admission, he had placed his hopes for too long in 'the false fleeting sweetness which the treacherous world gives' ('quel falso dolce fuggitivo / che 'l mondo traditor può dare'). Seeing what he was doing, and 'not deceived by an imperfect knowledge of the truth', he had loved a mortal thing 'with the faith that belongs to God alone' ('con tanta fede / quanto a Dio sol per debito convensi').[12] Just as culpably, he feared that he had aestheticized his erotic torments in order to gain glory. He revealed this by personifying glory in the same terms that he used to address Laura, as 'una donna più bella assai che 'l sole' ('a lady much more beautiful than the sun'), and also by ambiguously confusing the referents of the 'laurel' that served as a symbol for each of them.[13] In the *Rime sparse* Petrarch shows himself trying to rectify the situation by undergoing a belated Augustinian-like conversion after Laura's death, in which he seeks to purge himself of his worldly vanity by replacing its forms with spiritualized alternatives. Thus, 'Amor' is displaced as his governing master by God as 'mio Signore eterno' ('my eternal lord'), and his desire is recast as a purified spiritual love ('quella pura fede') which has left him convinced that his love for Laura is the root of his salvation ('la radice di mia salute') because her chastity has uprooted every low thought from his heart ('ch 'ogni basso penser del cor m'avulse').[14] Finally, Petrarch was moved to substitute the Virgin Mary for Laura as the object of his devotion:

> Vergine umana et nemica d'orgoglio:
> del comune principio amor t'induca

12 *Rime*, no. 264, ll. 28–9, 91–2, 99–100.
13 See, for example, *Rime*, no. 119, ll. 1, 103–5.
14 Ibid., no. 345, l. 14; no. 347, l. 7; no. 351, ll. 8, 14.

miserere d'un cor contrito umile;
ché se poca mortal terra caduca
amar con sì mirabil fede soglio,
che devrò far di te, casa gentile?

(Kindly Virgin, enemy of pride, let love of our common origin move you, have
mercy on a contrite and humble heart; for if I am wont to love with such mar-
vellous faith a bit of deciduous mortal dust, how will I love you, a noble thing?)

The _Rime sparse_ conclude with Petrarch affirming to his new mistress that he
will seek to consecrate and cleanse in her name his thought, wit and style,
tongue and heart, and his tears and sighs, and with him begging her to accept
his 'cangiati desiri' ('changed desires') so that Christ might receive his last
breath in peace.[15]

In spite of Petrarch's belated efforts to retrieve himself from the 'wretched
and vile state' ('mio stato assai misero et vile') into which his desires had led
him, the changes that Protestant English poets made to the Petrarchan mode
show that most of them remained highly uneasy about the spiritual illicitness
of Petrarchan eroticism when viewed from a Protestant perspective, especially
as the belatedness of Petrarch's recantation looked suspiciously like a desire to
have one's cake and eat it too. Almost invariably, they felt moved to acknowledge the moral dubiety of Petrarchan erotic experience in one way or another.
Some, like Henry Constable, adopted Petrarch's own expedient of showing an
abandonment of earthly love as the culminating movement of the sonnet
sequence itself. Others, like Barnabe Barnes, dealt with the matter more
crudely by driving a wedge between the secular (Italianate) and the sacred
(Protestant), so as to give free reign to sexual libertinism in the description of
a desire that did not pretend to be anything other than depraved, and which
could then be cancelled out by a baptizing of the muse following the poet's
subsequent 'conversion'. Thus, only two years after publishing the sexually
explicit rapist's fantasy of _Parthenophil and Parthenophe_ (1593), Barnes issued
A Divine Centurie of Spirituall Sonnets (1595), in which he repudiated the
earlier sequence as comprising 'lewde laies of lighter loves'. Instead, he offers
to the reader 'The severall passions of comforte and ghostly combates'
devised 'in earnest true motions of the Spirite'. The poems themselves are
presented as fruits of his repentance:

I know my fault, I did not as I should;
My sinful flesh against my soule rebel'd.[16]

---

[15] Ibid., no. 364, l. 9; no. 366, ll. 118–37.
[16] Barnabe Barnes, _A Divine Centurie of Spirituall Sonnets_, ed. Alexander B. Grosart (London,
1875), 'To the Favourable and Christian Reader'; sonnet no. 38, ll. 9–10. On Barnes' religious
sonnets, see Thomas P. Roche, _Petrarch and the English Sonnet Sequences_ (New York, 1989),
pp. 168–85. On literary recantation generally, see Patricia Berrahou Phillipy, _Love's Remedies:
Recantation and Renaissance Lyric Poetry_ (Lewisburg and London, 1995).

In true Calvinist fashion, Barnes seeks divine aid to assist him in casting off his former vices, including his erotic poetizing:

> To thee, my GOD! I turne my sinfull eyes,
> Whom I provoke with my remorsefull cries,
> Some succour for my vexed thoughts to show;
> That, as I have my native countrie changed,
> So likewise from the world I may bee weaned:
> And as my weede with nation is estranged,
> I may so shine in Christian armes unfeyned;
> And as I leave my nation's true language,
> My Muse may change for a diviner rage.[17]

This conversion of the muse to 'a diviner rage' was a strategy that many other English poets would adopt as their way of establishing a right relationship between Petrarchism and the Word.

Still other poets avoided the need for such a facile expedient by investing the Petrarchan discourse itself with a distinctively English-Protestant inflection. This can be observed by tracing the subtle differences of translation in the respective versions of Petrarch's *Rime* 224 by the French poet Philippe Desportes and by a poet in the Sidney circle, Samuel Daniel:

> S'una fede amorosa, un cor non finto,
> un languir dolce, un desiar cortese,
> s' oneste voglie in gentil foco accese,
> un lungo error in cieco laberinto,
>
> se ne la fronte ogni penser depinto,
> od in voci interrotte a pena intese
> or da paura or da vergogna offese,
> s' un pallor di viola et d'amor tinto,
>
> s' aver altrui più caro che se stesso,
> se sospirare et lagrimar mai sempre
> pascendosi di duol d'ira et d'affanno,
>
> s' arder da lunge et agghiacciar da presso,
> son le cagion ch' amando i' mi distempre:
> vostro, Donna, 'l peccato et mio fia 'l danno.
>
> (If faithfulness in love, an unfeigning heart, a sweet yearning, a courteous desire – if chaste desires kindled in a noble fire, a long wandering in a blind labyrinth –

---

[17] Barnes, *A Divine Centurie*, sonnet no. 41, ll. 6–14.

if to have all my thoughts written on my brow, or barely understood in broken words, or cut off by fear or shame – if a pallor like the violet's, tinted with love –

if to love another more than oneself – if to be always sighing and weeping, feeding on sorrow and anger and trouble –

if to burn from afar and freeze close by – if these are the causes that I untune myself with love, yours will be the blame, Lady, mine the loss.)[18]

Philippe Desportes follows Petrarch's original very closely in the eighth sonnet of *Les amours de Diane* (1573):

> Si la foy plus certaine en une âme non feinte,
> Un desir temeraire, un doux languissement,
> Une erreur volontaire, et sentir vivement,
> Avec peur d'en guarir, une profonde atteinte;
> Si voir une pensée au front toute depeinte,
> Une voix empeschée, un morne estonnement,
> De honte ou de frayeur naissans soudainement,
> Une pasle couleur, de lis et d'amour teinte;
> Bref, si se mespriser pour une autre adorer;
> Si verser mille pleurs, si tousjours soupirer,
> Faisant de sa douleur nourriture et bruvage;
> Si, loin estre de flamme, et de près, tout transi,
> Sont cause que je meurs par defaut de merci,
> L'offence en est sur vous, et sur moy le dommage.[19]

And here is Daniel's translation in the fifteenth sonnet of *Delia* (1592), which may itself have been based on Desportes' version:

> If that a loyal heart and faith unfeigned,
> If a sweet languish with a chaste desire,
> If hunger-starven thoughts so long retained,
> Fed but with smoke and cherished but with fire,
> And if a brow, with cares' characters painted,
> Bewrays my love, with broken words half spoken
> To her that sits in my thought's temple sainted,
> And lays to view my vulture-gnawn heart open;
> If I have done due homage to her eyes
> And had my sighs still tending on her name;
> If on her love my life and honour lies,

[18] Petrarch, *Rime*, no. 224, pp. 380–1.
[19] Philippe Desportes, *Les amours de Diane*, ed. Victor E. Graham, 2 vols, Textes Littéraires Français (Geneva and Paris, 1959), vol. 1, no. 8, pp. 36–7.

And she, the unkindest maid, still scorns the same;
Let this suffice, that all the world may see
The fault is hers, though mine the hurt must be.[20]

The substitutions introduced in the French and English translations are fascinating, as they reveal a pattern of transformation that is characteristic of English Petrarchism at large. Specifically, the English poet introduces an objectified framework of moral values that makes the erotic experience susceptible to interpretation in terms of the normative assumptions of English Protestantism. Neither the French nor the English poet is prepared to reproduce the connotations of Petrarch's 'fede amorosa' ('faithfulness in love', or 'amorous fidelity') in line 1. Desportes turns it into 'la foy plus certaine' ('absolute constancy'). Daniel alters the components of the line altogether, by switching Petrarch's descriptor 'non finto' ('unfeigned') from 'cor' ('heart') to 'faith', and by replacing the idea of 'fede amorosa' with that of a 'loyal heart'. The effect is to suppress the erotic condition of feeling suggested by 'amorosa', and to replace it with a more generalized notion of steadfastness and integrity that need not be applied to erotic experience at all. A similar thing happens in the translation of lines 2 and 3. Neither poet reproduces Petrarch's 'desiar cortese' ('courteous desire'), with its suggestion of the whole code of amorous flirtation inherent in the Provençal tradition, nor the somatic oxymoron of 'oneste voglie in gentil foco accese' ('chaste desires kindled in a noble fire'). Instead, Desportes replaces 'desiar cortese' with 'desir temeraire' ('reckless desire') and drops the third line completely, while Daniel conflates the two lines in order to substitute the idea of 'oneste voglie' for 'desir cortese', as 'chaste desire'. Again, the translation is moved further from the eroticism of the Italian source in order to intimate an emotion that is more permissible in Protestant terms. Through the rest of the translation, Daniel moves progressively further away from Desportes, and still further from Petrarch. Whereas Desportes gestures towards Petrarch's 'lungo error in cieco laberinto' ('a long wandering in a blind labyrinth') with 'une erreur volontaire', Daniel omits the idea altogether, replacing it with the morally less ambiguous 'hunger-starven thoughts so long retained, / Fed but with smoke and cherished but with fire', which exploits the pun on 'error' to affirm more explicitly the essential futility of the experience in which he has been involved. This explicit judgement is reinforced still further by the substitution of 'a brow, with care's characters painted' (l. 5) for Petrarch's 'ne la fronte ogni penser depinto' ('all my thoughts written on my brow'), which interprets the nature of the thoughts from a more censoriously judgemental perspective, and by the introduction of the idea of divine punishment (implicitly, for 'sin') with the Promethean allusion to his 'vulture-gnawn heart', for which there is

20 Samuel Daniel, *Daniel's Delia and Drayton's Idea*, ed. Arundell Esdaile, (London, 1908), no. 15, p. 15.

no suggestion in either Petrarch or Desportes. Subliminally, this idea of punishment may relate to the notion of idolatry implicit in the reference to 'her
that sits in my thought's temple sainted' (l. 7), another detail of Daniel's
invention that is present in neither of his sources.

Not content simply with identifying moral defects in himself, Daniel proceeds in the sestet to emphasize moral deficiencies in the lady as well. He does
this by shifting the focus in the first tercet from his own emotional turmoil
to the lady's scornful pride and 'unkindness', and, in the second tercet, by
inviting 'all the world' to 'see' – that is, to judge – that 'The fault is hers,
though mine the hurt must be' (l. 14). This evocation of an arena of public
judgement in which the lady will be perceived guilty represents a significant
shift from Petrarch's playfully paradoxical suggestion that the presence of a
lover's emotional turmoil in him indicates a sin ('peccato') in her (who is
innocent) for which he must bear the punishment ("l danno').

It is important to grasp the overall effect of these changes, subtle though
they may appear. By introducing an implicit moral framework against which
the status of the attitudes and predispositions depicted in the poem can be
judged, Daniel has, in fact, fundamentally altered the *mundus significans*, or
'signifying world', of his Italianate source to make it accord more readily with
the norms of his native Protestant discourse. Time and again, one can observe
a comparable process of discursive transformation occurring in the Italianate
imitations of English writers of the 1580s and 1590s, and when it does occur,
the authors who engage in it seldom feel a need to follow Barnes and his like
in repudiating the Italian mode altogether. In fact, the creation of a new
hybrid discourse through subjecting the Italianate one to a Protestant re-
inflection seems to have been motivated by a desire to avoid the need for just
such a repudiation.

All of the strategies mentioned so far – fictive recantation, dichotomizing
supersession and discursive transformation – are expedients designed to
acknowledge the moral dubiety of Petrarchism while preserving the right to
indulge in it. The three greatest Petrarchists of the period, Philip Sidney,
Edmund Spenser and William Shakespeare, took a much more thorough-
going approach to the problem of Petrarchan eroticism by making it one of
the main thematic preoccupations of the sonnet sequence itself. Petrarchan
imitation became a means of exploring the sources and effects of spiritual culpability in erotic experience in order to show not just the difficulty of finding an adequate way of remedying it, given the sinfulness inherent in human
nature, but also why there was a need to do so in the first place. The effect of
this new preoccupation is to turn the sonnet sequence into an instrument for
self-constitution, for it becomes a site where rival discourses can engage with
one another through the experience of individual subjects who discover a
need to reconcile them.

Sir Philip Sidney was the first poet after Wyatt to rediscover the usefulness of Petrarchan imitation for self-formation when his own experience as a frustrated lover impelled him into sonnet-writing in the summer of 1582. Following a period of voluntary rustication spent with his sister at Wilton, after his diplomatic efforts as ambassador to the German Emperor had failed to please the Queen, and his attempts to dissuade her from marrying the Catholic Duke of Alençon had positively antagonized her, Sidney had returned to court in 1581, actively participating in its affairs through most of that year.[21] His return coincided with the introduction at court of the Earl of Essex's younger sister, Penelope Devereux, who was soon to be affianced to Lord Rich in March 1581, marrying him eight months later. Although there is no evidence that his passion was actively requited, Sidney appears to have fallen in love with the newly married Lady Rich, for he goes to considerable lengths in *Astrophil and Stella* to identify himself with Astrophil and Lady Rich with Stella. Several years later, according to the report of George Gifford, the physician who attended him during his dying days, Sidney was still highly troubled by a guilty conscience regarding this affair. Gifford reports him as saying:

I had this night a trouble in my mind; for searching myself, methought I had not a full and sure hold in Christ. After I had continued in this perplexity a while, observe how strangely God did deliver me – for indeed it was a strange deliverance that I had! There came to my remembrance a vanity wherein I had taken delight, whereof I had not rid myself. It was my Lady Rich. But I rid myself of it, and presently my joy and comfort returned.[22]

Whether or not Sidney actually uttered these exact words, they attest to the fact that his contemporaries had been aware of his passion, and that they attributed to him a concern to restore the integrity of his moral being by purging himself of its traces. *Astrophil and Stella* confirms this intention. It appears to have been written as Sidney's attempt not only to reconcile himself to the reality that he could not attain the object of his desire, but also to reconstitute his spiritual being by clarifying the moral implications of his recent experience.

Sidney's strategy was to explore the respects in which his experience as a Petrarchan lover had been faulty. To do this, he established a rhetorical distance between Astrophil and himself through the use of comic, dramatic and structural irony, which enabled him systematically to de-romanticize most of the central Petrarchan commonplaces in order to expose a wilful self-

---

[21] See Philip Sidney, *The Poems of Sir Philip Sidney*, ed. William A. Ringler, Jr (Oxford, 1962), p. xliii.

[22] George Gifford, 'The Manner of Sir Philip Sidney's Death', in *The Miscellaneous Prose of Sir Philip Sidney*, ed. Katherine Duncan-Jones and Jan Van Dorsten (Oxford, 1973), p. 169.

deception in his fictive counterpart.[23] From the outset, Astrophil is depicted as immature. He recurrently speaks in figurative language that associates him with a schoolboy in a classroom who is in the process of trying to master a hard lesson, as when in the opening sonnet he is seen 'biting [his] trewand pen', or when, at the height of his self-deception, he interprets Stella's response to him in terms of 'grammer rules'.[24] The poetry he writes is self-advertisingly contrived in its use of rhetorical figures like *gradatio*, antithesis and *chiasmus*, and in the exaggeratedly histrionic nature of its poses:

> Flie, fly, my friends, I have my death wound; fly,
> See there that boy, that murthring boy I say,
> Who like a theefe, hid in darke bush doth ly,
> Till bloudie bullet get him wrongfull pray.[25]

Even Astrophil's conception of love betrays immaturity: far from being the 'powerful lord' who governs Petrarch, the god of love who ensnares Astrophil is presented as a child who gets up to mischief 'like wags new got to play'.[26] This emphasis on Astrophil's immaturity helps reinforce an impression that his passion is, to a large extent, 'constructed', as if it is produced by a desire to be in love as much as by any sincerity of emotion.

Astrophil, moreover, is shown to be perverse in refusing to heed the dictates of conscience when presented with a calling to correct his conduct according to the Protestant norm.[27] Sidney is careful to ensure that the norm is articulated on a variety of occasions. The first occurs when an unnamed friend warns Astrophil of the spiritual danger of countenancing desire. Astrophil, however, refuses to listen to him:

> Alas have I not paine enough my friend,
> ...
> But with your Rubarb words yow must contend
>   To grieve me worse, in saying that Desire
>   Doth plunge my wel-form'd soule even in the mire
> Of sinfull thoughts, which do in ruine end?
>   If that be sinne which doth the maners frame,
> Well staid with truth in word and faith of deed,

---

[23] For a useful survey of critical views on these matters, see Janet H. MacArthur, *Critical Contexts of Astrophil and Stella and the Amoretti* (Victoria, British Columbia, 1989).

[24] *Astrophil and Stella*, no. 1, l. 13; no. 63, l. 1, in Sidney, *The Poems of Sir Philip Sidney*, ed. Ringler. All references to *Astrophil and Stella* are taken from this edition.

[25] *Astrophil and Stella*, no. 20, ll. 1–4.

[26] *Astrophil and Stella*, no. 17, l. 13.

[27] For a similar view see Alan Sinfield, 'Astrophil's Self-Deception', *Essays in Criticism*, 28 (1978): 1–18; and Alan Sinfield, *Literature in Protestant England 1560–1660* (Totawa, New Jersey, 1983).

Readie of wit and fearing nought but shame:
If that be sinne which in fixt hearts doth breed
A loathing of all loose unchastitie,
Then Love is sinne, and let me sinfull be.[28]

In making this offhand remark, Astrophil little knows at this point how quickly his desire will indeed prompt him to abandon all scruples about avoiding 'loose unchastitie', thus proving this friend's warning to have been well warranted. The norm is again asserted when Astrophil's passion has reached the point where he is seeking physical gratification of his desire. In response to his importunities, Stella herself tries to instruct Astrophil on the need for self-restraint:

... this at last is her sweet breath'd defence:
That who indeed infelt affection beares,
So captives to his Saint both soule and sence,
That wholly hers, all selfnesse he forbeares,
Thence his desires he learnes, his live's course thence.[29]

Astrophil never takes these injunctions seriously, and Sidney shows this perversity as springing from an unwillingness to subordinate his physical desire to his awareness of higher spiritual obligations, or of Stella's own wishes. Like Petrarch, he recognizes that 'A strife is growne between *Vertue* and *Love*', but unlike Petrarch he sees a simple remedy for the problem:

Let *Vertue* have that *Stella's* selfe; yet thus,
That *Vertue* but that body graunt to us.[30]

This inclination to disassociate desire from virtue in order to pursue its gratification serves to focus attention more closely on the carnal dimension of Astrophil's desire, or what he describes as his 'boiling sprites', to a much greater extent than had ever been the case with Petrarch.[31] Astrophil himself confesses that 'Desire ... oft so clings to my pure Love, that I / One from the other scarcely can descrie',[32] and the force of it leads him to relinquish Petrarch's more complex (con)fusion of the erotic with the spiritual, and along with it the idealized exaltation of the lady that this fusion had maintained.

Sidney's imitation of *Rime* 248 ('Chi vuol veder quantunque po Natura') in the sonnet 'Who will in fairest booke of Nature know' illustrates how

[28] *Astrophil and Stella*, no. 14.
[29] *Astrophil and Stella*, no. 61, ll. 4–8.
[30] *Astrophil and Stella*, no. 52, ll. 1, 13–14.
[31] *Astrophil and Stella*, no. 16, l. 3.
[32] *Astrophil and Stella*, no. 72, ll. 1–3.

radically he transformed Petrarch's idealized love in re-inflecting it with Astrophil's carnal desire.[33] Not only does Astrophil reduce the scope and status of Stella's virtue in comparison with Petrarch's exaltation of Laura's, but the last line threatens to negate even as much perfection as he allows her to retain. For Petrarch, Laura represents 'all that Nature and Heaven can do among us' ('quantunque po Natura / e 'l Ciel tra noi'), having 'every virtue, every beauty, every regal habit, joined together in one body with marvelous tempering', which makes her able to be a sun not only for his eyes but for the blind world itself. Astrophil strips away any suggestion of supernal grace, and treats Stella as a strictly secularized version of Scripture in which the observer may read 'those faire lines, which true goodnesse show', 'How Vertue may best lodg'd in beautie be', and how all vices are overthrown 'Not by rude force, but sweetest soveraigntie / Of reason, from whose light those night-birds flie'. Even though he accords her this exemplary virtue, Astrophil instantly proves himself to be one of these same night-birds when he – in contrast to Petrarch, who turns Laura into an embodiment of the refining power of earthly beauty – declares his unwillingness to assimilate the lesson:

> So while thy beautie drawes the heart to love,
>   As fast thy Vertue bends that love to good:
>   'But ah,' Desire still cries, 'give me some food.'

The whole purpose of Sidney's imitation of *Rime* 248, it turns out, has been to show how Astrophil's physical desire subverts his ability, or even willingness, to follow Petrarch in seeking to convert his earthly love into a means of attaining grace. Sidney's depiction of desire, in fact, exemplifies the Calvinist view that original sin is 'concupiscence', and that 'everything which is in man, from the intellect to the will, from the soul even to the flesh, is defiled and pervaded with this concupiscence'.[34]

All of Astrophil's subsequent troubles, in fact, are shown to spring from the unbridled nature of his concupiscence. In the first instance, his determination to gratify his desire renders him vulnerable to self-deception. When Stella, responding to his craving of 'the thing which ever she denies / ... / Least once should not be heard, twise said, No, No', he wilfully misreads her reply as 'Yes', by concluding that 'in one speech two Negatives affirme'.[35] Similarly, when Astrophil suffers doubt as to whether his hopes are soundly based, he prefers to perpetuate the delusion rather than run the risk of

---

[33] *Astrophil and Stella*, no. 71. For further comment on Sidney's changes to the source, see David Kalstone, 'Sir Philip Sidney and "Poore Petrarchs Long Deceased Woes"', in *Essential Articles for the Study of Sir Philip Sidney*, ed. Arthur F. Kinney (Hamden, Connecticut, 1986), pp. 241–54.
[34] Calvin, *Institutes*, II.1.8, vol. 2, p. 293.
[35] *Astrophil and Stella*, no. 63, ll. 5–7, 14.

confronting reality: addressing his personified hopes, he resolves 'thy errour to maintaine, / Rather then by more truth to get more paine'.[36] And when, finally, Stella grants him her affection on condition that he pursue a 'vertuous course', he unscrupulously accepts the condition without any intention of honouring it: 'No kings be crown'd but they some covenants make'.[37] Consequently, Astrophil first steals a kiss while Stella is sleeping, and in spite of her anger, follows this up with an attempted full seduction (evoked in the Fourth song). Because he has not taken her earlier resistance seriously, he has no grounds for understanding why she repulses him, and his violent reaction to it shows male egotism in its nastiest guise.

Indeed, Sidney's dramatization of Astrophil's response to the failure of his attempted seduction seems designed to illustrate the psychopathology resulting from the sinful concupiscence in human nature – 'with no small argument to the incredulous of that first accursed fall of Adam', as Sidney might have said with respect to the effect of his sonnet sequence.[38] Astrophil's reaction is shown to be a combination of outrage, wounded pride and self-love, and spiteful vindictiveness. The self-serving shallowness of his unctuous poetic flattery is exposed by the swiftness with which his attitude is 'metamorphosd quite':

> For rage now rules the reynes, which guided were by Pleasure.
> I thinke now of thy faults, who late thought of thy praise,
> That speech falles now to blame, which did thy honour raise,
> The same key op'n can, which can locke up a treasure.[39]

In typical male fashion, he seeks to transfer to her the culpability for his own fault:

> I say thou art a Devill, though clothd in Angel's shining:
> For thy face tempts my soule to leave the heav'n for thee,
> And thy words of refuse, do powre even hell on mee:
> Who tempt, and tempted plague, are Devils in true defining.[40]

Both this attempt to shift blame and Astrophil's threat to denounce Stella publicly ('You see what I can say; mend yet your froward mind'), manifest a spiritual corruption that springs from concupiscent self-regard, in that both tactics are deeply manipulative in intent, being designed to coerce Stella into

---

[36] *Astrophil and Stella*, no. 67, ll. 13–14.
[37] *Astrophil and Stella*, no. 69, ll. 13–14.
[38] Philip Sidney, *An Apology for Poetry or The Defence of Poesy*, ed. Geoffrey Shepherd (London, 1965), p. 101/21–2.
[39] *Astrophil and Stella*, Fifth song, p. 213/15–18.
[40] Ibid., p. 215, ll. 70–84.

submission to his desire. It is not surprising, therefore, that when Astrophil receives confirmation of the finality of Stella's refusal, he lapses first of all into exaggerated self-pity ('she hates me, wellaway, / Faining love, somewhat to please me'), and then a leaden despair that clips the wings of his 'yong soule' and wraps him in night.[41] Quite deliberately, Sidney has shown Astrophil in this last third of the sequence living through the self-punitive consequences of remaining in an unregenerate condition.

There has been considerable debate concerning the extent to which Sidney can be separated from his fallen persona, ranging from the view that his attempts to distance himself from his speaker are 'at best limited',[42] to the assertion that Sidney is teaching morality by negative example.[43] There is no need to deny the existence of a rhetorical persona simply because it can be demonstrated that Sidney shared Astrophil's desire and 'impure persuasion' of Stella, so long as one understands the instrumental, self-constitutive function that Sidney intended the work to have – not only for himself, but also for the reader.[44] Clear evidence of this intention is furnished by the way he sets up the Eighth song to provide an objectified perspective on the experience of the lovers and how it is to be interpreted. The choric function of this song, which records a meeting during which Stella tries to explain the grounds of her refusal to consummate a physical love, is activated in several ways. First, it has a narrative frame that is couched in the past tense ('In a grove most rich of shade … *Astrophil* with *Stella* sweete, did for mutuall comfort meete'). Second, the exchange between the lovers is dramatically enacted in the present, which allows – and indeed prompts – the reader to make inferences that are quite different from those that Astrophil himself expresses in subsequent poems. In the course of the song, the reader, along with the author, is induced to see more about the experience depicted in it than Astrophil sees. Specifically, the reader sees that Stella genuinely loves him and, indeed, feels a reciprocal desire. It is only her sense of honour that leads her to refuse him:

> 'If thou love, my love content thee,
> For all love, all faith is meant thee.

> 'Trust me while I thee deny,
> In my selfe the smart I try,
> Tyran honour doth thus use thee,
> Stella's selfe might not refuse thee.'[45]

---

[41] Ibid., Ninth song, p. 222/41–2; sonnet no. 108.
[42] Heather Dubrow, *Echoes of Desire: English Petrarchism and its Counterdiscourses* (Ithaca and London, 1995), p. 101.
[43] Roche, *Petrarch and the English Sonnet Sequences*, pp. 195–7.
[44] For further comment on this matter, see the range of opinions surveyed in MacArthur, *Critical Contexts of Astrophil and Stella and the Amoretti*, pp. 56–64.
[45] *Astrophil and Stella*, p. 220/91–6.

By causing Stella to articulate a viewpoint that is self-denying rather than self-regarding – in accordance with norms that are taken to define honourable conduct – Sidney turns her into an exemplary measure by which Astrophil is to be judged and found wanting. Her attitude is accorded privilege by the fact that Astrophil's subsequent reactions are shown to involve a degree of self-deception that does not cloud Stella's own judgement. The reader is therefore left in a position from which he or she can sympathize with Astrophil, without needing to approve of his imprisonment in self-pitying self-regard.

The process of this rhetorical strategy offers a clue to the function of the sequence as a whole. It has been designed to serve as a tool for analytical self-exploration that, because of the self-admonition involved, can lay the foundations for a reformative self-reconstitution to be enacted in the real life of the author himself. That Sidney should have contrived *Astrophil and Stella* to have this instrumental role is entirely consistent with the view of poetry he enunciated in *An Apology for Poetry*, written at about the same time. In terms of Sidney's theory of poetry, his sonnet sequence had been designed to be a 'representing, counterfeiting, or figuring forth' of 'notable images of virtues, vices, or what else' through which men, including himself, would be moved to take goodness in hand, and 'know that goodness whereunto they are moved'.[46] The delight produced by the enterprise was to come from the artistry with which he was able to imitate the forms, themes, motifs and conventions of Petrarchism, while its teaching would result from the ability of the representation to lead the 'erected wit', both of the author and reader, into an understanding of how far short of perfection a man like Astrophil is liable to be kept by his 'infected will' in the absence of a willingness to 'grow in effect into another nature'.[47] Ultimately, the speaking picture that Sidney constructed out of his own earlier experience was designed to illuminate grounds of wisdom 'before the imaginative or judging power' that would be capable of moving him to reshape his attitude and actions according to the dictates of conscience – in spite of the undoubted continuance of the 'vanity' concerning Lady Rich from which he could not entirely free himself.[48]

If Sidney addressed the problem of Petrarchan eroticism by exposing Petrarch's 'desio' for what it was from a Protestant perspective – self-regarding sinful concupiscence – Edmund Spenser took a step further in his *Amoretti* by suggesting how it could be remedied. Spenser's motive for engaging in this act of self-reformation, as with Sidney, arose from a real-life situation: his courtship of Elizabeth Boyle leading to their marriage in June, 1594. As in Sidney's case, his experience moved him to show, through

---

[46] Sidney, *Apology for Poetry*, p. 101/34–5; p. 103/3–6, 29–30.
[47] Ibid., p. 101/21–4.
[48] Ibid., p. 107/32–4.

Petrarchan imitation, how he had addressed a need to intercept the sinful egotism promoted by erotic desire. His solution was to relocate Petrarch's fusion of the erotic and the spiritual to a context within which it could be legitimately realized to the spiritual benefit of the lovers: that is, within Christian marriage. Like Sidney, Spenser dramatizes the stages by which the male lover in his *Amoretti* comes to terms with the inadequacy of his Petrarchan expectations. There is an important difference, however, in that whereas Sidney portrays Astrophil as remaining a prisoner of his concupiscent egotism, Spenser shows his own persona evolving out of such egotism into a love that is selfless rather than self-regarding, and which, as such, imitates the love that moved Christ to sacrifice himself to redeem humanity. It is the selflessness of this Christian love, Spenser suggests, that licenses the gratification of desire, and it can take place only within the reciprocal commitment solemnized by the bonds of marriage.[49]

At the outset of Spenser's representation the male subject of the *Amoretti* is shown to be in the grip of the same libidinous state as any other conventional Petrarchan lover. He suffers from a 'love pinéd hart', resents his lady's cruelty in not requiting his love, and is determined to 'lay incessant battery to her heart' to convert her, or else to 'fall downe and dy before her'.[50] Spenser, like Sidney before him, establishes a critical perspective on this characteristic Petrarchan behaviour by having the lady doubt its sincerity, as the lover laments:

> ... when I pleade, she bids me play my part,
> And when I weep, she sayes teares are but water:
> And when I sigh, she sayes I know the art,
> And when I waile, she turnes hir selfe to laughter.
> So doe I weepe, and wayle, and pleade in vaine,
> Whiles she as steele and flint doth still remayne.[51]

The lady's scepticism serves to highlight the suggestion of a self-serving manipulative intent that underlies the lover's Petrarchan affectations.

More importantly, Spenser weaves a whole set of moral values drawn from Protestant theology into the web and woof of the sonnet sequence, in order to establish criteria by which the behaviour of both the lover and the lady can be judged.[52] For the most part, these values reside in images that evoke concepts of good and evil, heaven and hell, virtue and sin, and salvation and damnation.

---

[49] See Edmund Spenser, *Edmund Spenser's Poetry: Authoritative Texts and Criticism*, ed. Hugh Maclean and Anne Lake Prescott (New York and London, 1993), p. 639. All quotations from the *Amoretti* are taken from this edition.

[50] *Amoretti*, nos 2, 14.

[51] *Amoretti*, no. 18.

[52] For further comment on the Protestant doctrinal overtones that run through the *Amoretti*, see William J. Kennedy, *Authorizing Petrarch* (Ithaca and London, 1994), pp. 245–53.

One can observe Spenser putting them in place by tracing the modifications he makes to Petrarchan sources on the occasions when he imitates them directly, as when he reworks Petrarch's 'Passa la nave mia colma d'oblio' into Sonnet 34 of the *Amoretti*, 'Lyke as a ship that through the Ocean wyde'. In Petrarch's original, the analogy between the lover's state of mind and a ship passing through a stormy sea is developed in very specific terms to evoke the full range of complex, subjective feelings being experienced by the lover in response to his lady's unattainability:

Passa la nave mia colma d'oblio
per aspro mare a mezza notte il verno
enfra Scilla et Caribdi, et al governo
siede 'l signore anzi 'l nimico mio;

à ciascun remo un penser pronto et rio
che la tempesta e 'l fin par ch' abbi a scherno;
la vela rompe un vento umido eterno
di sospir, di speranze et di desio;

pioggia di lagrimar, nebbia di sdegni
bagna et rallenta le già stanche sarte
che son d'error con ignoranzia attorto.

Celansi i duo mei dolci usati segni,
morta fro l'onde è la ragion et l'arte
Tal ch' i' 'ncomincio a desperar del porto.

(My ship laden with forgetfulness passes through a harsh sea, at midnight, in winter, between Scylla and Charybdis, and at the tiller sits my lord, rather my enemy;

each oar is manned by a ready, cruel thought that seems to scorn the tempest and the end; a wet, changeless wind of sighs, hopes and desires breaks the sail;

a rain of weeping, a mist of disdain wet and loosen the already weary ropes, made of error twisted up with ignorance.

My two usual sweet stars are hidden; dead among the waves are reason and skill; so that I begin to despair of the port.)[53]

Spenser replaces this extremely personal, subjective representation of Petrarch's troubled state of thought and feeling with a much more generalized statement:

[53] *Rime*, no. 189, pp. 334–5.

Lyke as a ship that through the Ocean wyde,
By conduct of some star doth make her way,
Whenas a storme hath dimd her trusty guyde,
Out of her course doth wander far astray.
So I whose star, that wont with her bright ray,
Me to direct, with cloudes is overcast,
Doe wander now in darknesse and dismay,
Through hidden perils round about me plast.
Yet hope I well, that when this storme is past
My Helice the lodestar of my lyfe
Will shine again, and looke on me at last,
With lovely light to cleare my cloudy grief.
Till then I wander carefull comfortlesse,
In secret sorow and sad pensiveness.[54]

Instead of emphasizing the buffeting effects of the storm to evoke a turbulent emotional state as Petrarch had done, Spenser focuses on the location of the ship and the absence of sound navigational bearings to guide it on its voyage. He thus invests the representation with a more universalized quality in which the wandering 'far astray' of the ship in the absence of a 'trusty guyde' symbolically suggests the general propensity of human beings to stray from the right path when they lack sound guidance. To reinforce this idea, Spenser structures his reworking around a series of contrasts between images of light and images of darkness that serves to suggest a moral illumination that the poet has lost, and also a spiritual darkness into which he has fallen. When the lover expresses a hope that 'the lodestar of [his] life' will shine again 'With lovely light to cleare [his] cloudy grief', Spenser is intimating that he needs not only to recover his lady's favour but also his true sense of direction through a clarification of the moral and spiritual 'cloudiness' that has dimmed his understanding. The sonnet is thus, like the allegory of *The Faerie Queene*, made to function on several levels. At the simplest level, it signifies the misery that the lover feels as a result of the lady's disdain, as it had in the Petrarchan original. At another level – because of the presence of symbolic images that intimate the existence of a moral order – it also implies the regenerative process that would be necessary for the lover's misery to be properly assuaged.

Spenser subjects the lady herself to this moral scrutiny as well as the poet. Again, one can see this happening in Spenser's reworking of particular Petrarchan poems, as when he adapts Petrarch's madrigal 'Or vedi, Amor'. A playful urbanity marks Petrarch's poem:

Or vedi, Amor, che giovenetta donna
tuo regno sprezza et del mio mal non cura,
et tra duo ta' nemici è sì secura.

[54] *Amoretti*, no. 34.

Tu se' armato, et ella in treccie e 'n gonna
si siede et scalza in mezzo i fiori et l'erba,
ver me spietata e 'ncontr' a te superba.

I' son pregion, ma se pietà ancor serba
l'arco tuo saldo et qualcuna saetta,
fa di te et di me, signor, vendetta.

(Now see, Love, how a young woman scorns your rule and cares nothing for
my harm, and between two such enemies is so confident.

You are in armour, and she in a mere robe with loose hair is sitting barefoot
amid the flowers and the grass, pitiless toward me and proud toward you.

I am a prisoner, but if mercy has kept your bow whole and an arrow or two,
take vengeance, Lord, for yourself and for me.)[55]

Spenser loads his imitation with an additional weight of signification:

Unrighteous Lord of love, what law is this,
That me thou makest thus tormented be?
The whiles she lordeth in licentious blisse
Of her freewill, scorning both thee and me.
See how the Tyrannesse doth joy to see
The huge massácres which her eyes do make:
And humbled harts brings captives unto thee,
That thou of them mayst mightie vengeance take.
But her proud hart doe thou a little shake
And that high look, with which she doth comptroll
All this worlds pride bow to a baser make,
And al her faults in thy black booke enroll:
That I may laugh at her in equall sort,
As she doth laugh at me and makes my pain her sport.[56]

In Petrarch's version, the poem plays upon the paradox that the God of Love,
who is heavily armed and normally omnipotent, cannot overcome a simple
unarmed girl, whose erotic desirability should make her an easy victim of his
arrows. In the process of imitation, Spenser empties the poem of much of its
paradoxical play in order to establish a moralizing perspective – again,
through introducing figurative language that evokes the norms of Protestant
theology. Rather than being a simple, beautiful young woman sitting barefoot amid the flowers and the grass, largely unaware of the erotic effect she
produces, Spenser's lady is imaged as a powerful *guerriera*, or female warrior,

[55] *Rime*, no. 121, pp. 234–5.
[56] *Amoretti*, no. 10.

in her own right – a 'Tyrannesse' who 'lordeth in licentious blisse / Of her freewill', and who 'doth joy to see' the erotic conquests she is able to make. The effect of this change of character is to invest her 'pride' with a more sinister quality. Whereas Petrarch's Laura was 'proud' towards Love because of his inability to overpower her, the pride of Spenser's lady suggests a surrender to egotistical gratification that lends an extra depth of meaning to the reference to her 'licentious' blisse. It is licentious not merely because it is uncurbed by Cupid's law, but also because it contains a trace of spiritual intemperance. As such, it is worthy of being enrolled in Love's 'black booke' as a fault for which she deserves to be chastised. On the other hand, the vindictive desire of the lover to get even with her shows that his indignation springs equally from pride – in his case, wounded pride – while his use of the term 'unrighteous', with its parody of religion, implies the true righteousness by which these spiritual faults could be corrected. Spenser's adaptation of the original thus prepares for the movement out of this concupiscent self-absorption by the lovers that he will show taking place in the later parts of the sequence.

Indeed, both the lovers shed their pride as they come to realize its vanity. An admonition is offered to the lady in the form of a choric comment by the lover in which he warns her of the danger of 'fowly shaming' the gift of beauty that Nature has given her:

> ... if her nature and her wil be so,
> That she will plague the man that loves her most:
> And take delight t'encrease a wretches woe,
> Then all her natures goodly guifts are lost.
> And that same glorious beauties ydle boast,
> Is but a bayt such wretches to beguile,
> As being long in her loves tempst tost,
> She meanes at last to make her piteous spoyle.[57]

The lady, Spenser is saying, needs to realize that Nature's gifts are to be used well, and that this entails an obligation for her to consider seriously the suit of 'the man that loves her most', rather than abusing her beauty by converting its effects on others into a source of self-love. On another occasion, he also warns her of the folly of trusting in her own self-sufficiency:

> Weake is th'assurance that weake flesh reposeth
> In her owne powre, and scorneth others ayde:
> That soonest fals when as she most supposeth
> Her selfe assurd, and is of nought affrayd.
> All flesh is frayle, and all her strength unstayd,
> Like a vaine bubble blowen up with ayre:

---

[57] *Amoretti*, no. 41.

Devouring tyme and changeful chance haue prayd
Her glories pride that none may it repayre.[58]

The vulnerability of human beings to the destructive force of time and
mutability makes excessive trust in one's self-sufficiency misplaced, and
renders desirable the 'ayde' that can be derived from a mutually supportive
relationship.

On the other hand, the lover has to learn that the lady's 'selfe assurance',
rightly placed, supports a moral integrity and steadiness that he should value
more than he did at the outset. Such a woman will not swerve at either good
fortune or misfortune,

But like a steddy ship doth strongly part
The raging waves and keepes her course aright:
Ne ought for tempest doth from it depart,
Ne ought for fayrer weathers false delight.

Significantly, the steadiness of the lady, imaged in the undeviating line of the
ship's course, contrasts with the directionless wandering of the lover's ship (in
Sonnet 34) once its guiding star had become obscured. Spenser therefore
concludes the sonnet by suggesting a steadfastness of purpose in her that can
give form and direction to his own life:

Most happy she that most assured doth rest,
But he most happy who such one loves best.[59]

Having attained a realization of these truths, the two lovers are ready to enter
into betrothal in preparation for marriage. Once again, to mark this radical
departure from the conventional pattern of Petrarchan erotic experience,
Spenser creatively adapts another famous poem by Petrarch, 'Una candida
cerva'.[60] In this case, Spenser seems to have had uppermost in mind not just
Petrarch's poem, but more specifically Wyatt's negative imitation of it, 'Who
so list to hounte'.[61] His purpose is to show how loss may be converted into
gain through the giving over of self, and he uses the echoes of Wyatt's poem
to highlight the transformative difference that such a surrender of ego can
make. Spenser follows Wyatt in converting Petrarch's pursuit of the white doe
into a huntsman chasing a hind, and the lover in his poem experiences a

---

[58] *Amoretti*, no. 58.
[59] *Amoretti*, no. 59.
[60] *Rime*, no. 190.
[61] Other analogues by Tasso and Marguerite de Navarre are cited by Reed Way Dasenbrock,
Imitating the Italians: Wyatt, Spenser, Synge, Pound, Joyce (Baltimore and London, 1991), and by
Anne Lake Prescott, 'Allegorical Deer and *Amoretti* 67', in Spenser, *Edmund Spenser's Poetry*, ed.
Maclean and Prescott, pp. 809–13, but the echoes of Wyatt's poem seem far more distinct.

similar weariness from the 'vaine assay' ('vayne travaill' in Wyatt) of the chase. There the similarities end, however, for whereas Wyatt's deer is corrupted by venality, and 'wylde for to hold' though she seems tame, Spenser's lady is a 'gentle deare' who returns 'the selfe-same way' she fled, now willing to entrust herself into his power:

> There she beholding me with mylder looke,
> Sought not to fly, but fearelesse still did bide:
> Till I in hand her yet halfe trembling tooke,
> And with her owne goodwill hir fyrmely tyde.

The psychology that makes this willing surrender possible is neatly captured in the two-way referentiality of 'mylder looke': she sees him looking less predatory and threatening (because he has come to control the egotistical excesses prompted by his desire), which in turn gives her the confidence to allow her own desire to make her responsive to him:

> Strange thing me seemd to see a beast so wyld,
> So goodly wonne with her owne will beguyld.[62]

From the lady's willing, though residually apprehensive surrender, we can infer that she has come to trust in the vision of married love that the whole sonnet sequence has been designed to affirm. This vision is most explicitly articulated when the lover tries to assure her that the liberty she will lose when entering into the bond of marriage is more than counterbalanced by the advantages she will gain from it:

> Sweet be the bands, the which true love doth tye,
> Without constraynt or dread of any ill:
> The gentle birde feeles no captivity
> Within her cage, but singes and feeds her fill.
> There pride dare not approch, nor discord spill
> The league twixt them, that loyal love hath bound:
> But simple truth and mutuall good will
> Seekes with sweet peace to salve each others wound:
> There fayth doth fearlesse dwell in brasen towre,
> And spotlesse pleasure builds her sacred bowre.[63]

This is Spenser's ultimate answer to the Petrarchan dilemma. Desire can be fulfilled, but only when the self-regarding egotism that springs from concupiscence is replaced by a mutual good will and loyalty that is possible only

---

[62] *Amoretti*, no. 67.
[63] *Amoretti*, no. 65.

within the reciprocal commitment of marriage. Within such a commitment, sexual desire (symbolized in the phallic 'brasen towre') can be gratified in 'spotlesse pleasure' because of the 'fayth' that resides in it.

Some critics have doubted Spenser's confidence in this vision because the sequence ends not with the marriage it anticipates, but with 'an unresolved drama of temporary separation and anxiety'.[64] However, the anxieties expressed in the concluding sonnets merely consolidate the sense of a real situation in which the lover has to contend with his recognizably human emotions concerning potential impediments to the fulfilment of his relationship: his absence from the lady (Sonnets 78, 87, 88 and 89), the continuance of his own 'sensuall desyre', Sonnet 84), the pressure on him to finish *The Faerie Queene* (Sonnet 80), the fact that someone has tried to slander him to his lady (Sonnet 86), and so forth. The magnificent *Epithalamion* that concludes the volume in which the *Amoretti* was published in 1595 is clearly set up to celebrate 'the wishéd day [which] is come at last'. With its concluding prayer to the heavenly powers to pour blessings on the couple so that they might raise 'a large posterity' who will long possess the earth with lasting happiness, and mount to heaven to increase the number of the blessed saints, the *Epithalamion* consummates Spenser's Protestant reinterpretation of Eros as well as preparing for the actual consummation of the marriage it celebrates.

Apart from Sidney and Spenser, William Shakespeare was the other most notable Elizabethan poet to have tackled the problem of desire through a radical rewriting of Petrarch. Even more than his two forebears, Shakespeare seems to have been influenced by the Calvinist conviction that sexual desire was depraved, and he was certainly very perturbed by his own experience of it, as not merely the *Sonnets* but also many of his plays suggest. The most zealous puritan preacher of the time could not have surpassed Shakespeare in suggesting the sinful proclivities that attend lust as it drives a man to seek the release of a sexual climax:

Th'expence of Spirit in a waste of shame
Is lust in action, and till action, lust
Is periurd, murdrous, blouddy, full of blame,
Sauage, extreame, rude, cruell, not to trust

...

[Mad] in pursut and in possession so,
Had, hauing, and in quest to haue, extreame.[65]

---

[64] Kennedy, *Authorizing Petrarch*, p. 273.

[65] William Shakespeare, *Shakespeare's Sonnets*, ed. Stephen Booth (New Haven and London, 1977), no. 129. All references to Shakespeare's *Sonnets* are taken from the facsimile of the 1609 text reprinted in this edition, lightly repunctuated if necessary.

Equally, Shakespeare acknowledges the intemperate nature of his own desire
– real or imagined – in language that could have come from any number of
contemporary Protestant doctrinal treatises dealing with the evils of
concupiscence:

> My loue is as a feauer longing still,
> For that which longer nurseth the disease,
> Feeding on that which doth preserue the ill,
> Th'vncertaine sicklie appetite to please:
> My reason the Phisition to my loue,
> Angry that his prescriptions are not kept
> Hath left me, and I desperate now approoue,
> Desire is death, which Phisick did except.[66]

Throughout the *Sonnets*, in fact, repeated references to devils, saints, angels,
temptation, purity and pride, sin and punishment, and heaven and hell evoke
the normative concepts of contemporary Protestant discourse as the backdrop against which the psychomachia taking place on centre stage is to be
viewed.

Prompted by anxiety about the sinful baseness of carnal desire,
Shakespeare sought, like Sidney and Spenser before him, to work out a
response to the problem by engaging in Petrarchan imitation. To do so, however, he departed radically from the precedents established by either of his
predecessors – possibly because his perturbation concerning issues of
sexuality seems to have been very much deeper. Rather than simply seeking
to expose the inadequacy of the moral solipsism inherent in Petrarchism as
Sidney had, or to redeem it by leading his lovers through a regenerative transformation as Spenser had, Shakespeare attempted to separate out the different aspects of love that had been fused in Petrarch in order to reassign them
to two antithetically opposed types of love-relationship. His purpose was to
try to isolate a form of love that could be erotic without being tainted by the
corrupting influence of carnal lust.

Inevitably, he found that to pursue such a goal he needed systematically to
rewrite the Petrarchan archetype, and he did this with almost paradigmatic
thoroughness. His first tactic was to substitute a male lover for the conventional Petrarchan mistress, so that the love to be developed in this relationship need not be implicated in sexual lust – or so Shakespeare thought at an
early stage in the sequence when he acknowledged the youth as the 'Master
Mistris' of his passion.[67] Correspondingly, he found it necessary to invert the
presentation of the female mistress, in order to be able to contrast the nature
of his love for her with his love for the youth:

[66] *Sonnets*, no. 147.
[67] *Sonnets*, no. 20.

Two loues I haue of comfort and dispaire,
Which like two spirits do sugiest me still,
The better angell is a man right faire:
The worser spirit a woman collour'd il.[68]

As a result, the youth ends up with all the 'golden', 'sweet' 'loveliness' and beauty that was formerly attributed to the Petrarchan mistress, while the woman is given a blackness of hair and eyes, and a face that some who behold her say 'hath not the power to make loue grone'.[69] The advantage of this dichotomized opposition was that Shakespeare could treat the physical contrast between them as symbolically indicative of a moral difference, and then interpret his libidinous relationship with the corrupt woman as debasing, and his non-libidinous relationship with the pure man as ennobling and comforting.

A second major change Shakespeare made to the Petrarchan model was to show both loves as requited, rather than unrequited, which served to reinforce and clarify the distinction he wanted to affirm between a non-sexual reciprocal love and one based on reciprocal lust. Consequently, he put Petrarch's favourite device of oxymoron to a new use, using it not to evoke a suspended state of subjective decentredness but rather to suggest man's helpless inability to avoid surrendering to the lust he wishes afterwards he had been able to resist:

[Lust is] Inioyd no sooner but dispised straight,
Past reason hunted, and no sooner had
Past reason hated as a swollowed bayt,
On purpose layd to make the taker mad.
...
A blisse in proofe and prou'd [a] very wo,
Before a ioy proposd behind a dreame,
All this the world well knowes yet none knowes well,
To shun the heauen that leads men to this hell.[70]

There is nothing in Petrarch's imaginative repertoire that anticipates the application of oxymoron to such a specific purpose, and the fact that Shakespeare could have conceived of it attests to the revolution of mindset that had been wrought by the Protestant Reformation in England.

We can see, then, the lines of construction for the strategy Shakespeare felt inclined to use in order to reconcile eroticism with Protestant conscience. Nevertheless, no one with a mind as subtle as Shakespeare's was likely to be satisfied for long with such a crudely paradigmatic approach to a problem

---

[68] *Sonnets*, no. 144.
[69] *Sonnets*, no. 131, l. 6.
[70] *Sonnets*, no. 129.

that was too complex to be contained within its rigidities. Not surprisingly, the sequence as a whole shows him constantly probing the limitations of the paradigm by showing how experiential reality disrupts the neatness of its categories. Indeed, the dichotomized opposition between the youth and the woman tends to blur as the poet discovers problems in his relationship with the former, and a source of contentment in his relationship with the latter that its sensual baseness should theoretically preclude. By the end of the sequence, paradoxically, it is debatable as to which of the two relationships gives the greater comfort, and which the greater despair.

Problems arise with Shakespeare's attempt to idealize the relationship he has with the young man when the poet discovers deficiencies both in the youth and himself. The first shock occurs when he learns that the youth has committed a 'sensuall fault' – specifically, that he has been seduced by the poet's own mistress.[71] The emotional destructiveness of this event is conveyed in the images that Shakespeare uses to describe its effect on him. He characterizes it as inducing a feeling like that experienced by someone who is caught in a storm that he did not foresee, but should have been able to predict had he been less beguiled by the apparent promise of fair weather:

> Why didst thou promise such a beautious day,
> And make me trauaile forth without my cloake,
> To let bace cloudes ore-take me in my way,
> Hiding thy brau'ry in their rotten smoke.

Even the youth's regret cannot repair the damage,

> For no man well of such a salue can speake,
> That heales the wound, and cures not the disgrace.

The real problem for the poet is that his mistress's seduction of the youth confirms the reality of the truth from which he had been trying to escape: that even the best of human beings is susceptible to the corrupting influence of the concupiscence that is most manifest in sexual lust. How devastating this perception was for Shakespeare is implied in the comparison he draws between himself and Christ carrying his cross to Calvary to be crucified (for the sins of others):

> Nor can thy shame giue phisicke to my griefe,
> Though thou repent, yet I haue still the losse,
> Th' offenders sorrow lends but weake reliefe
> To him that beares the strong offenses [c]rosse.[72]

---

[71] *Sonnets*, no. 35, l. 9; nos 40, 41.
[72] *Sonnets*, no. 34.

Shakespeare tries to find excuses for the fact that this fall has happened, but the terms in which he propounds the excuse simply confirm the idea of the intrinsic corruption of human nature:

No more bee greeu'd at that which thou hast done,
Roses haue thornes, and siluer fountaines mud,
Cloudes and eclipses staine both Moone and Sunne,
And loathsome canker liues in sweetest bud.[73]

Even while the youth's 'sinnes' do not cause the poet to love him any the less, they do irrevocably destroy what he had hoped the younger man could mean to him.[74]

For his own part, Shakespeare finds that his love for the youth is not as free from the egotism of desire as he might have thought. He has to restrain his inclination to 'controule [the] times of pleasure' of the youth, and to require 'th' account of houres'. He also experiences something very akin to sexual jealousy when he is kept awake at night by his love, fearing that his lover may be with someone else:

For thee watch I, whilst thou dost wake elsewhere,
From me farre of, with others all to neere.[75]

The sexual basis of this jealousy, however sublimated it may have been in actuality, is further revealed in the sonnets in which Shakespeare records the advent of a rival who is also addressing verses to the youth. These sonnets contain various puns that intimate sexual activity – for example, in the reference to 'thy louely argument' that 'Deserues the trauaile of a worthier pen' in Sonnet 79, or the reference to the rival who 'vpon your soundlesse deepe doth ride' with a bark 'of tall building, and of goodly pride' in Sonnet 80. While the sexual sense of words like 'argument', 'pen' and 'pride' are not fully activated here, their concentration does, as Stephen Booth has noted, give these poems 'vague sexual overtones'.[76] The effect is to undermine the suggestion that the poet's homoerotic passion can ultimately be any more exempt from concupiscence than his fully sexual relationship with the woman can.

Moreover, Shakespeare discovers that he is just as capable as the youth of betraying their love when he, too, lapses into sexual infidelity. He tries to excuse his 'travelling' on the grounds that he was never false of heart, even

---

[73] *Sonnets*, no. 35.
[74] *Sonnets*, nos 94, 95.
[75] *Sonnets*, nos 58, 61.
[76] *Sonnet* 80, headnote (p. 273). See also Booth's comments on Sonnet 38.3n. (p. 196) and Sonnet 78.3, 7, 11n. (pp. 269–70). For an interpretation that does see a fully expressed homosexuality in Shakespeare's *Sonnets*, see Bruce R. Smith, *Homosexual Desire in Shakespeare's England: A Cultural Poetics* (Chicago, 1991).

though 'in my nature raign'd / All frailties that besiege all kindes of blood', and that these 'blenches' have, paradoxically, given him back another 'youth', both by reactivating his ability to love idealistically and by restoring his faith in the youth himself, since 'worse essays proved thee my best of love'.[77] In a less facetious mood, however, he more readily acknowledges the hurt his transgression may have inflicted:

> That you were once vnkind be-friends mee now,
> And for that sorrow, which I then didde feele,
> Needes must I vnder my transgression bow,
> Vnlesse my Nerues were brasse or hammered steele.
> For if you were by my vnkindnesse shaken
> As I by yours, y' haue past a hell of Time.

The only thing that shields him from the pain of remorse is that the youth's earlier trespass becomes a fee, so that, from the poet's perspective, 'Mine ransoms yours, and yours must ransome mee'.[78]

Even as Shakespeare becomes aware of the realities within his own nature and that of the youth that subvert the possibility of sustaining the vision he had tried to construct, he nevertheless seeks to salvage the selfless love that was to have been its foundation. The generalized statement that constitutes Sonnet 116 seems to have been contrived as a manifesto and is worth quoting in full, especially as it contains complexities that are often overlooked:

> Let me not to the marriage of true mindes
> Admit impediments, loue is not loue
> Which alters when it alteration findes,
> Or bends with the remouer to remoue.
> O no, it is an euer fixed marke
> That lookes on tempests and is neuer shaken;
> It is the star to euery wandring barke,
> Whose worths vnknowne, although his higth be taken.
> Lou's not Times foole, though rosie lips and cheeks
> Within his bending sickles compasse come,
> Loue alters not with his breefe houres and weekes,
> But beares it out euen to the edge of doome:
>   If this be error and vpon me proued,
>   I neuer writ, nor no man euer loued.

What is most remarkable about this poem is the way it affirms an ideal while intimating the experiential realities that might threaten the ideal. The ideal itself is captured in a critical rewriting of a Petrarchan commonplace. In the

[77] *Sonnets*, nos 109, 110.
[78] *Sonnets*, no. 120.

Rime sparse, Petrarch recurrently invokes Laura's eyes as the constellation from which he takes his bearings:

> Come a forza di venti
> stanco nocchier di notte alza la testa
> a' duo lumi ch' à sempre il nostro polo,
> così ne la tempesta
> ch' i' sostengo d'amor, gli occhi lucenti
> sono il mio segno e 'l mio conforto solo.

(As in the force of the winds the tired helmsman at night lifts his head to the two lights that our pole always has, thus in the tempest I endure of love those shining eyes are my constellation and my only comfort.)[79]

Whether or not Shakespeare was referring to this passage directly or indirectly, he reworks the motif so that it is love itself that provides the bearings for navigation, and not the lover in his or her own person. This modification to the referent of the image of the polar star marks a significant shift in the conception of love itself, away from self-regarding eroticism to its opposite. The love that Shakespeare is seeking to affirm is characterized, instead, by a generous, forgiving, selfless dilation of spirit that is more akin to the notion of charity, as the echo in line 12 of Saint Paul's hymn to 'Love' in the Geneva version of 1 Corinthians: 13 attests. Paradoxically, this charitable love is shown to arise out of the experience of the perturbing aspects of human sexually driven behaviour that have the power to destroy love – the 'impediments' that the poem is talking about. This paradox is intimated by the coexistence within the sonnet of two antithetical layers of reference at key points. Most immediately, it presents an affirmation of an ideal Christian, Platonic love, a 'marriage of true mindes'. At the same time, however, the poem offers, in Booth's words, 'a substratum of random bisexual references': in the intimations of a woman's loss of desire (line 3), of post-coital detumescence (line 4), of priapic bawdiness (lines 5–8) and of other sexual activity (suggested by the punning connotations of lines 9–10).[80] This half-concealed level of reference serves to imply the consequences of desire so as to relate the ideal of an immutable, spiritual love to the potentially debasing actualities in human experience that necessitate and prompt it, according to the Calvinist viewpoint that Shakespeare admits in the *Sonnets*. To put it another way, he shows that because the concupiscence in human nature will cause men and women to 'fall', and fall repeatedly, the love that Sonnet 116 describes is inseparably and symbiotically related to the fallibilities that it is designed to address, as

---

[79] *Rime*, no. 73, ll. 46–51; cf. no. 189 ('Passa la nave mia colma d'oblio').
[80] See Shakespeare, *Shakespeare's Sonnets*, ed. Booth, pp. 391–2. I disagree with Booth's conclusion that these sexual references are trivial or irrelevant.

awareness of these is precisely what moves people to experience the compassion that enables them to rise above self.

As if to confirm this perception, Shakespeare immediately follows his idealistic assertion in Sonnet 116 with several sonnets in which the poet's own ongoing transgressions are recorded. Being full of the youth's 'nere cloying sweetnesse', he had himself been unfaithful, having 'frequent binne with vnknowen mindes', and sickened by 'potions ... of *Syren* teares, / Distil'd from Lymbecks foule as hell within'.[81]

Shakespeare's vision of a transcendent charity of spirit generated by humane recognition of the fallen propensities of oneself and others is consolidated still further by the sonnets he addressed to the dark lady at the conclusion of the sequence. The carnal baseness of this relationship is exposed with shocking force, together with the promiscuity, lying, deception and self-deception in which the lovers engage, but in spite of the poet's recoil from it, he still finds within the experience a cause to love her. The complex diacritical coexistence of positives and negatives in this relationship is perhaps best summed up in the amazing series of puns of Sonnet 138, in which Shakespeare captures the ability of human beings to gain mutual sustenance from a relationship the character of which is marked by many of the vices that spring from the corruption of human nature. His mistress perjures herself when she swears that she is 'made of truth' (a loyal maid), while the poet's willingness to believe her, in spite of knowing that she 'lies' (sleeps with other men), is equally the product of his self-interest. As well as being 'in vain', his desire to have her believe that he is 'some untutored youth, / Unlearnèd in the world's false subtleties' not merely displays a disingenuity that is the opposite of what it professes, but also manifests the 'vanity' that comes from self-love. This willing tolerance of mutual deceit, however, is shown to spring from a motive deeper than that of sexual cupidity or vanity alone:

> On both sides thus is simple truth supprest:
> But wherefore sayes she not she is vniust?
> And wherefore say not I that I am old?
> O loues best habit is in seeming trust,
> And age in loue, loues not t'haue yeares told.
> > Therefore I lye with her, and she with me,
> > And in our faults by lyes we flattered be.

Mutual deception in this situation is a way of securing the illusion of security in the face of a mutability in the world and a fallibility in human nature that would otherwise be a cause for despair. As such, it actually expresses a kind

---

[81] *Sonnets*, nos 117, 118, 119. Booth notes that lines 1–2 of Sonnet 119 are suggestive of perverse sexual activity, whether construed as male homosexual fellatio or as cunnilingus (p. 400, 1–2n.).

of love, in that it manifests a willingness on the part of each of the lovers to provide some of the emotional support for the other that their respective vulnerabilities require, even while the dominant motive may be self-interest.

In typical fashion, then, by the time Shakespeare has reached the end of his sonnet sequence, he has discovered that the neatness of the paradigm that potentially might have given it a conclusive ideational structure has dissolved under his gaze into a confusion of the categories that he would have liked to keep oppositionally distinct. His ability to idealize his homoerotic love has become impaired by his recognition that it excites in him a jealousy and possessiveness that spring from the same self-regard that accompanies sexual lust. He also discovers that this relationship is just as susceptible to mutability as any sexual affair when, after three years, he finds himself waning in interest and turning to other company. Conversely, he discovers through his perturbing relationship with the dark-haired woman that 'cunt-science' may become the grounds for attaining the 'conscience' out of which true love is born.[82] The puns and *double entendre* that abound in the presentation of both relationships attest to the interchangeable similarities that underlie their more apparent differences. It is the poet's ultimate awareness of these similarities that enables him to attain, however temporarily, a love that transcends the limitations of his naive idealization of the youth, and the harshness with which he is inclined to condemn the woman and himself. Yet there is no sense of closure in the *Sonnets*, or that Shakespeare believes a final solution to the problem of desire has been found. What one is left with is the image of an experience that is militant and inconclusive. For Shakespeare, it is the process of attaining a compassionate understanding of human limitation through experiencing it that ennobles; he finally repudiates the idea that a product can be attained in which those limitations can be deemed to have been perfected.

For these three great authors, Sidney, Spenser and Shakespeare, Petrarchan imitation was more than just a fashion to be tried out. It was an instrument for seriously addressing the clash between two of the most powerful discourses of the day concerning the conduct of one's erotic life. None of them rejected Petrarchism outright, but they all subjected it to a radical modification in order to acknowledge the respects in which the Petrarchan archetype could be found wanting when viewed from the more demanding perspectives of Protestant doctrine. What they all share in common is a heightened sense of the sinfulness of desire and the secondary impulses it prompts, and the consequent need for these to be intercepted and restrained. To this end, Petrarchan imitation became a means for self-exploration and self-admonition, with a view to promoting self-reformation.

---

[82] For the pun on 'conscience' see Sonnet no. 151, and Booth's note to ll. 1, 2, 13 (p. 526).

It is significant, however, that only Spenser was prepared to show the process of interior reformation as being brought to fruition, and then only if one accepts that the *Epithalamion* celebrates the marriage foreshadowed in the *Amoretti*. Neither Sidney nor Shakespeare were so unguardedly optimistic. Sidney, one senses, lacked confidence in his ability to fulfil the implied injunctions with which his fiction had challenged Astrophil, even though he accepted the need for personal desire to be constrained by the dictates of an exteriorized social and religious code. Shakespeare, on the other hand, was too aware of the potential for everything to be turned inside out – like the Silenus in Erasmus' *Praise of Folly* – to be able to commit himself to any understanding that simplified through dogmatic definition. He had also taken on board the full load of anxiety over the sinfulness of sexuality that contemporary Protestant discourse was tending to promote, without any ability to believe that it could be allayed by an appeal to a solution that was less complex than the experience it purported to address. On the evidence of the *Sonnets*, Shakespeare appears to have been hampered by something else: an unwillingness to admit the strength of a latent homosexuality that he felt obliged to repress, without any ultimate ability to do so. The resulting pressures, one suspects, are responsible for the ambivalence of many of the sonnets, as well as the inconclusiveness of the sequence as a whole.

Engagement in Petrarchan imitation for the sake of self-constitution was merely one aspect of a much larger phenomenon. Protestant English writers found Italianate imitation equally valuable as a means for interpreting the significance of the emerging English nation-state in relation to what it could and should be. It is to the use of Italian pastoralism for this purpose that this investigation will now turn.

4

Ethic and Politic Considerations: Spenser, Sidney and the Uses of Italianate Pastoral

Apart from Petrarchan lyric poetry, a second major literary mode to be introduced into England during the sixteenth century was the Italian pastoral. One motive behind the sudden enthusiasm with which English poets took up this genre in the reign of Elizabeth was a desire to emulate writers on the Continent: to show – as a matter of national pride – that the English language was just as capable as any other European vernacular of attaining the evocative effects and *cantabile* of classical pastoral poetry. The poets were also concerned to demonstrate that the culture of the new Protestant nation was just as sophisticated as the cultures of the old order from which it had departed.

There was a deeper motive, however, prompting imitation of the Italian pastoral in its various guises. In *An Apology for Poetry*, Philip Sidney claimed that 'poetry' (that is, fictive representation) is the most effectual means for attaining 'the highest end of the mistress-knowledge, by the Greeks called *architectonike*, which stands ... in the knowledge of a man's self, in the ethic and politic consideration, with the end of well-doing and not well-knowing only'.[1] Italianate pastoral poetry, the English poets discovered, could achieve both these ends more effectually than many other literary kinds because of the unique blend of the erotic and political, and of the symbolic and allegorical, that it had acquired by the time they inherited it. To represent shepherds suffering unrequited love could serve just as effectively as Petrarchan lyric self-projection for exploring issues of will and desire, and hence for pursuing knowledge in the 'ethic consideration'. Equally, the potential for pastoral

---

[1] Philip Sidney, *An Apology for Poetry or The Defence of Poesy*, ed. Geoffrey Shepherd (London, 1965), p. 104.

conventions to take on a topical level of reference, whether through symbolic exemplification, as in Sidney's *Arcadia*, or allegorical correspondence, as in Spenser's *Shepheardes Calender*, made pastoralism a powerful tool for interpreting contemporary political situations and seeking to influence their outcome. Prompting both concerns, as usual, was the stimulus of the new state religion with its compelling ideological imperatives. The Elizabethan poets, therefore, imitated Italianate pastoral both to know themselves better in the light of their new-found Protestantism, and also to work towards the institution of the goodly society they aspired towards – with the end, as Sidney averred, 'of well-doing and not well-knowing only'. The rest of this chapter will explore why English writers found Italianate pastoral modes so congenial for these purposes, and the particular ways in which they put them to use.

By the time the Elizabethans inherited it, the Italianate pastoral had evolved into two divergent traditions, each of which embodied very different representational strategies. To complicate matters, the two writers who established the prototypes for all subsequent English pastoralists, Spenser and Sidney, each espoused a different type of Italianate pastoral mode, even though they shared many of the same poetic forms and themes. Before one can understand why the two architects of Renaissance English pastoralism should have differed in their choice of pastoral type, it is necessary to unravel some of the threads of the complicated skein that makes up the European pastoral tradition.

The main influence on Renaissance pastoral was that of the Roman poet Virgil, despite the fact that bucolic poetry had been invented by the Syracusan Greek poet Theocritus, writing more than 200 years earlier (in about 275 BC). Why Virgil rather than Theocritus should have been the dominant influence (beyond the contributing factor that more people knew Latin than Greek) can be explained by the changes Virgil made to the basic Greek model.[2] Virgil's first important alteration was to invest Theocritus' uncomplicated depiction of scenes in the lives of Sicilian shepherds with a new dimension: namely, a deeper level of intermittent autobiographical and political reference displaced into the details of pastoral life through symbolic transfer. This level of reference arose because the *Eclogues* were written during the political and social turmoil following the murder of Julius Caesar in March, 44 BC. Virgil expresses his concern at injustices he saw being perpetrated around him, such as the eviction of tenant farmers to reward demobilized soldiers with the land they had occupied. He also affirms his belief that

[2] For the evolution of pastoral, see Thomas G. Rosenmeyer, *The Green Cabinet: Theocritus and the European Pastoral Lyric* (Berkeley and Los Angeles, 1969); Walter W. Greg, *Pastoral Poetry and Pastoral Drama: A Literary Inquiry, with Special Reference to the Pre-Restoration Stage in England* (London, 1906); and Helen Cooper, *Pastoral: Mediaeval into Renaissance* (Ipswich, 1977).

justice, peace and prosperity could be restored through a return to the rule of a single man. Thus, in Eclogue I he alludes to a youth who is capable of restoring order (probably Octavius), 'for whom twice six days every year our altar smokes' ('quotannis / bis senos cui nostra dies altaria fumant').[3] Shifting tack in the famed messianic Eclogue IV, Virgil images the restored polity for which he hopes as a new golden age to be brought about by the birth of an extraordinary child to a noble pair – possibly Antony and Octavia – whose marriage the poem may have been intended to celebrate.[4] In many instances, the details of the pastoral world in the *Eclogues* are used to symbolize the felicity of the longed-for new political order, in sharp contrast to the 'traces of sin' ('sceleris uestigia nostri') that corrupt the condition of the present, as when Virgil addresses the infant whose birth he predicts:

> ipsae lacte domum referent distenta capellae
> ubera, nec magnos metuent armenta leones;
> ipsa tibi blandos fundent cunabula flores.
> occidet et serpens, et fallax herba ueneni
> occidet; Assyrium uulgo nascetur amomum.
> at simul heroum laudes et facta parentis
> iam legere et quae sit poteris cognoscere uirtus,
> molli paulatim flavescet campus arista
> incultisque rubens pendebit sentibus uua
> et durae quercus sudabunt roscida mella.
> pauca tamen suberunt priscae uestigia fraudis,
> quae temptare Thetim ratibus, que cingere muris
> oppida, quae iubeant telluri infindere sulcos.

> (She-goats unshepherded will bring home udders plumped
> With milk, and cattle will not fear the lion's might.
> Your very cradle will pour forth caressing flowers.
> The snake will perish, and the treacherous poison-herb
> Perish; Assyrian spikenard commonly will grow.
> And then, so soon as you can read of heroes' praise
> And of your father's deeds, and know what manhood means,
> Soft spikes of grain will gradually gild the fields,
> And reddening grapes will hang in clusters on wild brier,
> And dewy honey sweat from tough Italian oaks.
> Traces, though few, will linger yet of the old deceit,
> Commanding men to tempt Thetis with ships, to encircle
> Towns with walls, to inflict deep furrows on the Earth.)[5]

---

[3] Virgil, *The Eclogues: The Latin Text with a Verse Translation and Brief Notes*, ed. Guy Lee (Harmondsworth, 1980), Eclogue I, ll. 42–3.
[4] Ibid., p. 55.
[5] Eclogue IV, ll. 21–33 (ibid., pp. 56–7).

The purpose of such passages is to give readers a symbolic correlative for the state to be desired which, through the imaginative associations that inhere in the images, is capable of marshalling emotions to the support of the idea. It is this 'moving' power of symbolic pastoral imagery that made the pastoral mode, as developed by Virgil, into a potent vehicle for political commentary and intervention.

A second modification destined to have a profound influence on Renaissance poets was Virgil's demonstration of how states of feeling could be communicated through establishing a subjective relationship between a man and his perception of the natural setting in which he found himself. In Theocritus, nature is presented merely as a backdrop against which the actions of the lover are enacted. When the love-sick shepherd in the third Idyll, for example, wishes he were a bee, it is not because he senses any direct correspondence or contrast between the bee and himself, but for the sake of being able to fly into a cave through the ivy and fern behind which his dark-browed Amaryllis has taken refuge.[6] In Virgil, on the other hand, the pastoral details that the lover chooses to describe, together with the emotion he invests in their description, usually serve as a subjective index to the state of his own feelings. The second Eclogue, in which Corydon expresses his longing for the beautiful slave-boy, Alexis, illustrates how effectively Virgil reveals the tormented condition of the lover through this strategy:

> 'O crudelis Alexi, nihil mea carmina curas?
> nil nostri miserere? mori me denique coges.
> nunc etiam pecudes umbras et frigora captant,
> nunc uiridis etiam occultant spineta lacertos,
> Thestylis et rapido fessis messoribus aestu
> alia serpyllumque herbas contundit olentis.
> at mecum raucis, tua dum uestigia lustro,
> sole sub ardenti resonant arbusta cicadis.'

> ('O cruel Alexis, have you no time for my tunes?
> No pity for us? You'll be the death of me at last.
> Now even the cattle cast about for cool and shade,
> Now even green lizards hide among the hawthorn brakes,
> And Thestylis, for reapers faint from the fierce heat,
> Is crushing pungent pot-herbs, garlic and wild thyme.
> But I, while vineyards ring with the cicadas' scream,
> Retrace your steps, alone, beneath the burning sun.')[7]

---

[6] Theocritus, Idyll III, in *Greek Pastoral Poetry: Theocritus, Bion, Moschus, the Pattern Poems*, trans. Anthony Holden (Harmondsworth, 1974), pp. 57–8.
[7] Virgil, Eclogue II, ll. 5–13.

The details in this scene are not incidental. Corydon registers the search of the cattle and lizards for coolness and shade, and the herbal restoratives that Thestylis is preparing, because of his awareness that there is no relief for him, whether from the literal heat of the noon-day sun – reinforced by the image of the singing cicadas – or from the metaphoric 'heat' of the frustrated desire that he feels for the youth. All of Virgil's poetic description in the *Eclogues* works in this way, achieving a remarkably powerful effect through a fusion of the sensuous apprehension of the pastoral world with various states of emotional feeling.

Virgil's introduction of a topical level of reference into bucolic poetry, and his demonstration of how pastoral elements could be used to realize the subjective condition of particular emotional states – especially those relating to love – were to influence all subsequent writers of pastorals in Europe, but the forms in which this influence would be felt were to depend upon the further mediation of a number of key Renaissance Italian poets who provided the immediate models for pastoral imitators in other European vernaculars. In brief, the two main innovations that Virgil made to Theocritus became the foundations for two distinct schools of pastoral writing. The first, led by Petrarch in his *Bucolicum carmen* (1344–50), picked up the political strain in Virgil and developed it into an overriding concern with allegory of a satirical and polemical complexion. The second, following the example established by Boccaccio in his *Ameto* (1341–2), focused on the preoccupation with love in Virgilian pastoral, and enhanced its expressive potential by adding a linking prose narrative drawn from the genre of romance. The contrast between the fictive worlds that were created by these rival pastoral modes was very great indeed.

For Petrarch, allegory was the essence of pastoral, and the purpose of allegory was to turn men and women away from vice towards the virtuous path to heaven. Consequently, Petrarch's pastoral landscape is populated with admonitory figures like John the Baptist (in the figure of 'a hirsute youth') and Christ (in the figure of Apollo) (Eclogue I), tearful mothers who grieve over the delinquency of their children (Eclogue V), along with corrupt Popes (like Mitio in Eclogue VI) and cardinals imaged as lustful he-goats (Eclogue VII) who live in the increasing darkness of their vices. Similarly, far from being characterized by idyllic tranquillity, the life of shepherds is filled with infected flocks, calloused hands, fearful thunderstorms and tornados, theft, rapine, pillage, pain, loss, grief and other mishaps that attest to the harshness of fortune and the fallen nature of the world. Presiding over all is a dark sense of the 'remorseless pursuit' of the Black Death – the lethal bubonic plague that was sweeping through Italy at the time Petrarch was writing. Petrarch's pastoral world is a grim, unrelieved one that figures forth a deeply pessimistic view of life. The only way out of his nightmare vision is summed up in the advice that Theophilus offers to Philogeus at the conclusion of Eclogue IX:

Accipe consilium propere; cuntatio namque
Lenta fuit semper subitis inimica periclis:
Huc, huc volve oculos; hec est via recta sine ullis
Insidijs, predura quidem calcataque paucis,
Sed super aerios arcto que tramite colles
Perferat et sistat fessum in regione quieta.
Illic vita habitat; leva sed olentis averni
Sulphureis stant stagna vadis; ibi lurida mortis
Signa vides, atroque polum nigrescere fumo.
Hoc evade lacus; dextrum michi prende cacumen.

(Take my advice and hasten always in imminent danger
Lengthy delay has proved fatal. Turn your eyes hither, I bid you,
Hither. You'll see the right path, though many have left it untrodden.
Free of all traps it will lead you by a narrow way to the airy
Summits and bring you at last to a place that gives rest to the weary.
There life eternal abides. To your left lie the swamps of Avernus,
Stinking with sulphurous pools. There, raising his hideous ensigns,
Death reigns supreme and the lowering skies are charged with dark vapors.
Shun those grim lakes, take the road on my right that leads to the
mountain.)[8]

Pastoral, for Petrarch, serves not to enhance enjoyment of the world but to prepare men and women for leaving it.

When Boccaccio began writing Latin eclogues, in about 1341, he seems to have been inclined to eschew political topicality and satire altogether in favour of the erotically expressive strain in Virgil,[9] but once he was shown Petrarch's 'Argus' eclogue (Eclogue II), in which his mentor mourned the death of King Robert of Naples, Boccaccio felt obliged to revise his conception of the genre, thereafter using the eclogue as a medium, first, for attacking corruption in Petrarch's manner, and then for dealing with religious themes of a Dantesque sort.[10] The net effect of Petrarch's all-powerful influence was to force Boccaccio to vacate the eclogue as a form in which he could develop the other strain in Virgilian pastoral, causing him to seek scope for that endeavour in a new genre of his own invention.[11] He found what he was

---

[8] Petrarch, Eclogue IX, ll. 88–97. All references are to Francesco Petrarca, *Petrarch's Bucolicum Carmen*, trans. Thomas G. Bergin (New Haven and London, 1974). For further comment on the defining characteristics of Petrarchan pastoral, see Cooper, *Pastoral*, pp. 36–46.

[9] He conceded later that Eclogues I and II of his *Buccolicum carmen* 'openly bear on the outside my youthful lusts as it were' ('fere iuveniles lascivias meas in cortice pandunt'). See Giovanni Boccaccio, *Eclogues*, trans. Janet Levarie Smarr, vol. 11, Garland Library of Medieval Literature (New York and London, 1987), p. xxxv.

[10] Ibid., pp. xxxiii–l.

[11] In the letter to Fra Martino da Signa which accompanied the final version of his *Buccolicum carmen*, Boccaccio reveals his awareness of the difference of natural inclination between Petrarch

looking for, in writing his *Ameto*, by placing a romance narrative within a pastoral *locus amoenus*, or pleasance, and then interweaving passages of prose narrative with lyric songs in *terza rima* in which each of the seven nymphs that the shepherd Ameto meets while hunting tells the story of her loves.[12] Moreover, he secured a respectful distance from Petrarch by writing in Italian rather than Latin. These expedients left him largely free of the burden of didactic expectation with which Petrarch had loaded the medieval eclogue, and free to explore the expressive aspects of Virgilian pastoral that had been largely suppressed. The *Ameto* still ends up with an allegorical *significatio*, but it is a largely factitious one, being arbitrarily applied at the conclusion of the work when Ameto belatedly realizes that the seven nymphs who have kindled his desire are really the seven virtues, whose effects are turning him from a brute animal into a man.[13] Up to that point, however, Boccaccio develops the fiction as if it is to be apprehended solely at the literal level, through the senses – as, indeed, Ameto apprehends the nymphs. Pastoral detail is used not to suggest an allegorical level of reference but to represent and elicit a highly charged condition of sensuous and emotional arousal that is unlike anything in Petrarch's *Bucolicum carmen*, but very reminiscent of Virgil (and certain other Roman poets, such as Ovid). This can be illustrated from the moment when Ameto urges Lia to lie down with him in the shade:

> Tu se' lucente e chiara più che 'l vetro;
> e assai dolce più ch'uva matura
> nel cor ti sento, ov'io sempre t'impetro.
>   E, sì come la palma in vèr l'altura
> si stende, così tu, vie più vezzosa
> che 'l giovinetto agnel nella pastura.
>   E se' più chiara assai e graziosa

---

and himself, and sees his own practice as closer to the classical original: 'Theocritus, a poet of Syracuse, was the first, we are told by ancient writers, to develop the pastoral mode in Greek poetry, and he intended nothing beyond what the outer meaning of the words conveyed. After him Virgil wrote in Latin, but he concealed some further meanings beneath the surface, though he did not invariably want us to understand anything else under the names of his characters. After him others also wrote, but they are insignificant and not worthy of attention, with the exception of my famous teacher Francis Petrarch, who has raised the style a little above what is usual and who continually gives his speakers significant names according to the subjects of his eclogues. Of these writers I have followed Virgil, in that I have not always been concerned to conceal a further meaning in all my characters' names'. I quote the translation given by Cooper, *Pastoral*, p. 217, n. 59.

[12] For the Italian text, see Giovanni Boccaccio, *Decameron; Filocolo; Ameto; Fiammetta*, ed. Carlo Salinari, Enrico Bianchi and Natalino Sapegno, vol. 8, La Letteratura Italiana: Storia e Testi (Milan and Naples, 1952); for an English translation, see Giovanni Boccaccio, *L'Ameto*, trans. Judith Serafini-Sauli, vol. 33, Garland Library of Medieval Literature, Series B (New York and London, 1985).

[13] Ibid., Italian text, p. 1051; English text, p. 139.

che le fredde acque a' corpi faticati
o che le fiamme a' freddi o ch'altra cosa.
E' tuo cape' più volte ho simigliati
di Cerere alle paglie secche e bionde,
dintorno, crespi, as tuo capo legati.[14]

(You are glittering and shining more than glass, and within my heart, where I always implore you, I hold you far sweeter than ripe grapes; and even as the palm tree stretches upward, so do you; and you are far more graceful than the youthful lamb in pasture. You are more welcome and sweet than cold waters to tired bodies, or flames to the cold, or anything else; and often I have compared your hair, waving and bound around your head, to the ripe blond straw of Ceres.)

The allegorical frame of reference is very remote in a passage like this. What is uppermost is a rapid movement from one sense to another – sight, taste, somatic sensation – in images that suggest not just beauty but also the idea of a 'fruition' that reflects the object of the lover's desires. The connection with allegory seems even more tenuous in the lubricious descriptions that some of the nymphs give of their sexual encounters, as, for example, when Agapes recounts the revulsion she felt when her aged husband 'tried in vain to cultivate the gardens of Venus ... seeking to cleave the earth of those gardens, which longed for gracious seeds, with an old ploughshare ... [which] refused to carry out its due office in the firm fallow'.[15] Even when the allegorical intention resurfaces – in the encounter between Agapes (Charity) and the youthful Apiros (Without Fire), arranged by Venus – the intimations of their literal lovemaking are at least as important as the allegorical message, especially when its ardour is contrasted with the 'cold embraces' of Agapes' aged husband ('i freddi abbracciamenti del vecchio marito') which she thereafter eschews.[16]

By the end of the Trecento, therefore, two rival traditions of pastoral had been established in Italy, each defined by the relative priority of the topical and expressive elements to be found in Virgil. The one was embodied in the eclogues of Petrarch, in which the pastoral world existed to be a cipher for establishing a corrective view of vices in the real world. The other was realized in the pastoral romance of Boccaccio, in which the fictive world had its

---

[14] Ibid., Italian text, p. 923; English text, p. 19.

[15] The full passage reads: 'O ninfe, abbiate ora compassione alle mie noie. Poiché egli ha gran parte della notte tirata con queste ciance, gli orti di Venere invano si fatica di cultivare; e, cercante con vecchio bomere fendere la terra di quelli, disideranti li graziosi semi, lavora indarno; però che quello dall'antichità roso, come la lenta salice, la sua aguta parte volgendo in cerchio, nel sodo maggese il debito ufizio recusa d'adoperare' (ibid., Italian text, pp. 1000–1; English text, p. 90).

[16] Ibid., Italian text, pp. 1006; English text, p. 90.

own experiential reality as well as being a vehicle for the communication of more abstract ideas. Petrarch's didactic high seriousness meant that the eclogue in Latin as he shaped it inevitably became espoused by Renaissance humanists as a tool for promoting reform. By linking the idyllic aspects of the pastoral world to prose romance, Boccaccio inadvertently ensured that his new hybrid form would thereafter be the province of the vernacular. Both these traditions were to descend to the writers of sixteenth-century Europe, but by way of two further mediators whose impact it is vital to grasp if the dynamics of English pastoralism in the Renaissance are to be properly understood.

The mediator of the Petrarchan didactic eclogue was the Italian Carmelite monk Baptista Spagnuolo Mantuanus (1448–1516), whose *Adolescentia* (1498) became a highly influential textbook for educators across most of Europe.[17] All ten of Mantuan's eclogues are didactic, touching on many of the themes covered by Petrarch, and adopting many of the Petrarchan attitudes. Semi-naturalism prevails, with emphasis on the hardships of rustic life, natural disasters and the corruption of the world. Both women and love are satirized, while scorn is heaped on the faults of members of contemporary society, such as the failure of rich men to offer patronage to poets (Eclogue V), or the bestial lusts, drunkenness, homicides and thefts perpetrated by those (Mantuan has his eye particularly on Rome) who dwell in the fetid air of the city (Eclogue VI).[18] As with Petrarch, the world signified by his pastoral fictions is a fallen place whose corruption can ultimately be cured only in heaven; in the meantime, it is to be exposed for what it is and excoriated, and that is the bitter function which, for Mantuan, pastoral serves.

Mantuan's influence was enormous – in his own time he was considered superior to Virgil[19] – and it was through him that the classical pastoral came to England. Some time before 1514 Alexander Barclay translated two eclogues from the *Adolescentia* which, together with a verse paraphrase of Aeneas Sylvius' *Miseriae curialium* cast as three further eclogues, eventually appeared as *Certayne Eglogues of Alexander Barclay Priest* in 1570. While Barclay mentions Theocritus, Virgil, Petrarch and Boccaccio in his 'Prologe', it is Mantuan that he singles out as 'The best of that sort since Poetes first began'. Moreover, his reference to Petrarch as writing 'playne and meryly' in his pastorals shows that he had no first-hand knowledge of the *Bucolicum carmen*, and while he seems to know by hearsay that Boccaccio wrote pastorals, the fact that he alludes only to the *Genealogia deorum* suggests that he did not know that author's *Buccolicum carmen* either.[20] It appears that Barclay found

17 On Mantuanus, see Cooper, *Pastoral*, pp. 108–11.
18 The text of the *Adolescentia* may be found in Baptista Spagnuolo Mantuanus, *The Eclogues of Baptista Mantuanus*, ed. W.P. Mustard (Baltimore, 1911).
19 See Cooper, *Pastoral*, p. 108.
20 Alexander Barclay, *The Eclogues of Alexander Barclay*, ed. Beatrice White, vol. 175, Early English Text Society, Original Series (London, 1928), p. 2, ll. 31–42.

Mantuan's version of the Petrarchan eclogue sufficient for what he was look-ing for – a moral instrument for praising virtue and condemning vice:

> If any suche [i.e. backbiter] reade my treatise to the ende
> He shall well perceyue, if he thereto intende,
> That it conteyneth both laudes of vertue,
> And man infourmeth misliuing to eschue,
> With diuers bourdes and sentences morall,
> Closed in shadowe of speeches pastorall,
> As many Poetes (as I haue sayde beforne)
> Haue vsed longe time before that I was borne.[21]

Half a century later, when the general interest in Italian literature exploded in the 1560s, Barclay's example was followed by other writers. The pastorals in Barnabe Googe's *Eglogs, Epytaphes, and Sonettes* (1563) are largely mod-elled on Mantuan's *Adolescentia* and have the same didactic bias. Fortified by extreme Protestant convictions, Googe takes an even sterner attitude towards human shortcomings. Love is denounced as a 'fervent humour' whose poison 'infects the blood about / and boils in every part' until all senses decay and the oppressed lover is left imprisoned in a mindless frenzy that subjects him to all the torments of hell.[22] Correspondingly, shepherds are exhorted to 'leave Cupido's camp, / the end whereof is vile', and love God with their whole hearts in order to avoid the monster in hell whose 'greedy mouth ... always feeds / upon the sin-drowned soul', and 'Whose greedy paws do never cease in sinful floods to prowl'.[23] It is not surprising that Googe should seize upon the allegorical potential of pastoralism to denounce the persecution of the faithful by the Marian bishops of the previous reign, alluding specifically to the burning of Cranmer, Latimer and Ridley:

> Such sheep as would not them obey,
>   but in their pasture bide,
> With cruel flames they did consume
>   and vex on every side.
> And with the sheep, the shepherds good
>   (O hateful hounds of hell)
> They did torment, and drive them out
>   in places for to dwell.
> There dièd Daphnes for his sheep,
>   the chiefest of them all,
> And fair Alexis flamed in fire
>   who never perish shall.[24]

---

[21] Ibid., p. 3, ll. 95–102.
[22] Barnabe Googe, *Eclogues, Epitaphs, and Sonnets*, ed. Judith M. Kennedy (Toronto, 1989), 'Egloga prima', ll. 65–84.
[23] Ibid., 'Egloga octava', ll. 41–2, 221–8.
[24] Ibid., 'Egloga tertia', ll. 129–40.

If Googe's use of pastoral seems a grotesque perversion of the genre, it merely represents a chick born of the egg that Petrarch had laid and Mantuan had hatched. Moreover, the influence of Mantuanesque pastoral persisted beyond Googe with barely diminished force. George Turbervile translated Mantuan's eclogues in 1567, and when Spenser attempted pastoral, with *The Shepheardes Calender* (1579), it was to Mantuan he chiefly turned, both through direct imitation and also by adapting the work of one of Mantuan's French imitators, Clement Marot. Potentially, therefore, this Mantuanesque strain of pastoral might have dominated English pastoral right through the Renaissance had Sidney not become aware of the existence of an alternative: the distinctive version of Boccaccio's pastoral-romance evolved by the other major Italian intermediary of the late fifteenth/early sixteenth century, Jacopo Sannazzaro.

Picking up where his forebear had left off, Sannazzaro, in *Arcadia* (1504), developed Boccaccio's hybrid *prosimetrum* into a form of pastoral that would ultimately have a far greater impact on Renaissance English consciousness than the alternative tradition of didactic pastoral. To an even greater extent than Boccaccio, he enhanced the beauty of the natural world in order to oppose the natural against the artificial as a superior source of pleasure. Furthermore, the beauty and tranquillity of the pastoral setting are used as a backdrop to intensify a pervasive mood of eroticism: nearly all of Arcadia's shepherds, and the narrator himself, are love-sick, or have recently been so. Sannazzaro's Arcadia, in fact, is a country of the mind – a source of comfort into which the suffering individual can retreat to seek refuge from the troubles of the outer world. As such, it is associated with the perfection of the golden age – a time when fields were held in common, when there were no poisonous plants, and when wrath and jealousy were unknown – which is recalled in order to highlight the corruption of the contemporary age, with its faithlessness, depravity, greed, injustice and progressive degeneration. This can be seen in the lament Opico shares with Serrano in Eclogue 6:

Ov' è 'l valore, ov' è l'antica gloria?
    u' son or quelle genti? Oimè son cenere,
    de le qual grida ogni famosa istoria.
I lieti amanti e le fanciulle tenere
    givan di prato in prato ramentandosi
    il foco e l'arco del figliuol di Venere.
Non era gelosia, ma sollacciandosi
    movean i dolci balli a suon di cetera,
    e 'n guisa di colombi ognior basciandosi.
O pura fede, o dolce usanza vetera!
    Or conosco ben io che 'l mondo instabile
    tanto pèggiora più, quanto più invetera;

tal che ogni volta, o dolce amico affabile,
ch'io vi ripenso, sento il cor dividere
di piaga avelenata et incurabile.

(Where is the valor, where is the ancient glory?
Where now are those people? ay me, they are ashes,
they of whom every famous history cries aloud.
The happy lovers and the tender maidens
went from meadow to meadow renewing in their minds
the fire and the bow of the son of Venus.
There was no jealousy, but pleasuring themselves
they trod their sweet dances to the sound of the cither,
and in the manner of doves exchanging kisses.
O unspotted faith, O sweet venerable custom!
Now do I well know that the unstable world
worsens so much the more, the more it ages.
So that every time – O sweet affable friend –
that I think upon you, I feel my heart is pierced
with an empoisoned and incurable wound.)[25]

In short, Sannazzaro reverses the direction of the Petrarchan treatment of pastoral by consciously aestheticizing the pastoral world so as to turn it into a source of consolatory pleasure.

One consequence of this frank acceptance of aesthetic pleasure as a legitimate goal in its own right was Sannazzaro's decision to break free of the tyranny of Latin dactylic hexameters and recast the pastoral eclogue in a variety of popular Italian verse measures of the day, including the *frottola*, the *barzelletta* and *madrigal*, the *canzone*, the *sestina*, *terza rima sdrucciola* and *terza rima piana*.[26] Not only did this range of verse forms allow Sannazzaro greater scope for lyricism, it also enabled him to differentiate between the different types of eclogue he imitated from Virgil – the singing match, funeral elegy, panegyric, exchange of insults, lover's complaint and so forth – more effectively. The making of beautiful poetry in itself becomes a part of the recreation, both for the shepherds in the fiction and for Sannazzaro in real life, and later poets were quick to see the challenging possibilities that this simple but (for the time) fairly radical perception opened up for them.

Sannazzaro's other major innovation was to introduce an alienated outsider, Sincero, into the Arcadian setting, which has the effect not merely of

[25] Eclogue 6, ll. 100–14. References to *Arcadia* are to Jacopo Sannazzaro, *Opere de Iacopo Sannazzaro*, ed. Enrico Carrara (Turin, 1952) for the Italian text, and Jacopo Sannazzaro, *Arcadia & Piscatorial Eclogues*, trans. and ed. Ralph Nash (Detroit, 1966) for the English translation.

[26] For more detailed discussion of these measures, see William J. Kennedy, *Jacopo Sannazzaro and the Uses of Pastoral* (Hanover and London, 1983), pp. 96–7.

expanding the narrative interest, but also of generating a dynamic tension between the pastoral beauty and tranquillity he encounters and his own melancholic awareness of the problems which await him back in the outer world. The whole work, in fact, functions like an extended oxymoron in which sadness is derived from pleasure, and pleasure from sadness. The aestheticization of sadness in *Arcadia*, however, is not merely gratuitous; Sannazzaro shows it prompting his persona, Sincero, to re-engage with the outer world, once he has been led from Arcadia through a phantasmagorical subterranean landscape to emerge at the foot of the hill in Naples where he now realizes his love lies dead. This lesson, too, would not be lost on Sidney: that pastoral need not rely on didactic allegory for a profundity of moral effect, which could be equally, and possibly even more effectually, achieved through the imaginative experience of a fully realized literal fiction enhanced by all the aesthetic pleasure that poetic art could supply.

We are finally in a position, then, to ascertain how and why the Elizabethan poets responded to the varieties of Italianate pastoral that were available to them in the sixteenth century. As in other matters, Edmund Spenser and Philip Sidney led the way, with the former favouring the Mantuanesque variety of pastoral, and the latter developing the Sannazzaran kind. The primary impetus for their pastoral imitations appears to have arisen, as in the case of their Petrarchism, from their Protestant concerns. In the Mantuanesque allegorical eclogue Spenser found an appropriate vehicle for denouncing the irresponsibility of the neo-Roman clergy, and for warning against the subversive presence of unreformed elements within the Church of England. Simultaneously, he discovered that other conventions of the Virgilian pastoral, such as the topos of the grieving lover, could be invested with a deeper level of signification that allowed them, too, to be used for indirect comment on the contemporary political situation. Sidney, developing cues he found in the pastoral romance of Sannazzaro, evolved an entirely new genre of pastoral that allowed him to explore with great imaginative profundity not simply issues of personal and political governance, but also the larger meaning of contemporary English experience in the context of divine providence. In both cases, these poets were led by their Protestant inclinations to reconfigure the Italianate models that they inherited, Sidney by 'contaminating' the pastoral with elements from Greek romance and epic in order to depict a more tragic sense of the human situation, and Spenser by blending Mantuanesque pastoral satire with a Sannazzaran/Virgilian love-sickness that could, when dressed up in native English trappings, be read as signifying his own frustration at being denied the effectual role in the new polity that he believed his learning and expressive talents equipped him to play.

With *The Shepheardes Calender* Spenser burst upon the Elizabethan literary scene, simultaneously announcing his arrival as a major new poet and his support of the puritan drive for a more thorough-going reformation of the English Church.[27] The religious Settlement of 1559 had left the Church predominantly Calvinist in doctrine, but with traces of Catholicism in many of its practices – particularly its episcopal system of governance, and its use of elaborate vestments and rituals. To many ardent Protestants, the 1559 religious Settlement was a temporary compromise for the sake of expediency, not the lasting *via media* that the Queen and some of her ministers were determined it should be. By 1579, when *The Shepheardes Calender* was published, people with puritan sympathies were becoming seriously worried. Some progress towards reform had been made following the appointment of Edmund Grindal to the See of Canterbury in 1575 – Grindal permitted the Geneva Bible, with its Calvinist glosses, to be printed in England and defended the priority of preaching and the Word – but Grindal's moderate puritanism had alarmed Elizabeth and Burghley and he was soon removed from office, to be replaced by the reactionary John Whitgift. Spenser's main purpose in writing *The Shepheardes Calender* was to voice the concern felt by many that the consolidation of the Protestant Reformation in England was about to be aborted, not merely because reactionary forces were gaining control of policy but also – and more dangerously – because the Queen herself appeared to be slackening in her willingness to defend the interests of her Protestant subjects. The prospect that Elizabeth might contract a marriage with the Catholic Duke of Alençon cast a particularly sinister shadow on events at this time.

Given Spenser's support of the puritan reformist position, it is not difficult to see why the allegorical pastoral should have appealed to him. The genre had already become associated with the reform of ecclesiastical abuse as a result of Petrarch's denunciation of the Avignon papacy in the *Bucolicum carmen*, and Mantuan's attack on the corruption of the Roman clergy in Eclogue 8 of his *Adolescentia*, 'quae dicitur Falco de moribus Curiae Romanae'. Moreover, the values of the reformed ecclesiastical polity that Spenser and other English puritans wished to see instituted in the Elizabethan Church were already symbolically implicit in the imagery and topoi of pastoral poetry. The picture of shepherds living a life of humble simplicity, devoted to the care of their flocks and vigilantly protecting them against the predations of rapacious wolves, could readily be made to signify the clerical ideal that many believed the English clergy were failing to observe. By adopting an archaic English diction and giving his characters names like 'Colin Clout' and 'Piers', which recalled an earlier tradition of rustic

---

[27] On the extent of Spenser's support of a moderate puritan position see David Norbrook, *Poetry and Politics in the English Renaissance* (London, 1984), pp. 61–9, and John N. King, *Spenser's Poetry and the Reformation Tradition* (Princeton, 1990).

complaint, Spenser was able to dress the Continental pastoral tradition in native attire and thus enlist its moral force to the support of the reformist cause.

Spenser's main strategy was to follow Mantuan in investing pastoral images with allegorical significance for the purpose of exposing clerical abuse, especially in the three 'moral' eclogues that form the backbone of *The Shepheardes Calender* – 'Maye', 'Iulye' and 'September' – which, as E.K. warns the reader, contain an admixture of 'Satyrical bitternesse'.[28] In 'Maye', for instance, he draws a contrast between Palinode and Piers as two different shepherd types. Palinode wishes to join in the Maying festivities:

> Yougthes folke now flocken in euery where,
> To gather may buskets and smelling brere:
> And home they hasten the postes to dight,
> And all the Kirke pillours eare day light,
> With Hawthorne buds, and swete Eglantine,
> And girlonds of roses and Sopps in wine.[29]

Piers, in contrast, disapproves of shepherds who neglect their sheep in order to pass their time in 'lustihede and wanton meryment', denouncing them as 'shepeheards for the Deuils stedde' (ll. 42–3). As the introductory 'Argument' makes clear, Palinode is the type of the neo-Catholic priest who takes excessive delight in the sensuous trappings of religion, symbolized in the delights of May, at the expense of his spiritual responsibilities, while Piers (whose name suggests the humility of his famous forebear, Piers Plowman) is a type of the true Protestant pastor who is aware that 'shepheard must walke another way, / Sike worldly souenance [i.e. remembrance] he must foresay' (ll. 80–1). Similarly, just as Spenser invests his shepherd types with a deeper allegorical relevance, so too does he transform the conventional pastoral topos of a vanished golden age to which he makes Piers allude:

> The time was once, and may againe retorne,
> (for ought may happen, that hath bene beforne)
> When shepeheards had none inheritaunce,
> Ne of land, nor fee in sufferaunce:
> But what might arise of the bare sheepe,
> ...
> Nought hauing, nought feared they to forgoe.
> For Pan himselfe was their inheritaunce,

---

[28] Edmund Spenser, *The Works of Edmund Spenser: A Variorum Edition*, ed. Charles Grosvenor Osgood, Edwin Greenlaw, Frederick Morgan Padelford and Ray Heffner, 11 vols (Baltimore, 1932–57), vol. 1: *The Minor Poems*, 'The generall argument of the whole booke', p. 12. All subsequent references to *The Shepheardes Calender* are to this edition.

[29] *Shepheardes Calender*, pp. 46–7, ll. 9–14.

And little them serued for their mayntenaunce.
The shepheards God so wel them guided,
That of nought they were vnprouided,
Butter enough, honye, milke, and whay,
And their flockes fleeces, them to araye.
But tract of time, and long properitie:
That nource of vice, this of insolencie,
Lulled the shepheards in such securitie,
That not content with loyall obeysaunce,
Some gan to gape for greedie gouernaunce,
And match them selfe with mighty potentates,
Louers of Lordship and troublers of states.

(ll. 103–23)

In Spenser's hands, the motif of the golden age is turned into a symbol of the pristine ideal that the Catholic priesthood has betrayed in becoming corrupted by worldliness and pride.

Spenser misses no opportunity, in fact, to exploit the potential for pastoral commonplaces to be invested with the deeper allegorical resonance that Petrarch and Mantuan had shown they could have. In 'Iulye' he borrows the motif of a debate between an upland and a lowland shepherd that Mantuan had used in his eighth eclogue, in order, once again, to expose the difference between responsible and negligent priests. Morell, the upland shepherd (who represents, in the words of E.K.'s argument, 'proude and ambitious Pastours'), extols the hills as being 'higher heuen' (l. 89), while Thomalin, the lowland shepherd, who is a type of the good priest, affirms the superiority of the dales:

To Kerke the narre, from God more farre,
    has bene an old sayd sawe.
And he that striues to touch the starres,
    oft stombles as a strawe.
Alsoone may shepheard clymbe to skye,
    that leades in lowly dales,
As Goteherd prowd that sitting hye,
    vpon the Mountaine sayles.

(ll. 97–104)

Significantly, Spenser has radically altered the symbolism that he found in his source. Mantuan's uplander easily prevails with his account of the marvels of the mountains, whereas Spenser transfers the moral advantage to the more humble lowlander. Spenser's association of the contrast between hill and dale with one between pride and humility, in fact, reflects the transition from a Catholic sensibility to an English puritan one.

In other respects, Spenser's polemical eclogues show some striking departures from his Italian models. The story that Piers tells in 'Maye' of a fox who tricks a kid into unbarring the door by pretending to be a sheep and peddling 'a trusse of tryfles at hys backe' (l. 239) is like nothing in Mantuan or Petrarch, but does recall the beast fables of medieval English literature, and also the polemical discourse of the earlier Henrician and Edwardian reformers, as found in works like William Turner's *The Hunting and Fyndyng out of the Romishe Fox.* Likewise, the passage that concludes 'Iulye', in which Spenser alludes to the recent fall of 'Algrind' (alias Grindal) by describing how an eagle dropped a shellfish on his bared white head, thinking it was chalk, has no antecedent in the pastoral tradition, but is reminiscent of the allegorical symbolism to be found in the scores of political prophecies that circulated around England during the sixteenth century. We thus see Spenser deliberately trying to domesticate the Italian political eclogue by hybridizing it with native English kinds. This reflects not simply his desire to be well received by English readers, but also the literary nationalism that is signalled in E.K.'s dedicatory epistle to Gabriel Harvey.[30]

While the pressure of Spenser's reformist commitment led him to imitate Mantuan's use of the eclogue for political allegory, he was too much of a humanist not to know that the Virgilian archetype had contained a much greater variety than was to be found in the recension of his Carmelite predecessor. Accordingly, Spenser sought to achieve some of this variety by including eclogues in various Virgilian kinds that are classified as 'Plaintiue' and 'recreatiue', in addition to the 'Moral' ones.[31] Even here, however, Spenser seeks to move his imitation of the Virgilian love-complaint and funeral elegy closer towards the allegorical mode of Mantuan in order to make them serve his political purposes, which are to express frustration at being excluded from a meaningful role in national affairs, and to utter an indirect admonition concerning Elizabeth's failure to fulfil her role as the defender of the Protestant nation.

His method is to lace the plaintive and recreative eclogues with hints that they may contain a deeper level of meaning – accessible if their symbolic displacements are decoded – which is never made explicit. It is extremely difficult, if not impossible, to identify the 'generall dryft and purpose' of the eclogues (as a long history of divergent scholarly speculations attests), for as E.K. reminds us in the dedicatory epistle to Gabriel Harvey, Spenser had 'laboured' to conceal it.[32] Nevertheless, Spenser does indicate the presence of a topical level of reference by developing a number of relationships centring on Colin Cloute, under whose name, E.K. informs us, Spenser 'secretly

30 *Shepheardes Calender*, pp. 8–9.
31 'The generall argument of the whole booke', *Shepheardes Calender*, p. 12.
32 *Shepheardes Calender*, p. 10.

shadoweth himself'.[33] These relationships are progressively brought into collocation with one another until the concerns of each begin to become associated with those of each of the others, thus adding up to a cumulative impression of a determinate view held by Spenser himself that the discerning and receptive reader is invited to share.

The Shepheardes Calender begins and ends with two love-complaints that voice Colin's despair over the fruitlessness of his suit to a country lass called Rosalind. Such utterances had become commonplace in the pastoral tradition, and there is nothing at the outset of the work to suggest a topical level of reference apart from the peculiar intensity with which Spenser develops the correlation between the sterility of the winter landscape and Colin's inner emotional condition:

> You naked trees, whose shady leaues are lost,
> Wherein the byrds were wont to build their bowre:
> And now are clothd with mosse and hoary frost,
> Instede of bloosmes, wherwith your buds did flowre:
> I see your teares, that from your boughes doe raine,
> Whose drops in drery ysicles remaine.
>
> All so my lustfull leafe is drye and sere,
> My timely buds with wayling all are wasted:
> The blossome, which my braunch of youth did beare,
> With breathed sighes is blowne away, and blasted,
> And from mine eyes the drizling teares descend,
> As on your boughes the ysicles depend.
>
> (ll. 31–42)

As the work proceeds, other eclogues supply additional information about Colin that prompts one to suspect that his grief may arise from more than love-melancholy alone. In 'Aprill' the shepherds Thenot and Hobbinol acknowledge Colin's love for Rosalind, but when they aim to demonstrate how 'trimly dight' his 'ditties' are (l. 29) it is Colin's ode to Elisa, 'Queene of shepheardes all', that they sing, not any praise of Rosalind. Indeed, at no point in *The Shepheardes Calender* is Rosalind ever accorded an expression of devotion equal to that which Colin bestows on Elisa:

> To her will I offer a milkwhite Lamb:
>   Shee is my goddesse plaine,
>   And I her shepherds swayne,
> Albee forswonck and forswatt I am.
>
> (ll. 96–9)[34]

---

[33] *Shepheardes Calender*, gloss to 'Januarye', p. 18, note to l. 1.

[34] E.K. glosses 'forswonck and forswatt' as 'ouerlaboured and sunneburnt' (*Shepheardes Calender*, p. 43, note to l. 99).

Equally, in the 'Iune' eclogue, when Hobbinol offers Colin a remedy for his lack of success in 'love', it consists not of advice on how to overcome Rosalind's resistance but of an exhortation for him to

> Leaue me those hilles, where harbrough nis to see,
> Nor holybush, nor brere, nor winding witche:
> And to the dales resort, where shepheards ritch,
> And fruictfull flocks bene euery where to see.
>   (ll. 19–22)

In other words, Hobbinol's remedy for Colin's love-sickness is for him to come to London where the opportunities for gaining patronage are much greater than in the country, a proposal that subtly shifts the grounds of the argument. Similarly, the reiterated pretexts that Spenser finds for diverting the discussion to the topic of the Queen make it pretty clear what kind of patronage he would prefer: a position at court. Cumulatively, Spenser's handling of Colin's love-melancholy allows one to infer that, whether or not Colin's unrequited love for Rosalind signifies an actual love affair, its more important function within the overall fiction is to serve as a generalized figure for Spenser's discontent at his lack of advancement within the Elizabethan political establishment.

In spite of his decision to make the deeper 'dryft and purpose' of *The Shepheardes Calender* intentionally obscure, Spenser may have become fearful that he had overdone the concealment, for he seeks to make the deeper level of signification relating to his personal frustration more explicit in the 'October' eclogue. To do so, he reverts to the simpler allegorical mode of Mantuan, this time imitating Eclogue 5 of the *Adolescentia* to construct a dialogue between Cuddie, a frustrated poet who 'little good hath got, and much lesse gayne' (l. 10), and Piers, who believes that 'the prayse is better, then the price' (l. 19), and that the supreme reward of the poet is to have his mind lifted up to heaven in the course of poetic inspiration. In spite of his belief that the transcendence achieved through poetic creativity is its own reward, Piers also believes that 'Princes pallace' is 'the most fitt' place for 'peerless Poesy' (ll. 79–82), and outlines for Cuddie a poetry-writing programme designed to procure him advancement. Cuddie is first to abandon pastoral poetry for epic and 'sing of bloody Mars, of wars, of giusts', then to proceed to panegyric (Piers suggests that Leicester, the Queen's favourite, would be a suitable subject), and finally to write 'Of love and lustihead'.[35] The fact that Spenser himself followed this programme closely in the years ahead, producing *The Faerie Queene*, the *Prothalamion*, and the *Amoretti* and *Epithalamion*, to match the kinds that Piers recommends, confirms how

---

[35] *Shepheardes Calender*, p. 97, ll. 37–54.

important his desire for patronage really was. It is a sad irony that, after Spenser had mounted the most ambitious campaign for patronage in the English Renaissance, the belated recognition it eventually achieved him came too late to do him any real good.[36]

We are presented, then, with a work in which Spenser uses the conventions of Italianate pastoral for the purpose of voicing personal and political discontents through decorous displacement. This indirection culminates in the enigmatic 'Nouember' eclogue, in which he tackles the subject closest to his heart. Ostensibly, the poem is a funeral elegy in which, according to E.K., Spenser laments the death of 'some mayden of greate bloud, whom he calleth Dido'.[37] Critics have long suspected, however, that Dido may represent Queen Elizabeth herself, and that the elegy may be a lament for her 'death' to England as a result of the French marriage that seemed imminent in 1579.[38] Several important aspects of the poem support this surmise. In the first place, 'Nouember' is based very closely on Clement Marot's *Eglogue sur le Trespas de ma Dame Loyse de Savoye, Mere du Roy Françoys, premier de ce nom*, a poem dealing with the death of a queen, and Spenser reinforces the regal stature of his subject by giving her the name of another famous queen upon whose actions the fate of a nation depended, Dido. When E.K. observes in the 'Argument' to the eclogue that 'The personage is secrete, and to me altogether vnknowne, albe of him selfe [i.e. Spenser] I often required the same' (p. 104), he is pointing to a fundamental incongruity: anyone who had recently died, and who was of sufficiently 'greate bloud' to warrant this elevated treatment, is unlikely to have been so totally unknown at the time as E.K. confesses is the case. The absence of a well-known candidate to whom the terms of the elegy could be literally applied may in itself have been designed to prompt a figurative interpretation.[39] Second, the elegy for Dido (Virgil's 'Elissa') in 'Nouember' appears to have a close relationship with the eulogy of Elisa in 'Aprill'. Colin is the author of each, the complicated stanzaic forms he uses are variants of one another, and when he exhorts the shepherds' daughters to 'sing no moe / The songs that Colin made in her prayse' (ll. 77–8), within the context of the work as a whole it is his earlier panegyric of Elisa that springs to mind. Finally, there are specific local allusions within the eclogue that support a topical identification of Dido with

---

[36] See Alistair Fox, 'The Complaint of Poetry for the Death of Liberality: the Decline of Literary Patronage in the 1590s', in *The Reign of Elizabeth I: Court and Culture in the Last Decade*, ed. John Guy (Cambridge, 1995), pp. 229–57, esp. pp. 235–8.

[37] *Shepheardes Calender*, 'Nouember', Argument, p. 104.

[38] See, in particular, P. McLane, *Spenser's Shepheardes Calender: A Study in Elizabethan Allegory* (Notre Dame, 1961), pp. 47–60.

[39] For a summary of speculations on Dido (variously identified as a daughter of Lady Sheffield, Ambrosia Sidney, and Susan Watts), see Spenser, *The Works of Edmund Spenser*, ed. Greenlaw and others, vol. 1, 'Commentary', pp. 402–4.

Elizabeth. Spenser's apostrophe to the 'greate shepheard Lobbin', for whom Dido once made nosegays and 'knotted rushrings', and deemed nothing too dear (ll. 113–17), almost certainly contains an anagram that refers to '[R]obbin L' – Robert Dudley, the Earl of Leicester, known as 'Robin', who had been the Queen's favourite until his secret marriage with Lettice Knollys was revealed to Elizabeth in 1578 by Simier, agent of the Duke of Alençon.[40] Even more tellingly, the nature of Spenser's modification of some key lines in Marot suggests that he was tailoring them to warn of the consequences should Elizabeth fail to protect her Protestant subjects. Extolling the beneficial rule of Louise de Savoie as regent during the captivity of François I in Madrid, Marot writes:

> Tant bien sçavoit en seurté confermer
> Tout le Bestail de toute la Contrée,
> Tant bien sçavoit son Parc clorre & fermer
> Qu'on n'a point veu les Loups y faire entrée.[41]

(All the animals throughout the whole country knew that they were completely protected, for they knew that their park was so impregnably enclosed and locked up that it was impossible for any wolf to gain entry into it.)

In imitating this passage, Spenser alters it significantly:

> The feeble flocks in field refuse their former foode,
> And hang theyr heads, as they would learne to weepe:
> The beastes in forest wayle as they were woode,
> Except the Wolues, that chase the wandring sheepe:
> Now she is gon that safely did hem keepe.
>
> (ll. 133–7)

Whereas the source had portrayed the security of the beasts resulting from Louise's good government, Spenser focuses on their vulnerability in the absence of the protection that Dido once afforded them. Moreover, far from being barred entry to the park, the wolves are now rejoicing at the prospect of being able to pursue the 'wandering' sheep freely, especially now that the flocks are enfeebled through refusing their former food. Spenser's reworking invests the passage with a depth of religious symbolism that is altogether lacking in the source: the 'food' that the sheep are refusing is the Word as

---

[40] Spenser again used the anagram 'Lobbin' to refer to Leicester in *Colin Clouts Come Home Againe* (1591), in which he has Hobbinol (Gabriel Harvey) describe how he went to court 'To wait on *Lobbin* (*Lobbin* well thou knewest)' (ll. 735–6).
[41] Clement Marot, *Œuvres lyriques*, ed. C.A. Mayer (London, 1964), Eglogue I, p. 331, ll. 145–8. For further comment on Spenser's use of Marot, see Annabel Patterson, *Pastoral and Ideology: Virgil to Valery* (Berkeley, 1988), pp. 106–32.

interpreted in Calvinist doctrine, while the rejoicing 'Wolues' are closely allied to the crafty wolves and foxes that are denounced in the 'Maye', Iulye' and 'September' eclogues – that is, the popish clergy. Spenser has thus converted the pastoral elegy to a new purpose in using it to suggest what will happen to Protestant England if Elizabeth persists in the course upon which she seemed set in 1579. Moreover, by placing the elegy in parallel with the earlier eulogy of Elisa, Spenser is offering Elizabeth an option as to which view of herself she wants to have sung by her people: she can remain adored by her grateful subjects, or lamented as their defaulting protector should the French marriage proceed.

Spenser's experiment with Italianate neo-classical pastoral has seldom been judged entirely successful, in spite of the dexterity with which he handles an impressive array of metrical forms.[42] Given the certitude of his Protestant convictions, together with the allegorical temper of his literary instincts, it was inevitable that he would be drawn to the Petrarchan bucolic mode as developed by Mantuan rather than the alternative variety evolved by Boccaccio and Sannazzaro, but having chosen it, Spenser had difficulty overcoming its limitations. The first problem he encountered was to find a way of making the basic Virgilian pastoral kinds carry the burden of allegorical expectation that Petrarch and Mantuan had thrust upon them. Because the love-plaint, the singing match and the funeral elegy had not originally been designed to carry this burden, there was an intrinsic mismatch between their forms and the weightiness of what Spenser wanted to use them to say. In short, the Petrarchan/Mantuanesque pastoral had a limited representational capacity in spite of the potential for allegory that it seemed to promise. When Spenser attempted to use pastoral in this way the result was a confusion – rather than variety – of voices, and a degree of obscurity that has hindered readers from perceiving his 'dryft' rather than stimulating their interest in it (especially in the plaintive and recreative eclogues). Spenser himself appears to have found that his experiment had led to a dead end, for when he returned to the writing of pastoral a little over a decade later, with *Colin Clouts Come Home Againe*, he reverted to the simpler, more direct native mode to be found, for example, in John Skelton's *Collyn Clout*, the title of which Spenser's poem echoes. To escape entirely from the limitations of the representational cul-de-sac into which Mantuan had led him, Spenser had to switch genres completely, which he did by moving from pastoral to epic with the composition of *The Faerie Queene*.

The contrast between Philip Sidney and Spenser in their response to Italianate pastoral could not be greater, and it is extremely instructive.

---

[42] For comment on Spenser's metrical virtuosity, see Paul Alpers, 'Pastoral and the Domain of Lyric in Spenser's *Shepheardes Calender*', *Representations*, 12 (1985): 83–100.

Whereas Spenser followed Mantuan, Sidney opted for the alternative mode created by Boccaccio and Sannazzaro and developed it into an entirely new form of epic pastoral romance. The reasons for this divergence can be traced back to a difference of aesthetic inclination which in turn arises out of a contrasting conception of the extent to which knowledge is able or likely to be translated into action, whether by the individual or the state, in a world dominated by sin.

While both men showed strong Calvinist leanings, Spenser appears to have been far less troubled by the implications of his religion than his contemporary, particularly with respect to the degree to which the will is able to be freed from its sinful bondage. Spenser's works suggest that he was far more willing than Sidney to accept the existence of determinate solutions for the problems in human experience that he addressed. In the *Amoretti*, for example, he shows how sexual desire can be reconciled with spirituality within the bond of marriage. Likewise, in *The Faerie Queene* most of his knights are shown to be successful in completing their quests: the Red Cross Knight slays the dragon, Sir Guyon destroys the Bower of Bliss, Britomart frees Amoret and restores her to Scudamour, and so on. No matter how frequently the protagonists are diverted from their course by false turnings or overpowered by enemies, their destination is never in doubt, and the right path to it is always clearly identified as such once the wayfaring knight has recovered it. The pattern of experience undergone by the Red Cross Knight in Book I is paradigmatic, in Spenser's view, of what is possible for all men and women: naive, wilful and overconfident at the beginning of his quest, the Red Cross Knight inevitably falls through pride to the point where he becomes susceptible to despair, but with the intervention of grace and the guidance of true religion he is able to be restored to a regenerate wholeness that enables him to fulfil his earthly quest and prepares him to enter into the New Jerusalem in the next life. For Spenser, there is always a 'right form' for every human belief and action that can be perceived through reason illuminated by faith, and which can be attained through responsible self-control informed by the teachings of religion and assisted by grace. The process may be militant, but the outcome, should men and women be prepared to cooperate with God, is assured.

For Sidney, on the other hand, the argument for 'the first accursed fall of Adam' and the reality of 'man's infected will' always seems more compelling than the idea that regeneration is likely to be readily achieved. His heroes usually display a force of desire that is stronger than any ability they have to control it, and their failure to do so is shown to produce disastrous consequences. In *Astrophil and Stella*, for example, Astrophil refuses to listen either to the dictates of his own conscience or to the injunctions of Stella in seeking to gratify an illicit passion. Similarly, Amphialus, in *Arcadia*, is led through the encouragement of the evil Cecropia and his desire for Philoclea to mount a rebellion that unleashes a series of tragic events that disrupt the order of the commonwealth and end in his own near ruin. To put it bluntly, Sidney believed – in the words with which he would translate Philippe du Plessis-Mornay's *The Trewnesse of the Christian Religion* – that even while 'the most part of us ... preach the kingdome of heaven, ... [we] have our groynes ever wrooting in the ground'.[43] For this reason, Sidney was seldom prepared to show problematical issues being brought to a point of resolution and closure in the way that Spenser usually does, and on the one occasion he attempted to do so, with the contrived ending of the *Old Arcadia*, the result was manifestly unsatisfactory and may have prompted his decision to recast the work entirely.

These fundamental differences in outlook between Spenser and Sidney underpinned their respective choices of pastoral mode. Spenser, with his more resolute view of things, was looking for a form of pastoral that could be used for purposes that were primarily polemical and declamatory, rather than exploratory, and for this the Petrarchan/Mantuanesque tradition of allegorical pastoral suited him admirably, being monological rather than dialogical in its signifying processes. Sidney, on the other hand, was looking for a form that would assist 'well-knowing' to be translated into 'well-doing'. According to the aesthetic that he propounds in the *Apology for Poetry*, fictive representation is effectual in achieving this end because the image it presents to the mind is able to activate its powers to make wise discriminations and judgements, and also to 'move' the reader into translating 'gnosis' into 'praxis' through its affective force. Sidney's belief in the vital importance of the psychological and emotional responses induced by fictive imitation made him less receptive than Spenser to the tradition of allegorical pastoral, as allegory tended to limit the freedom of choice made possible by the less regulated kind of imaginative participation that he valued. It was perfectly consistent with his religious and aesthetic outlook, therefore, that he should prefer the more fully mimetic pastoral mode that Sannazzaro had developed out of Boccaccio.

What, then, induced Sidney to take up pastoral in the first place, and what potentiality did he see in the Sannazzaran pastoral? It has been said that writers write about what they need to know about most, and that the mind will find the medium for the message it desires. In Sidney's case, both these apophthegms are particularly true. Between 1577 and the spring of 1581 (by which time the first version of *Arcadia* was complete),[44] Sidney had come to have very pressing reasons for needing to know himself 'in the ethic and

---

[43] Philip Sidney, *The Prose Works of Sir Philip Sidney*, ed. Albert Feuillerat, 4 vols (Cambridge, 1963), 'Preface to the Reader', p. 190.

[44] On the date of composition of the *Old Arcadia*, see Philip Sidney, *The Countess of Pembroke's Arcadia (The Old Arcadia)*, ed. Jean Robertson (Oxford, 1973), pp. xv–xix. All subsequent references to the *Old Arcadia* are to this edition.

politic consideration', and the Sannazzaran pastoral yielded itself admirably to the creation of the kind of fictive representations through which he could explore the implications of his situation. Because the *Arcadia* is the product of an extremely complex intrication of personal, moral, religious, political and aesthetic issues, it is worth taking some time to establish the factors that were involved.

By 1580 Sidney and his family had fallen out of royal favour, and at the time of writing *Arcadia* Sidney was chafing with discontent at his deliberate exclusion from power by Elizabeth and her administration.[45] His marginalization had resulted from a number of compounding causes. In February 1577 he had been given his first major diplomatic assignment, having been appointed to lead an embassy to the Emperor Rudolph II.[46] Ostensibly, his mission was to convey the Queen's condolences to Rudolph and the two Counts Palatine, Ludwig and Casimir, on the deaths of their fathers, but his covert purpose had been to sound out a number of Protestant princes, including William of Orange, on the possibility of a defensive league against Spain. Upon his return, Sidney was dismayed to find that the Queen refused to commit herself to the aid of Casimir and William of Orange, with whom he had negotiated, and that she viewed his performance very coolly. Elizabeth was displeased at Sidney's aggressiveness of policy, and when it turned out that he had been excessively optimistic about the results that it would produce, she was not impressed.[47] It is also probable that, at a deeper level, Elizabeth did not trust him, and may even have perceived him as a potential threat. On his mother's side he was descended from the Dudleys, being the Earl of Leicester's nephew and designated heir (until the Earl produced a legitimate son in 1581). Another uncle, Guildford Dudley, had been executed with Lady Jane Grey as a usurper of the throne, and Leicester himself had been viewed during the earlier 1570s as a likely consort for the Queen. Philip Sidney's own eligibility as a candidate for a princely match was strikingly demonstrated on the embassy of 1577, when William of Orange opened negotiations for him to marry his daughter, Marie of Nassau, which would have entailed Sidney becoming governor of the provinces of Holland and Zeeland. In addition, there is some evidence that he had explored the possibility of marriage with a German princess, possibly Elizabeth of Anhalt, or, alternatively, John Casimir's sister.[48] With the prospect of an alliance

---

[45] The influence of Sidney's dissatisfaction on the composition of *Arcadia* is admirably traced in Richard C. McCoy, *Rebellion in Arcadia* (New Brunswick, 1979), many of whose conclusions I follow.

[46] For a detailed account of Sidney's 1577 mission, see Katherine Duncan-Jones, *Sir Philip Sidney: Courtier Poet* (New Haven and London, 1991), pp. 120–34.

[47] See the comments of William Ringler, in Philip Sidney, *The Poems of Sir Philip Sidney*, ed. William A. Ringler, Jr (Oxford, 1962), p. xxvi.

[48] See Duncan-Jones, *Sir Philip Sidney*, pp. 132–4.

between the Dudley family and these foreign powers through such a match, Queen Elizabeth could not support the Continental Protestant princes without committing herself to a more aggressively Protestant foreign policy than she could wish, nor could she afford to allow Sidney to advance to a position where he might threaten her. Sidney's ambitions were high, and the Queen's determined efforts to contain them must have filled him with frustration, testing his loyalty and patience to the limit.

Growing evidence of the Queen's disfavour towards the Sidneys came when Sir Philip's father, Henry Sidney, then Lord Deputy Governor of Ireland, was recalled in 1578 to defend himself against accusations of misgovernment involving the imposition of a land tax in kind or provisions on those Irish lords living in the English 'Pale'.[49] The situation grew worse in July of 1579 when Jean de Simier, the Duke of Alençon's envoy, revealed to Elizabeth the fact of Leicester's secret marriage to Lettice Knollys, which had taken place six months earlier. The Queen's rage extended to other members of Leicester's circle, including the Sidneys, and Sidney's mother was obliged to withdraw from court.[50] To make Sidney's humiliation complete, the Queen supported the Earl of Oxford against Sidney in a serious quarrel between the two in late August 1579. The quarrel arose when the Earl ordered Sidney off the tennis court at Greenwich Palace, claiming precedence on the grounds that he, Oxford, was 'born great, greater by alliance, and superlative in the prince's favour'.[51] When Elizabeth intervened, following a trading of insults that seemed destined to lead to a duel, she appears to have turned the incident into a further pretext for putting Sidney in his place, reminding him of 'the difference in degree between earls and gentlemen; the respect inferiors owed to their superiors; and the necessity in princes to maintain their own creations, as degrees descending between the people's licentiousness and the anointed sovereignty of crowns'.[52] To a man of Sidney's pride, this condescension must have seemed intolerable, particularly in the light of the expectations that many people were entertaining of him.

The event that finally sealed the Queen's hostility towards Sidney, however, was the stunningly forthright letter he wrote to her sometime between late August and October 1579 expounding the reasons why she should not marry the Duke of Alençon. In essence, this letter warned her that the only benefit the marriage could give her was children, which in any case she could have by another man, and that even this blessing would be at the cost of the deep love her subjects presently bore towards her, together with the loss of England's independence and security. It would be better for Elizabeth, Sidney

[49] Ibid., p. 136.
[50] Ibid., p. 160.
[51] Fulke Greville, *The Prose Works of Fulke Greville, Lord Brooke*, ed. John Gouws (Oxford, 1986), p. 38.
[52] Ibid., p. 39.

concluded, if – in standing alone as the only protector of God's Church – she remained 'the example of princes, the ornament of this age, the comfort of the afflicted, the delight of your people, the most excellent fruit of all your progenitors, and the perfect mirror to your posterity'.[53] Although he suffered no direct reprisals for this criticism of the proposed match – unlike the unfortunate John Stubbes, whose right hand was cut off with a butcher's cleaver for writing a propaganda piece attacking the French marriage – Sidney's candour cost him any remaining shreds of favour that the Queen may have been prepared to bestow on him. For over a year Sidney was systematically excluded from advancement or any position of importance, and he soon found it expedient to withdraw from court to the circle of his sister, the Countess of Pembroke, at Wilton. It was during the eighteen months between autumn 1579 and the spring of 1581 that much of the first version of *Arcadia* was written, a large part of it while Sidney was rusticated at Wilton.

Sidney's overwhelming need by the time of his rustication in late 1579 was to come to terms with the existence of obstacles between him and the attainment of his desire. This desire manifested itself in two ways. At one level, Sidney was motivated by religious zeal, a profound conviction of the worth of his abilities, and aristocratic pride to desire an active role in the political affairs of the nation, not only to satisfy ego but also to ensure that the Protestant cause was advanced both at home and abroad. At another level, as *Astrophil and Stella* would soon confirm, Sidney was also possessed of a high level of sexual libido for which he found it difficult to secure legitimate satisfaction. Sidney seemed doomed by the intensity of his desire to be imprisoned in a situation in which prevailing circumstances made the attainment of his aspirations impossible, partly because of his own temperamental extravagance and partly because his way was blocked by a queen who was determined to keep him in a disempowered position. The result, unsurprisingly, was an intense conflict in Sidney: on one hand he felt tempted to find ways of throwing off the shackles that restrained him; on the other, his Calvinist conscience warned him of the reality of humanity's 'infected will', and reminded him of the spiritual culpability of surrendering to such intemperate desires. Sidney needed, therefore, to reconcile these two contradictory imperatives, and being the poet he was, he decided to do it by creating a fictive representation in which the issues could be explored through symbolic displacement.

For this purpose, the Boccaccesque/Sannazzaran pastoral romance was ideal. The erotic element in it was very much greater than in the countervailing tradition of pastoral that Spenser had chosen, because Boccaccio had used the pastoral setting as a frame in which the nymphs of the *Ameto* could

---

[53] Philip Sidney, *The Miscellaneous Prose of Sir Philip Sidney*, ed. Katherine Duncan-Jones and Jan Van Dorsten (Oxford, 1973), pp. 51–7.

tell the diverse stories of their loves, while Sannazzaro had deepened the love interest still further by turning his love-sick Arcadian shepherds into Petrarchan lovers who often speak in phrases borrowed from the *Rime sparse*. This expanded preoccupation with love in the pastoral romance enabled Sidney to create a fable in which, through the love interest, issues relating to desire and its fulfilment could be symbolically objectified. Indeed, Sidney focuses attention on the topic of desire in the *Old Arcadia* by multiplying and compounding the number of love-relationships, and by showing its empire as extending across generational boundaries. Not only does he double the main love-relationship, presenting not one but two princes, Pyrocles and Musidorus, tormented by love for two royal sisters, Philoclea and Pamela, but he also makes Pyrocles himself the object of lust for the ruler of Arcadia, Basilius (who is deceived by Pyrocles' disguise as an Amazon), and his wife Gynecia (who realizes that Pyrocles is a man in spite of his disguise).

The prose narrative that linked the verse eclogues in Sannazzaro's *Arcadia* also lent itself to Sidney's purpose, for it enabled him to generate an extended action through which he could explore not only the dynamics of choice, but also the consequences of specific choices, especially those involving bad faith. In order to make the narrative achieve this end, Sidney needed to develop it far beyond anything attempted by Sannazzaro or his imitators (such as Jorge de Montemayor, whose *Diana* (*c.*1560) was also known to Sidney). He did this by inventing a multiple action in accordance with the principles being prescribed for romances by Italian theorists such as Giraldi.[54] Moreover, the plot of the *Old Arcadia* is also constructed in accordance with the five-act structure of classical drama: 'The First Book or Act' consists of the exposition (describing Basilius' decision to withdraw into the country to evade events predicted by an oracle he has consulted) and the initiation of the action (showing the onset of the respective love pursuits); 'The Second Book or Act' presents the unfolding of the action (by showing how the pursuits develop); 'The Third Book or Act' complicates the action (by showing the deceptions perpetrated by the princes to outwit Basilius and Gynecia so that they can abduct the princesses); 'The Fourth Book or Act' presents a series of reversals that frustrate the stratagems of the four lovers, leaving them in a state of mortal danger and the country in a state of near anarchy; and 'The Last Book or Act' presents a denouement that is averted from being a catastrophe at the last moment by an unexpected anagnorisis and peripeteia. In effect, by further adding a set of comic characters comprising Dametas and his family, Sidney was able to conflate a serious double-plot with a comic underplot to form the kind of dynamic action that could suit his thematic purpose.[55]

---

[54] See Giambattista Giraldi Cinthio, *Giraldi Cinthio on Romances: Being a Translation of the Discorso intorno al comporre dei romanzi with Introduction and Notes by Henry L. Snuggs*, ed. Henry L. Snuggs (Lexington, 1968), pp. 11, 21–3.

[55] See *Old Arcadia*, pp. xx–xxi.

A third reason for Sidney's preference for the Sannazzaran model lay in its uniquely distinctive pastoral world. With the beauty and tranquillity of its natural landscape, the stability and harmony of its shepherd society, and the joyful rustic recreations of its inhabitants, the Arcadia created by Sannazzaro could serve as a symbolic backdrop to the problematical human issues being dealt with in the foreground. Sidney could thus use it to highlight the perversity of the main characters' actions and the destructive consequences they beget, while simultaneously intimating the ideal condition that England should be striving to attain, but which would be beyond its reach should its governors continue to replicate the behaviour of the protagonists in his fiction.

Fourth, Sidney could exploit Sannazzaro's depiction of the alienated outsider to construct a symbolic image of his own personal situation. Sannazzaro had represented his persona, the melancholy Sincero, as having taken refuge in Arcadia to seek relief from his own political misfortunes and the deep perturbation he feels at his awareness that the woman he loves, and who requites his love platonically, is unaware that his love for her is accompanied by sexual desire.[56] Sidney similarly shows his own persona, Philisides, seeking to find refuge in Arcadia in response to unrequited 'love', which in his case represents his lack of favour with Queen Elizabeth as much as any literal love affair. Commenting on the recreations of the Arcadian shepherds, Sidney writes:

> the peace wherein they did so notably flourish, and especially the sweet enjoying of their peace to so pleasant uses, drew divers strangers, as well of great as of mean houses, especially such whom inward melancholies made weary of the world's eyes, to come and live among them, applying themselves to their trade: which likewise was many times occasion to beautify more than otherwise it would have been this pastoral exercise.[57]

Philisides is one such melancholy stranger, and symbolically his entry into Arcadia signifies not only the attempt of his creator to escape from his own troubles in the real world of Elizabethan morality and politics by withdrawing to his sister's house at Wilton, but also the attempt of Sidney-the-artist to find refuge in the creative activity of composing the *Old Arcadia* itself.

A final reason for the appeal of the Sannazzaran pastoral to Sidney is that imitating Sannazzaro's *prosimetrum* gave him an ideal opportunity to display his virtuosity as a poet. The eclogues that Sannazzaro had interspersed through his prose narrative were cast in the most popular Italian verse measures of the day – the *frottola*, the *barzelletta* and *madrigal*, the *canzone*, the *sestina, terza rima sdrucciola* and *terza rima piana* – most of which had not

56 Sannazzaro, *Arcadia*, trans. Nash, chap. 7, p. 71.
57 *Old Arcadia*, p. 57.

been previously attempted in English. Sidney must have felt that this was one domain in which he could range freely and excel without restriction, for he not only reproduces Sannazzaro's most elaborate measures but tackles a range of classical quantitative metres as well.

One Italian verse form that he attempts for the first time in English was the notoriously difficult *frottola*, involving lines of eleven syllables (in Sidney's case ten syllables) whose fifth syllable (in Sidney's case the fourth syllable) rhymes with the last syllable of the preceding line. Sannazzaro had written *frottole* of exceptional grace and fluidity:

> vide un bel lume   in mezzo di quell'*onde*
> che con due *bionde*   trecce allor mi *strinse*
> e mi *dipinse*   un volto in mezzo al core.

> (I saw in the midst of those waves a lovely sight / that bound me then with two golden locks / and painted in the middle of my heart a face.)[58]

Sidney imitated this measure in the dialogue in which the aged, wise Geron exhorts Philisides to shake off his melancholy:

> *Geron.* Up, up, Philisides,   let sorrows *go*,
>   Who yields to *woe*   doth but increase his *smart*.
>   Do not they *heart*   to plaintful custom *bring*,
>   But let us *sing*,   sweet tunes do passions *ease*,
>   An old man hear,   who would thy fancies raise.

> *Philisides.* Who minds to please   the mind drowned in *annoys*
>   With outward *joys*,   which inly cannot *sink*,
>   As well may *think*   with oil to cool the *fire*;
>   Or with *desire*   to make such foe a *friend*,
>   Who doth his soul   to endless malice bend.[59]

An equally difficult Italian form is *terza rima sdrucciola*, consisting of tercets with lines of twelve syllables in which the rhyming stress falls on the ante-penultimate syllable, as distinct from the easier *terza rima piana*, which has lines of eleven syllables in which the rhyming stress falls on the penultimate syllable. Sannazzaro writes *sdrucciole* with consummate ease:

> Perisca il mondo, e non pensar ch'io trepidi;
>   ma attendo sua ruina, e già considero
>   che 'l cor s'adempia di pensier più lepidi.

[58] Sannazzaro, *Arcadia*, Eclogue I, ll. 62–4 (my emphases).
[59] *Old Arcadia*, 'The First Eclogues', p. 72, ll. 4–13 (emphases added).

(Let the world perish, and never think that I tremble, / but I await its downfall and already consider / that my heart is filled with thoughts that are pleasanter.)[60]

Sidney attempts to match Sannazzaro's skill with *terza rima sdrucciola* in another dialogue, this time involving an exchange between the jealous shepherd Dicus and his mistress, Dorus:

> *Dicus.* Dorus, tell me, where is thy wonted motion
> To make these woods resound thy lamentation?
> Thy saint is dead, or dead is thy devotion.
> For who doth hold his love in estimation,
> To witness that he thinks his thoughts delicious,
> Seeks to make each thing badge of his sweet passion.
>
> *Dorus.* But what doth make thee, Dicus, so suspicious
> Of my due faith, which needs must be immutable?
> Who others' virtue doubt, themselves are vicious.
> Not so; although my metal were most mutable,
> Her beams have wrought therein most sure impression:
> To such a force soon change were nothing suitable.[61]

To top off his bravura display of prosodic skill, Sidney even attempts a double sestina, uttered by Strephon and Klaius ('Ye goat-herd gods, that love the grassy mountains'), in imitation of Sannazzaro's double sestina in Eclogue IV of the *Arcadia*.[62] Even more than Spenser, Sidney seems to have been determined to equal, if not overgo, his Continental predecessors so as to make good a claim that the English language could rival other European vernaculars as a vehicle for poetic expression.[63] Indeed, the energy he put into creating his spectacular display of poetic virtuosity may suggest that poetic ambition had become for him, at this time, a substitute for other forms of ambition that he felt blocked from realizing in the real world of Elizabethan politics.

In essence, then, Sidney chose to imitate Sannazzaran pastoral because its elements gave him the means of addressing his concerns in a displaced symbolic representation. It allowed him to objectify and explore the dynamics and consequences of 'unbridled desire'; it enabled him to depict the discrepancy between what ought to be and the imperfect reality of what is; it permitted him to explore the implications of his own alienation; and it allowed him an outlet for his own frustrated ambition. What it could not do in the

---

[60] Sannazzaro, *Arcadia*, Eclogue I, ll. 40–2.
[61] *Old Arcadia*, 'The Second Eclogues', p. 137, ll. 11–22.
[62] *Old Arcadia*, 'The Fourth Eclogues', pp. 328–30.
[63] See Sidney, *Apology for Poetry*, pp. 140–1.

form in which he inherited it, however, was to represent adequately Sidney's Calvinist sense of the sinfulness of the human condition. He therefore needed to subject the mode to substantial modification.

He did this primarily by exploiting the dramatic structure he had created in the *Old Arcadia* to show a reiterated experiential pattern in the main characters, in which they undergo progressive degeneration as a result of failing to bridle desire. Overwhelmed by the urgings of passion, they are led to betray their better selves by premeditating or performing acts that affront either their moral conscience or the law, and usually both. Their misdeeds, whether actual or intended, bring them to the point of near ruin, following which they are redeemed only through some unanticipated, and unearned, providential intervention.

This pattern can be observed in the members of the older generation. Basilius, who has been a good ruler in the past, is led by 'the vanity which possesseth many who, making a perpetual mansion of this poor baiting place of man's life, are desirous to know the certainty of things to come, wherein there is nothing so certain as our continual uncertainty' into superstitiously consulting an oracle. Misled by his interpretation of the prophecy, and 'making his will wisdom', he surrenders his reason to superstition and, worse, abandons his responsibilities as a ruler in order to take refuge in a pastoral retreat, against all good advice.[64] Progressively surrendering to self-indulgence, Basilius ends up the victim of degrading self-deception when, thinking he has committed adultery with the object of his illicit desire, Cleophila (who unbeknown to him is really a man in any case), he discovers he has actually slept with his own wife. Similarly, Gynecia, who has hitherto been a good and virtuous wife to the Duke, gets carried away 'with the violence of an inward evil' when she becomes possessed by desire for Pyrocles, whom she has perceived to be a man under his Amazonian disguise.[65] Her passion brings her into despair and self-detestation when, with Basilius apparently dead from having drunk the aphrodisiac she had prepared for Cleophila/Pyrocles, she believes she has become a murderess.

The princes fare no better. Overmastered by his desire for Pamela, Musidorus first persuades her to run off with him, and is only prevented from breaking his promise to preserve her chastity by the interruption of twelve clownish villains. He sinks to the depths of degradation when Euarchus denounces him as ravisher and a thief, and condemns him to be beheaded. Pyrocles' degradation is even more visibly blazoned when, having become infatuated with Philoclea, he renders himself effeminate to gain access to her. Inevitably, he contrives an opportunity to commit the act that Musidorus only attempted, and having violated the laws of Arcadia by having premarital

[64] *Old Arcadia*, pp. 5, 9.
[65] *Old Arcadia*, p. 48.

sex with Philoclea, renders her life forfeit as well as his own. In condemning him to death for the wickedness of his lust, Euarchus denies him the excuse of love, pointing out that there is not a crime that could not be veiled under the name of love: 'For as well he that steals might allege the love of money, he that murders the love of revenge, he that rebels the love of greatness, as the adulterer the love of a woman; since they do in all speech affirm they love that which an ill-governed passion maketh them to follow'.[66] Although the misdeeds of the two princes seem more excusable because they are motivated by a sincere and reciprocal romantic passion, Sidney ensures that when they are subjected to the judgement of Euarchus' stern reason, their actions are seen to arise from the same unlawful concupiscence of will that motivates the other characters. Their deeds are only different in appearance, not in their intrinsic quality.

By the end of the work, all of these characters have been brought to the point where they are helpless to save themselves from the mortal consequences of their surrender to unbridled desires. The mimesis, therefore, 'figures forth' symbolically Sidney's Protestant view that, given the concupiscent infection that corrupts the human will, salvation is unearned and bestowed only through God's grace. This dispensation is symbolically figured in the *Old Arcadia* only in the last three pages of the final Book, when the confusions are unravelled with the revival of Basilius, and Euarchus realizes that 'all had fallen out by the highest providence' so as to fulfil the oracle in the true sense concealed within its equivocation, thus turning the potential tragedy into a comedy.[67]

Apart from patterning the action to show a progressive deterioration in the moral being of his characters once they surrender to their desire, Sidney also introduced a series of episodes that suggested a more pervasive imperfection in the human situation at large. Near the end of Book I a monstrous lion and a fierce she-bear attack the royal party; towards the end of Book II Cleophila (alias Pyrocles), Philoclea and Gynecia are overtaken by an unruly, riotous mob; the action of Book III is similarly disrupted by a band of rebels; Book IV ends with 'all the whole multitude fallen into confused and dangerous divisions' in the absence of their King, with 'tumult upon tumult arising';[68] and Book V threatens to conclude with Euarchus, King of Macedon, father to Pyrocles and uncle to Musidorus, executing his own son and nephew for the 'abominable and inexcusable' deeds that their 'unbridled desire' has led them to commit.[69] Not only do these episodes mirror emblematically the progressively worsening disorder (moral and political) caused by the protagonists' surrender to their libidinous inclinations, but, as one critic has aptly put it, 'in each case, the fragile expectations of self-contentment created by

[66] *Old Arcadia*, pp. 406/34–407/2.   [67] *Old Arcadia*, p. 416.
[68] *Old Arcadia*, pp. 320, 326.   [69] *Old Arcadia*, pp. 406/30, 407/35–408/1, 415ff.

the protagonists in their artificial vacuum are swept away by violence and malice springing from obscure recesses on the margin of social organization and moral righteousness'.[70] In short, these very un-Arcadian episodes – unprecedented in Sidney's Italian sources – serve to signify the presence of a mutability in the nature of things, and a force of disruptive evil resulting from human sinfulness, that truly attest to the reality of a fallen world.

What relevance to his own situation did Sidney see in this mimesis? Clearly, there are elements of self-projection in all of Sidney's main characters. All of them embody his temptation to surrender to the impulses of desire, and their withdrawal into the pastoral world mirrors his own withdrawal from active affairs, about which he felt guilty and defensive, as the correspondence between him and his humanist mentor, Hubert Languet, attests.[71] Sidney's self-projection is most strikingly visible in Pyrocles, who, having been 'formed by nature and framed by education to the true exercise of virtue', runs the risk of betraying his potential if he allows himself to succumb to dishonourable actions in pursuit of his desire. His friend, Musidorus, recognizes this when he learns of Pyrocles' intention to disguise himself as a woman:

> O sweet Pyrocles, separate yourself a little, if it be possible, from yourself, and let your own mind look upon your own proceedings; so shall my words be needless, and you best instructed. See with yourself how fit it will be for you in this your tender youth (born so great a prince, of so rare, not only expectation, but proof, desired of your old father, and wanted of your native country, now so near your home) to divert your thoughts from the way of goodness to lose, nay to abuse, your time; lastly, to overthrow all the excellent things you have done, which have filled the world with your fame (as if you should drown your ship in the long-desired haven, or like an ill player should mar the last act of his tragedy).[72]

This exhortation, with its embedded layer of autobiographical reference, suggests the function of the work for Sidney. The displaced fictive representation was a means for him to gain an interpretive distance from himself in order to appraise his own 'proceedings' for the sake of being 'best instructed'. In particular, he desired to gain an imaginative grasp of the likely consequences should he seek to fulfil his aspirations through illicit means. Several forebears

---

[70] Franco Marenco, 'Double Plot in Sidney's Old *"Arcadia"*', in *Essential Articles for the Study of Sir Philip Sidney*, ed. Arthur F. Kinney (Hamden, Connecticut, 1986), pp. 287–310.

[71] See McCoy, *Rebellion in Arcadia*, p. 54. Languet wrote to Sidney expressing alarm at his protégé's 'desire to fly from the light of your court and betake yourself to the privacy of secluded places to escape the tempest of affairs by which statesmen are generally harassed' (Philip Sidney, *The Correspondence of Sir Philip Sidney and Hubert Languet*, ed. Steuart A. Pears (London, 1845), p. 155).

[72] *Old Arcadia*, pp. 18–19.

on his mother's side had been brought to the block when their political ambitions had led them into open rebellion, and as the tragic example of the Earl of Essex would shortly prove, Sidney was not the only aristocrat in the uncertain world of the final years of Elizabeth's reign who would succumb to their belief that they could do a better job of governing the realm. The *Old Arcadia*, in fact, and even more so the *New Arcadia*, is really about the process whereby Sidney sought to bring the temptation to resolve his frustrations through dishonourable means under the control of his faith and reason.[73]

His chief strategy was to work out imaginatively the consequences of such behaviour in terms both of the morally corrosive effect on the individual, and also of the escalating disorder it generated in the body politic. At the same time, he used his exemplum to explore the likely consequences should a ruler like Elizabeth (figured in Basilius) abandon her responsibilities out of infatuation for Alençon (figured in the disguised Cleophila). The pattern of escalating disorder he depicts in the unfolding action confirmed for him not only the wisdom of refraining from imitating the princes, but also of discountenancing rebellion: however bad the situation when Basilius is neglecting his responsibilities as ruler, it is even worse when the state is at the mercy of those who aspire to take his place. Sidney learnt from his cautionary exemplum that there was good reason for him to bridle his desires, restrain his ambition and submit to the constraints imposed upon him by his sovereign and his God – even though the wish-fulfilment fantasy-ending of the *Old Arcadia* hinted at a residual desire to have his cake and eat it too.

Very soon after completing the *Old Arcadia*, which must have happened around October 1580, when Sidney wrote to his brother Robert promising him a copy of his 'toyful' work as soon as possible, he became dissatisfied with it – to the point where he recast it into an entirely new version.[74] Sidney must have begun writing the *New Arcadia* in late 1581 or early 1582, for in November 1586 Fulke Greville reported to Walsingham that he had sent Sidney's wife a correction of the 'old arcadia', 'done 4 or 5 years sinse, which he left in trust with me, wherof ther is no more copies, and fitter to be printed then the first, which is so common'.[75] This new version had been left incomplete, interrupted in the middle of a sentence in Chapter 29 of Book 3 by Sidney's death on 17 October 1586.

The *New Arcadia* is so radically different from the *Old Arcadia* as practically to constitute a new work. Sidney changes the narrative technique so that there is a mixture of action in the present, interspersed with extended

---

[73] My conclusions in this regard are not dissimilar to those reached by McCoy, *Rebellion in Arcadia*, although our emphases and perspectives differ.
[74] See William Leigh Godshalk, 'Sidney's Revision of the *Arcadia*, Books III–V', in *Essential Articles for the Study of Sir Philip Sidney*, ed. Kinney, pp. 311–26, esp. p. 313.
[75] Quoted by Godshalk, ibid.

reported accounts of episodes that have taken place in the past. His new narrative manner more resembles that of Heliodorus in the *Aethiopian History* (which Sidney seems to have had very much in mind) than that which he had used to create the dramatic mode of the *Old Arcadia*. He also vastly complicates the narrative by adding new characters and episodes which are, following Heliodorus, intricately interwoven. The action begins *in medias res* with the shipwreck of Musidorus and Pyrocles, and Sidney also describes in full the heroic adventures of the two princes in other countries that were barely mentioned in the *Old Arcadia*, and there is a much greater emphasis on tragic events that involve accidental death, bereavement, unrequited love, adultery, treachery, inconstancy, disfigurement, torture, revenge and executions. Sidney also introduces a full-scale rebellion led by two major new characters – Amphialus and his scheming mother, the evil Cecropia – that occupies the whole of the new Book 3. By introducing these changes, Sidney has, in effect, altered the whole genre and mode of his pastoral from essentially romantic and (tragi-)comic, to epic and tragic. Why should this have occurred?

As might be expected, the answer is largely to be found in Sidney's changed circumstances during 1580–2. Sidney's first shock came with the birth of a legitimate son, Robert Dudley, to the Earl of Leicester some time between autumn 1580 and early 1581. This effectively displaced Sidney as his uncle's heir.[76] The effect on him can be gauged from a letter Sidney wrote to Sebastian Pardini in Paris on 29 November 1580 declaring that he is suffering from 'illness and melancholy' – which probably relates to his feelings concerning the birth of Leicester's heir.[77] Further evidence is provided by Camden's account of how 'Sir Philip Sidney, who was a long time heir apparent to the Earl of Leicester, after the said Earl had a son born to him, used at the next tilt-day following ~~SPERAVI~~ [I have hoped] thus dashed through, to show his hope therein was dashed', which must refer either to the Accession Day tilt of 17 November 1580 or that of 1581.[78]

This severe disappointment was soon compounded by another equally devastating reversal of expectation. It had been the wish of the recently deceased Walter Devereux, Earl of Essex (d. 1576), that his elder daughter, Penelope, should be married to Philip Sidney, a highly desirable match so long as he was heir apparent to Leicester and Warwick.[79] When in January 1581 the Countess of Huntingdon brought Penelope Devereux, now her ward, from Ashby-de-la-Zouch to present her at court, Sidney had every reason to believe that a marriage between them was likely. On 27 February 1581, however, the old Lord Rich died, leaving his twenty-year-old son, Robert, with wealth and a title that made him a much more attractive

---

[76] See Duncan-Jones, *Sir Philip Sidney,* p. 194.
[77] Ibid., pp. 324–5, n. 2.
[78] Quoted by Duncan-Jones, *Sir Philip Sidney,* p. 194.
[79] Ibid., p. 196.

marriage prospect than Sidney, now that the latter had no prospects of inheriting Leicester's dignity and fortune. Inevitably, by 10 March 1581 the Earl of Huntingdon had written to Burghley proposing a match between the young Lord Rich and Penelope Devereux, and the marriage took place in November 1581. Sidney, who by this time had developed the genuine passion for Penelope Devereux that he records in *Astrophil and Stella* (probably written during another period of withdrawal from court between mid-December 1581 and March 1582), felt deeply bitter about this event, having lost his foreshadowed fiancée to someone of greater wealth and rank to himself.

To top it all off, Sidney was desperately short of cash without any means of gaining it in the absence of the emoluments of office that Elizabeth was withholding from him. In the words of his biographer, the barrage of begging letters that punctuate the autumn of 1581 – to Burghley, to Sir Christopher Hatton, the Lord Chamberlain, and to Thomas Ratcliffe, Earl of Sussex, the Vice-Chamberlain – show him to have been 'dispirited and nervous'.[80] Indeed, by the end of 1581 he must have felt that all the stars were conspiring against him, and the depression generated by his compounding misfortunes was undoubtedly one of the main factors that led him to revise a fiction which, when viewed in the light of his new misfortunes, would have seemed excessively self-deceptive in its optimism.

Accordingly, Sidney sought to construct a new image of the world as he was coming to understand it by repainting the picture he had presented in darker tones to suggest the more sinister aspects of the human situation. He emphasizes human evil to a much greater extent, incorporating many new instances of brutality and violence, such as the vengeful disfigurement of Parthenia by Demagoras, who rubs poison all over her face, or the flogging of Philoclea by Cecropia, which is described in terms that suggest the crucifixion of Christ:

> The sun drew clouds up to hide his face from so pitiful a sight, and the very stone walls did yield drops of sweat for agony of such a mischief: each senseless thing had sense of Pity; only they that had sense were senseless. Virtue rarely found her worldly weakness more than by the oppression of that day.[81]

Treachery abounds. The world of the *New Arcadia* is populated by perfidious lovers, adulterers, fathers who, like the King of Iberia, are willing to put their son to death, and wicked sons, like Plexirtus, the bastard of the Prince of Paphlagonia, who, 'with as much poisonous hypocrisy, desperate fraud, smooth malice, hidden ambition and smiling envy as in any living person

---

[80] Ibid., p. 218.
[81] Philip Sidney, *The Countess of Pembroke's Arcadia*, ed. Maurice Evans (London, 1987), Book 3, chap. 20, p. 552. Unless otherwise noted, references to the *New Arcadia* are to this edition.

could be harboured', turned his father against his legitimate brother, usurped his throne, put out his eyes and then turned him out to make his way through the dark world as best he could.[82] Throughout the *New Arcadia*, characters re-enact the primal crimes from which humanity can only be redeemed through the redemptive sacrifice of Christ for which Philoclea's scourging serves as a figure.

This darker, less romanticized depiction of the human condition provides a context in which Sidney undertakes a new and more profoundly searching exploration of himself. In the *Old Arcadia*, he had attempted to objectify his inclinations by displacing them symbolically into the erotic pursuits of the characters. In the *New Arcadia* he no longer restricts the representation of desire to sexual desire but extends it explicitly to encompass political desire as well. Locked into a state of helpless frustration in real life, Sidney turned to the new fiction he was making to explore both the positive and negative aspects of rebellion as a means for the oppressed to throw off their subjection. Consequently, whereas the subject of rebellion had been merely touched upon in the *Old Arcadia*, in the *New Arcadia* it becomes a major thematic preoccupation, along with an almost obsessive concern with the rights of subjects and the responsibilities of good government.

In many of the new episodes describing the overthrow of unjust rulers, one senses that Sidney may have been indulging fantasies concerning his belief that he himself had the talent to rule, and therefore should not be denied a place in the governing power elite by an aging, jealous queen. On three occasions the princes commit tyrannicide in the revised version, leading in two instances to their election by rebellious subjects as the new king. Musidorus, narrowly escaping being put to death by the King of Phrygia, who (like Elizabeth in Sidney's eyes) was 'fearful, and never secure, while the fear he had figured in his mind had any possibility of event [with] a toad-like retiredness and closeness of mind', provokes an insurrection and slays the King in battle, following which the grateful Phrygians offer him the crown.[83] Similarly, Pyrocles is offered the crown of Pontus after he and Musidorus have conquered the country to avenge a wrong done to their servants and Musidorus has slain the Prince.[84] On another occasion the two princes kill Tiridates, King of Armenia, to rescue Antiphilus, 'a young man but of mean parentage' in the court of Lycia, while Pyrocles is chosen by the Helots to be the commander of their rebellion against the oppressive Lacedaemonians in Laconia.[85] Even though Sidney shows each of the two princes declining to accept a crown when the offer arises, in other respects the presence of displaced wish-fulfilment fantasy elements in these episodes is barely concealed:

[82] *New Arcadia*, Book 2, chap. 10, pp. 277–8.
[83] *New Arcadia*, Book 2, chap. 8, pp. 269–70.
[84] *New Arcadia*, Book 2, chap. 9, pp. 272–3.
[85] *New Arcadia*, Book 2, chap. 13, pp. 302, 306; Book 1, chaps 6–7, pp. 99–103.

in the deeds of Pyrocles and Musidorus Sidney projected an image of himself that was commensurate with his conviction of his own worth. He was also able, in them, to experience vicariously a liberation from subjection that he could not hope for in the real world of Elizabethan politics unless he were literally to follow their example.

It was to contemplate the awesome implications of this latter possibility that Sidney made his other most striking change to the old version, by introducing the two major new characters: Amphialus and his scheming mother, the wicked Cecropia. If Pyrocles and Musidorus in the new episodes reveal Sidney's positive self-image, Amphialus represents Sidney in his victimized aspect – unlucky in love, politically unlucky, and constantly deprived of his good intentions by the vicissitudes of an unpredictable and uncontrollable ill fortune. He was also developed as a character to instruct Sidney as to why he could not afford to indulge his inclinations beyond the level of fantasy.

If the misfortunes Sidney suffered between late 1580 and early 1582 are borne in mind, the elements of self-projection in his portrayal of Amphialus become clear. Amphialus' love for Philoclea, who is his cousin, mirrors that of Sidney for Penelope Devereux, likewise his cousin (through Leicester's marriage to her mother, the widowed Countess of Essex). The terms in which Amphialus woos Philoclea also evoke the relationship that Sidney had depicted in *Astrophil and Stella* a few months earlier. Like Astrophil, Amphialus pleads the tyranny of love as his excuse for refusing her entreaties: 'It is love, it is love, not I which disobey you'.[86] Like Stella, Philoclea is prepared to accord him some provisional favour on the condition that he remain virtuous, telling him 'that where now she did bear him goodwill, she should, if he took any other way, hate and abhor the very thought of him'.[87] Later in the work, the narrator tells us that 'she had ever favoured him and loved his love, though she could not be in love with his person'.[88] These resemblances suggest that Sidney contrived Amphialus' hopeless desire for Philoclea as a symbolic representation of his loss of Penelope Devereux, who had been put beyond his reach by her marriage to Lord Rich.

Self-projection is equally apparent in Sidney's construction of Amphialus' political role, this time not as a reflection of what had actually happened but of what Sidney felt tempted to as a remedy for his own political frustration. The true architect of the rebellion is Amphialus' mother, Cecropia, who hates Basilius for having deprived Amphialus, his nephew, of the Arcadian succession – by having married late and begotten an heir of his own (just as Leicester had). Cecropia now turns out to have been responsible for all the previous mishaps that have threatened the lives of Philoclea and Pamela, whom she wishes to remove from the succession to make way for Amphialus.

---

86 *New Arcadia*, Book 3, chap. 3, p. 451.
87 Ibid.
88 *New Arcadia*, Book 3, chap. 24, p. 572.

In this way, she hopes 'to pull us out of the mire of subjection'.[89] Just as the motivation for the rebellion suggests Sidney's personal situation, the justification that Amphialus causes to be distributed to the people contains views that are likely to have been close to Sidney's own concerning the political scene in England. Amphialus appeals to the contemporary Huguenot doctrine of the subaltern magistracy, arguing that 'the weal-public was more to be regarded than any person or magistrate that thereunto was ordained' (for example, a queen), and that in a situation where the good of the realm was threatened, 'the care ... did kindly [i.e. 'naturally'] appertain to those who, being subaltern magistrates and officers of the crown, were to be employed as from the prince, so for the people'. Amphialus further interprets himself as one who, 'finding that his uncle had not only given over all care of government, but had put it into the hands of Philanax (a man neither in birth comparable to many, nor for his corrupt, proud, and partial dealing, liked of any)', has found it necessary to take matters into his own hands by removing the princesses from danger into his own protection.[90] In spite of the self-serving sophistry of Amphialus' justification – he is motivated as much by his desire for Philoclea as anything else – one can detect here traces of Sidney's own view of Elizabeth's political irresponsibility and one possible remedy for it.

Amphialus is not allowed to prevail, however, and in showing him as a failed negative version of Pyrocles and Musidorus with respect to both his erotic and political ambitions, Sidney also shows that he drew back from condoning the treason to which Amphialus succumbed. Nevertheless, he presents Amphialus empathetically (and with no small degree of projected self-pity) as a tragic figure who is more sinned against than sinning, largely because he is unable to control his fate or determine the outcome of his intentions, even when they are good. This is powerfully illustrated by the string of unintended deaths for which he is responsible. When, out of friendship for Philoxenus, the only son of his dear foster-father, he tries to woo Helen, Queen of Corinth, on Philoxenus' behalf, he ends up killing him in self-defence (when Philoxenus attacks Amphialus out of jealousy because Helen has fallen in love with him).[91] When, in battle, Amphialus pities the youthful Agenor for his beauty and bravery, and tries to spare his life by lowering his lance, the lance splinters 'with an unlucky counterbuff' and pierces Agenor in the face, 'giving not only a sudden, but a foul death'.[92] The list of such tragically ironic events compounds, with the killing of Argalus and his beloved wife Parthenia (who disguises herself as the 'Knight of the Tomb'),

[89] *New Arcadia*, Book 3, chap. 2, p. 446.
[90] *New Arcadia*, Book 3, chap. 4, p. 452. For further comment on the doctrine of subaltern magistracy, see McCoy, *Rebellion in Arcadia*, pp. 38–9.
[91] *New Arcadia*, Book 1, chap. 11, pp. 124–6.
[92] *New Arcadia*, Book 3, chap. 7, p. 468.

until Amphialus finds himself responsible for the death of his own mother. When, in despair, he advances on to the roof of the castle with his sword drawn to kill himself in his mother's presence, she, 'stricken with the guiltiness of her own conscience', 'went back so far till, ere she were aware, she overthrew herself from over the leads, to receive her death's kiss at the ground'.[93] In repeatedly subjecting Amphialus to tragic situations that were not of his own making, Sidney, one feels, was displacing his own anguish into the experience of his literary creation.

Indeed, by 1582 Sidney could no longer allow himself to believe that human desire was likely to be gratified in the way that he had signified in the arbitrary comedic ending of the *Old Arcadia*. Instead, he was forced to seek an answer to his dilemma in a religious explanation of the human situation and its processes. This, too, he projected into one of his characters – this time Pamela, who is given a greatly enhanced role in the *New Arcadia* in several crucial new episodes.

The first occurs when Pamela, having been imprisoned, utters a long prayer as she is about to face her ordeal at the hands of Cecropia. Appealing to God 'to limit out some proportion of deliverance unto me, as to Thee shall seem most convenient', Pamela nonetheless allows that there may be some deeper purpose to her suffering, in terms that may suggest a new understanding in Sidney of his own situation:

> But yet, my God, if in Thy wisdom, this be the aptest chastisement for my unexcusable folly; if this low bondage be fittest for my over-high desires; if the pride of my not-enough humble heart be thus to be broken, O Lord, I yield unto Thy will, and joyfully embrace what sorrow Thou wilt have me suffer.[94]

At the level of faith, Sidney needed to accept that his predicament was designed to work to his spiritual good according to a providential purpose.

This religious conviction was worked out at even greater length in the second major new episode involving Pamela, when she expounds her belief in providence to counter the *carpe diem* argument Cecropia uses to try to procure her for Amphialus. In response to Cecropia's atheistical view that human beings should cast off religious superstition, making natural wisdom their God and natural felicity their heaven, Pamela asserts that the order of the natural world proves 'that there is a constancy in the everlasting governor', and that 'this goodly work of which we are, and in which we live, hath not his being by chance'. Given the omnipotence and omniscience of the Creator, nothing can happen in the world that is not encompassed within his providence:

---

[93] *New Arcadia*, Book 3, chap. 24, p. 573.
[94] *New Arcadia*, Book 3, chap. 6, p. 464.

If his power be infinite, then likewise must his knowledge be infinite; for else there should be an infinite proportion of power which he should not know how to use ... and if infinite, then must nothing, no not the estate of flies ... be unknown unto him. For if it were, then there were his knowledge bounded and so not infinite. If his knowledge and power be infinite, then must needs his goodness and justness march in the same rank; for infiniteness of power and knowledge, without like measure of goodness, must necessarily bring forth destruction and ruin, and not ornament and preservation.[95]

Pamela's long disquisition is pure Calvinism, and its closeness to the argument of the first four chapters of Philippe du Plessis-Mornay's Calvinist treatise, *De la vérité de la religion Chrestienne* (Antwerp, 1581), which Sidney was translating about this time, suggests that Pamela may have been a mouthpiece for the expression of views that Sidney was developing for himself. By representing in her an exemplary faith, virtue, fortitude and constancy, Sidney was imaginatively formulating the pattern of response that he knew he needed to adopt if he were to avoid the tragic fate he had depicted in Amphialus.

How the *New Arcadia* would have ended had Sidney lived to complete it we do not know. Two endings are possible. Had Sidney chosen to perpetuate the mocking of expectation that Amphialus suffers, the work would have ended as a bleak tragedy. Had he chosen to work through the implications of Pamela's beliefs, he might have shown a concealed providence working itself out in events, as he does with the death of Cecropia. Whether conscious or unintentional, the suspension in which Sidney left the new version – in the middle of a sentence a little over half-way through the work – reflects a profound ambiguity at its centre. Sidney had no means of knowing whether to furnish his pastoral epic with a comic or a tragic ending, as life had not yet presented him with sufficient evidence for him to be able to make the choice.

By the time Sidney laid down his pen for the last time in the *New Arcadia* he had thoroughly transformed the Italian pastoral archetype that he had begun by imitating, but in a way that was unrepeatable. Partly this is owing to the idiosyncratic nature of his personal concerns, and partly to the passing of the historical moment that motivated English writers to imitate the Italians. As with Petrarchan imitation, imitation of both the Mantuanesque and Sannazzaran varieties of pastoral in England during the sixteenth century was inseparably bound up with the rise of Protestantism in its formative stages. In the context of the 1570s and 1580s the innate religious symbolism of pastoral conventions made it an ideal vehicle for the likes of Googe and Spenser for advancing the cause of evangelical reform. Equally, Sannazzaran Arcadianism – with its melancholy awareness of the incongruity existing

---

[95] *New Arcadia*, Book 3, chap. 10, pp. 488–92.

between the values of a lost golden age and the realities of the fallen human condition – provided someone like Sidney with an ideal imaginative stimulus for working out how he was going to reconstitute himself in the face of the troubled world of Tudor politics. Once the historical moment that invited these responses was over, pastoral writing migrated into different forms that had little to do with the models used by Sidney and Spenser. Interest in pastoral would revive two decades later when English dramatists sought to satisfy the taste of the Jacobean court for pastoral tragi-comedy under the influence of Tasso and Guarini. In the meantime, however, writers turned their attention to other forms that could answer to the pressing needs of the times. Spenser, following good classical precedent, moved from pastoral to epic, and when he did so, predictably, it was primarily to Italian models that he turned, with consequences that will be explored in the following chapter.

5

Epic and the Formation of National Identity: Ariosto, Tasso and *The Faerie Queene*

Even before he had completed *The Shepheardes Calender* Edmund Spenser was contemplating leaving behind his 'Oaten reede' in order to 'sing of bloody Mars, of wars, of giusts' – in other words, to move from the writing of pastoral to epic in order to tackle subjects of a more serious, public nature.[1] It is not surprising that he should have done so. From Virgil onwards such a progression had been considered natural for poets who wished to extend their talents. Moreover, epic was the appropriate mode for tackling topics such as the rise of the noble house, race or nation to which a poet professed allegiance, or for celebrating the events and values that had led a community to define itself.[2] Spenser had already tried using pastoral to address issues of broader concern, but with limited success because of the intrinsic incongruity between the mode he had chosen and the political and polemical functions he wanted to make it perform. It was therefore predictable that he should want to attempt a genre that gave him greater scope for public comment.

Spenser also had a compelling personal reason for writing *The Faerie Queene*: he was desperate to secure patronage in England – preferably that of the Queen, or, failing that, of members of her aristocratic elite at court.[3] To do so, he wrote the most stupendous exercise in flattery that British literature has ever seen: a praise of the values of Protestant England, imagined as being embodied in the person of Gloriana, the 'faery queene' – alias Elizabeth I –

[1] 'October', ll. 39–40, 56.
[2] See Andrew Fichter, *Poets Historical: Dynastic Epic in the Renaissance* (New Haven, 1982).
[3] See Alistair Fox, 'The Complaint of Poetry for the Death of Liberality: the Decline of Literary Patronage in the 1590s', in *The Reign of Elizabeth I: Court and Culture in the Last Decade*, ed. John Guy (Cambridge, 1995), pp. 235–8.

and her knights. By prefacing the work with a string of sonnets addressed to the Queen's chief ministers and courtiers – people such as Sir Christopher Hatton, the Lord High Chancellor; Burghley, the Lord High Treasurer of England; the Earl of Oxford, the Lord High Chamberlain of England; the Earls of Northumberland, Cumberland, Essex, Ormond and Ossory, Hunsdon, and Buckhurst, among others; knights such as Sir Francis Walsingham, Sir John Norris and Sir Walter Raleigh; and court ladies such as the Countess of Pembroke and Lady Carew – Spenser undoubtedly hoped to declare his credentials for court patronage by presenting them with a work which blazoned the values to which they were committed.

Given the political nature of Spenser's intent, the most interesting aspect of *The Faerie Queene* may be the imaginative strategies that he employed to achieve his aim. Significantly, his approach embodies the principles that had animated the religious Settlement of 1559, and which were continuing to animate the policies and actions of the Elizabethan administration itself in the later decades of the sixteenth century. Spenser's approach involved, specifically, the accommodation of a range of potentially incompatible cultural and intellectual possibilities through an eclectic but discriminatory selection of sources, which were then aligned with Elizabethan Protestant values through corrective modification where necessary.

Before the nature of his thematic and aesthetic strategies can be appreciated, it is necessary to recognize why Spenser, in an age when classical imitation was extremely important, chose as his primary models the Italian romantic epics of Ludovico Ariosto and Torquato Tasso rather than the classical epics of Homer and Virgil.[4] This chapter will explain the reasons for his choice, showing how Spenser's imitation of the Italian epic sprang from his realization that it could be more useful to him than the pure Virgilian model for the construction of a distinctively Protestant vision of the values that both he and the aristocrats to whom his work was addressed believed should inform the policies and procedures of the new English state, as well as the lives of each one of the Queen's loyal subjects.

In order to understand why Spenser preferred the Italian romantic epic to the classical form of epic it is necessary to recall the nature and evolution of the former. By the time Spenser came to compose *The Faerie Queene* the sixteenth-century Italian epics had acquired characteristics that differentiated them sharply from the classical archetype. Rather than being based primarily on the ancient models, the Italian genre had had its roots in the French *chansons de geste* of the twelfth century – tales recounting the deeds of Charlemagne and his knights, especially Roland, in their defence of Europe

---

[4] Edmund Spenser, *The Faerie Queene*, ed. Thomas P. Roche, Jr (Harmondsworth, 1978), p. 15. All references to *The Faerie Queene* are to this edition.

against the invading Moors.[5] Another important influence had been the Arthurian prose romances that also flourished in France at this time. By the second half of the thirteenth century, both the Arthurian romances and the epic tales of Charlemagne had been introduced into Italy by troubador poets, and by the fourteenth century the Carolingian epic had been naturalized in the Tuscan vernacular by minstrels called *cantastorie* – so called because they divided their epics into *canti*, units composed in *ottava rima* stanzas that were designed to be sung in the course of an hour or so. The true Italian romantic epic came into being when Matteo Maria Boiardo (1441–94), a member of the Estensi court at Ferrara, fused the Carolingian and Arthurian traditions inherited from France by turning Roland into the exemplar of Arthurian romantic love in his *Orlando innamorato* (1483). His successor, Ludovico Ariosto (1474–1533), another Ferrarese poet, consolidated this metamorphosis by fusing the classical tradition with the already fused medieval traditions in his *Orlando furioso* (1532), as his title – echoing Seneca's tragedy, *Hercules furens* – implies.

As a result of its complex genealogy, the *Orlando furioso* had acquired a form and appearance that was quite different from those of the classical epics by Homer, Virgil or Statius. While it retained many traces of classical features – thanks to Ariosto's imitation of passages and events from the *Aeneid*, and of similes, *sententiae* and images from classical poets such as Catullus, Horace and Ovid – its subject matter was distinguished by an emphasis on chivalric adventures, amatory episodes, enchanters and enchantresses, miracles, magic, and the fatally irresistible power of the heroine(s). In structure, it was organized as much around the romantic interests of its chief characters as the completion of an epic endeavour, and rather than being focused on a single, noble action it consisted of a multitude of plot strands woven into an elaborate tapestry: tales are constantly arrested, with their completion being deferred for cantos at a time to allow for the pursuit of other narrative interests; there is a rapid succession of incidents that pass from the sublime through the pathetic to the bawdy and ridiculous. Stylistically, the *Orlando furioso* was distinguished by its multitude of overlapping stylistic levels and tones, with Ariosto being at times grandiose and elevated, at times light-heartedly comic or calculatedly pedestrian, and at other times serious and tragic.[6] And for the first time in epic the author presents himself through a fully developed narrative persona who, with his ironic *sorriso* (smile),

---

[5] For the origins of the Italian romantic epic, see Ernest Hatch Wilkins, *A History of Italian Literature*, revised by Thomas G. Bergin (Cambridge, Massachusetts, 1974), pp. 5–9, 37, 158–65, 172–3, 186–92; and Graham Hough, *A Preface to the Faerie Queene* (London, 1962), pp. 14–24.

[6] See C.P. Brand, *Ludovico Ariosto: Preface to the Orlando furioso*, vol. 1, Writers of Italy Series (Edinburgh, 1974), chap. 8, 'The Arts of Poetry', pp. 142–59.

constantly intrudes to involve his readers in the contrivance of his literary creation and to guide their perception of human behaviour and the ways of the world in accordance with his own liberal, humane vision.

Between the mid-1560s and the mid-1570s the Italian genre underwent one final modification when Torquato Tasso (1544–95) 'corrected' Ariosto in his *Gerusalemme liberata* (1581). By the mid-Cinquecento Aristotle's *Poetics* had been translated into Latin (1536), and neo-classical theorists in Italy had grown dissatisfied with the way that the narrative discontinuities of the *Orlando furioso* violated Aristotelian formal principles.[7] Counter-Reformation moralists had also found fault with the sexually explicit episodes in the work and its pervasive irreverence. Concerned to avert such criticism, Tasso sought to rectify these purported faults by writing *Gerusalemme liberata* according to a prescription recorded in his *Discorsi dell'arte poetica e del poema eroico* (written probably about 1561–2). Instead of Ariosto's multiplicity of actions, there was to be a single main action, 'noble, great, and perfect' – the siege and capture of Jerusalem in 1099 by Godfrey of Boulogne – which would be narrated 'in the loftiest verse, with the aim of giving profit through delight'.[8] Moreover, the poet would eschew all 'low, common, indecent things': 'They merit no praise at all ... who have described amorous embraces in the fashion of Ariosto depicting Ruggiero with Alcina, or Ricciardetto with Fiordispina'.[9] Tasso did, however, compromise to the extent that he retained many of the most attractive elements of the Ariostean form: loves and marvels, an extremely seductive enchantress, evil wizards, good hermits, pagan beauties, digressive incidents focusing on chivalric adventure or romantic pathos, and the traditional octaves and canto structure.[10] In the event, Tasso was able to demonstrate how most of the essential characteristics of the Ariostean epic romance could be retained without offending against neo-Aristotelian canons concerning the need for formal unity and thematic high seriousness.

Both the Ariostean and Tassonian versions of the Italian romantic epic had a profound influence on the writing of *The Faerie Queene*. From Ariosto Spenser drew the multi-strand plot structure and interwoven narrative that is found in Books III, IV and VI, and his imitation of Ariosto's narrative

---

[7] See Daniel Javitch, *Proclaiming a Classic: The Canonization of Orlando furioso* (Princeton, 1991), pp. 86–105.

[8] Torquato Tasso, *Discourses on the Heroic Poem*, trans. Mariella Cavalchini, ed. Irene Samuel (Oxford, 1973), Book 1, p. 14. The first three Books of the *Discorsi* were published in 1587 and the rest in 1594.

[9] Ibid., Book 2, p. 54; Book 1, pp. 10–11.

[10] For further comment on Tasso's compromise between heroic, serious and didactic elements and the fanciful and romantic, see C.P. Brand, *Tasso: A Study of the Poet and His Contribution to English Literature* (Cambridge, 1965), pp. 80–1.

manner extended to the creation of a fully personalized narrator who speaks directly to the reader at the beginning of each canto. Similarly, he created a specially adapted version of Ariosto's *ottava rima* stanza by adding a ninth, twelve-syllable line. Spenser's greatest debt, however, was for the basic motifs and archetypes that inform his epic narrative. Most of the key characters and episodes in *The Faerie Queene* are, in fact, drawn from the *Orlando furioso*. Ariosto's enchanter, Atlante, reappears as Archimago, while his enchantress, Alcina, is metamorphosed into the guileful and duplicitous Duessa. Spenser even creates his own *guerriera* (female warrior) in the person of Britomart, who, in her quest to be united with Artegall, imitates the quest of Ariosto's Bradamante to be united with her lover, the pagan Ruggiero. Many of Spenser's other main female characters are based on the antithetical Ariostean type of heroine: the vulnerable woman of great beauty who becomes the innocent object of male lust. Angelica fleeing from her various enamoured pursuers finds her counterpart in the hapless Florimell, who is similarly forced to flee from a string of would-be rapists and monsters (*Faerie Queene*, Book III). Isabella, whom Ariosto imprisons in the cave of some robbers, becomes Spenser's Amoretta, who is imprisoned in Lust's Cave, and, later, Pastorella, who falls into the hands of brigands in Book VI of *The Faerie Queene*.[11] Even Olimpia makes her appearance in Spenser's epic when he replicates her naked exposure to the Orc by the Ebudans in the exposure of Serena's naked beauty by the Salvage Nation as they are about to sacrifice her to their god.[12] Countless other narrative details and incidents are drawn directly from the *Orlando furioso*. Arthur's magic shield is the shield with which Atlante stuns his victims, while the horn that Arthur's squire blows when his master challenges the giant Orgoglio derives from the horn that Logistilla presents to Astolfo. Similarly, Britomart's enchanted ebony spear is modelled on the spear that Astolfo passes over to Bradamante.[13] When Britomart's feminine beauty is revealed as she removes her helmet and armour in Malbecco's castle, she is merely re-enacting the comparable moment when Bradamante displays her golden hair in the Rocca di Tristano,[14] and when Artegall overpowers the cruel saracen Pollente who exacts unjust tolls at a bridge, he is re-enacting Orlando's battle with

---

[11] *Orlando furioso*, 12.89–13.4–14; *Faerie Queene*, IV.vii.8ff.; *Faerie Queene*, VI.x.39–xi.42. All references to the *Orlando furioso* are to Ludovico Ariosto, *Orlando furioso*, ed. Marcello Turchi, 2 vols (Milan, 1982) for the Italian text, and to Ludovico Ariosto, *Orlando furioso (The Frenzy of Orlando)*, trans. and ed. Barbara Reynolds, 2 vols, Penguin Classics (London, 1975) for the English text.

[12] *Orlando furioso*, 11.33–4, 67–71; *Faerie Queene*, VI.viii.41–4.

[13] For Atlante's shield see *Orlando furioso*, 2.55–6; for the horn see *Orlando furioso*, 15.14–15 and *Faerie Queene*, I.viii.3–4; for the enchanted spear see *Orlando furioso*, 23.15 and *Faerie Queene*, III.i.7.

[14] *Faerie Queene*, III.ix.20–4; *Orlando furioso*, 32.79–80.

Rodomonte, who also tries to exact tolls from travellers in order to decorate the sepulchre he has built for Isabella with trophies and expiate his crime.[15] To catalogue Spenser's borrowings exhaustively would be like numbering grains of sand; suffice it to say that, from beginning to end, *The Faerie Queene* draws its very sustenance from matter that Spenser derived from the *Orlando furioso*.

Spenser's debt to Tasso is of a somewhat different nature. It is signalled in the 'Letter of the Authors expounding his whole intention' addressed to Sir Walter Raleigh that Spenser appended to *The Faerie Queene* when the first instalment was published in 1590. This prefatory letter attributes to the work a comprehensive, consistent allegorical intention and a tight formal design that reflect the influence of principles that Tasso had expounded in his *Discorsi*, and exemplified in the *Gerusalemme liberata*. Tasso is explicitly named, along with Homer, Virgil and Ariosto, as one of the epic writers in whose footsteps Spenser is following, and Spenser's observation that Tasso had depicted 'the vertues of a priuate man' in his Rinaldo and the qualities of 'a good gouernour' in his Godfredo indicates that he had probably read the '*Allegoria*' that Tasso had composed in 1576 for the *Gerusalemme liberata*, and which had appeared in the edition published in 1581.[16] In the '*Allegoria*', Tasso had identified Goffredo as allegorically signifying the Understanding, with the other princes representing other powers of the soul. This is likely to have suggested to Spenser the governing idea he declares in the 'Letter' of making Arthur stand for Magnificence, while his other knights are to stand for each of the virtues that comprise it.[17] Certainly, it is to Tasso that Spenser owes the overarching design of the whole work, its concern for structural unity, its moral high seriousness, and its pervasive allegorical character. In particular, the tight structure of Books I, II and V of *The Faerie Queene* – all of them focusing on a single quest undertaken by a single hero – imitates the unified linear structure devised by Tasso in the *Gerusalemme liberata*, rather than the multivarious, interwoven structure of the *Orlando furioso*.

---

[15] *Faerie Queene*, V.ii.4–19; *Orlando furioso*, 29.33–48.

[16] *The Faerie Queene*, ed. Roche, p. 15. For further comment on Spenser's knowledge of the '*Allegoria*', see Brand, *Tasso*, pp. 230–1. Some critics have assumed that by 'Rinaldo' Spenser was alluding to Tasso's earlier chivalrous romance, *Rinaldo* (1562), but given Spenser's extensive imitation of the episodes in the *Gerusalemme liberata* in which Rinaldo is first seduced by Armida and then undergoes regeneration after his choice to leave her, it seems more likely to me that Spenser viewed Tasso as dealing with the 'Ethice' and 'Politice' in the two persons of Rinaldo and Goffredo within the one work.

[17] See Torquato Tasso, *Godfrey of Bulloigne: A Critical Edition of Edward Fairfax's Translation of Tasso's Gerusalemme Liberata*, ed. Kathleen M. Lea and T.M. Gang (Oxford, 1981), p. 89. All references to the English text of *Gerusalemme liberata* are to this edition; references to the Italian text are to Torquato Tasso, *Torquato Tasso, Poesie*, ed. Francesco Flora, vol. 21, La Letteratura Italiana: Storia e Testi (Milan and Naples, 1952).

There is evidence, in fact, that *The Faerie Queene* may have undergone substantive revision in order to make a version that was originally closely modelled on *Orlando furioso* conform more closely to the formal and moral pattern prescribed for the epic by Tasso. In a letter written to Spenser in 1580, Gabriel Harvey refers to a draft of 'that *Eluish Queene*' in which Spenser would 'seeme to emulate and hope to ouergo' Ariosto's *Orlando furioso*.[18] There is no mention in this letter of Tasso, nor of the elaborate and highly serious allegorical scheme that Spenser would later announce in his prefatory 'Letter ... to Sir Walter Raleigh'. This, together with the striking contrast between the Ariostean Books III, IV and VI and the Tassonian Books I, II and V, has led scholars to surmise that Spenser may have changed his conception of the work in about 1582, recasting it to conform more closely to the new, more serious model devised by Tasso once the 1581 edition of *Gerusalemme liberata*, with its accompanying '*Allegoria*', had become available to him.[19] The end product is a poem in which the characteristic elements of both Ariosto's and Tasso's great works are startlingly in evidence, quite overpowering the direct influence of Virgil or Homer, except where the traces of these classical writers are transmitted through the Italian intermediaries.

Why should Spenser have been moved to imitate the Italian romantic epics so extensively? The reasons range from the simple and obvious to the complex and buried. In the first place, he was responding to fashion. By the second half of the sixteenth century the Italian epics, especially the *Furioso*, had become immensely popular throughout Europe. In Italy alone, the second version of the poem (published in 1521) had been reissued at least fifteen times, and the final version (published in 1532) had been republished sixteen times by 1540. The Venetian publisher Gabriel Giolito had published twenty-seven editions of the *Orlando furioso* between 1542 and 1560, while a rival publisher in Venice, Vincenzo Valgrisi, published a further seventeen editions between 1556 and 1579.[20] Copies of Ariosto's masterpiece in Italian flooded into other European countries and were consumed by an avid readership, particularly at the royal courts of France, Spain and England, where the governing elite were trying to emulate the style and sophistication of their Italian counterparts. The prevailing enthusiasm for the work is reflected in the claim of Sir John Harington, the first English translator of the *Furioso*,

---

[18] Edmund Spenser, *The Works of Edmund Spenser: A Variorum Edition*, ed. Charles Grosvenor Osgood, Edwin Greenlaw, Frederick Morgan Padelford and Ray Heffner, 11 vols (Baltimore, 1932–57), vol. 9: *Spenser's Prose Works*, ed. Rudolf Gottfried, p. 471.

[19] For speculations on the composition of *The Faerie Queene*, see Josephine Waters Bennet, *The Evolution of the Faerie Queene* (Chicago, 1942); Hough, *Preface to The Faerie Queene*, pp. 84–9; and Brand, *Tasso*, pp. 230–1.

[20] I draw this information from Javitch, *Proclaiming a Classic*, p. 10.

that 'whatsoever is prayseworthy in *Vergill* is plentifully to be found in *Ariosto*', and, indeed, that the Italian poet is to be greatly preferred over his classical predecessor by virtue of the 'infinit places full of Christen exhortation, doctrine, and example' that are to be found sprinkled throughout the *Furioso*.[21]

Apart from being popular, the *Orlando furioso* had set a new standard of artistic achievement in the vernacular, which challenged writers in other European languages to emulate it. Ariosto's work was hailed in Italy as the first and only epic written in a vernacular since the time of the Romans that had been able to equal the great epics of antiquity.[22] As such, it allowed Italians to assume the superiority of their language and culture over those of the rest of Europe. To a patriotic Protestant Englishman like Spenser in a nation seeking validation for its newly independent identity, the urge 'to emulate and hope to ouergo' Ariosto that he confessed to Gabriel Harvey must have been irresistible.

Spenser could also hope that by imitating Ariosto he might deliver to Queen Elizabeth the flattering compliment for which he was aiming. Following a precedent established by Virgil, who designed the *Aeneid*, in part, as a compliment to the Emperor Augustus, Ariosto had contrived the *Furioso* as a dynastic epic designed to flatter his patrons, Alfonso I, Duke of Ferrara, and his brother, Cardinal Ippolito d'Este. Ariosto accomplished this flattery by portraying the female warrior Bradamante and the epic hero Ruggiero as the legendary founders of the Este dynasty, which he sees as destined to restore Italy to the pride and glory of its former years (*Orlando furioso*, 3.17–18). Spenser replicates this strategy and overgoes it by trebling the significance of Elizabeth I. First, he presents her in her political role as the prophesied descendant from the marriage of Britomart and Artegall who would reclaim the crown for 'Briton bloud' after centuries of Saxon rule, and restore Britain to a 'sacred Peace' after the tribulations of civil war, uniting nations in an 'eternall union'.[23] Second, he represents Elizabeth symbolically in her royal person as Gloriana, the Queen of Faeryland, who epitomizes the ideals and magnificence of Protestant England. Third, he depicts her in her private person as Belphoebe, the embodiment of personal beauty matched with exemplary chastity.[24] Had he lived to finish *The Faerie Queene*, Spenser would have gone still further to depict in the marriage of Arthur and the Faery Queen the fulfilment of England's historical destiny in the union of the virtues with glory under its Tudor monarch. In the event, Spenser was to be bitterly disappointed: his staggering achievement would eventually be

---

[21] Ludovico Ariosto, *Orlando furioso, Translated into English Heroical Verse by Sir John Harington (1591)*, ed. Robert McNulty (Oxford, 1972), 'Preface', pp. 10–11.
[22] See Javitch, *Proclaiming a Classic*, p. 16.
[23] See *Faerie Queene*, III.iii.48–9.
[24] See Spenser's prefatory 'Letter', *The Faerie Queene*, ed. Roche, p. 16.

rewarded with a handsome annual payment of £50, but getting it paid in the face of Burghley's stern disapprobation proved difficult, and Spenser never achieved the kind of court preferment in England for which he longed. In this respect, the precedent set by Ariosto was to lead him into false expectations.

Despite these practical reasons, Spenser had a still more compelling reason for imitating the Italian epics. It had to do with his recognition that the Italian genre contained fictive elements that were uniquely suited for catering to the needs of the time. By 1580, these needs were real and pressing: having broken from Rome, Protestant English men and women felt a need to orientate themselves in time – to work out what their separation meant in terms of the pattern of history; they also needed to identify their values, and especially the implications for moral and political conduct of the religious beliefs to which they and the nation had committed themselves. In the course of doing this, they needed to locate themselves in relation to the Continental cultural systems from which they were separating. At some point, Spenser realized that the Italian epics contained signifying possibilities that allowed him to address these needs more effectively than he could by imitating the classical epic in its pure form. The rest of this chapter will be spent in analysing the sources of this superior signifying potential, as well as the use Spenser made of it.

The contextual and conceptual frameworks of Spenser's twin Italian sources provided him with suggestions as to how he could accomplish his first task – to establish the historical significance of the new Elizabethan religio-political order. Both the *Orlando furioso* and the *Gerusalemme liberata* had as their backdrop the ongoing contest between Christendom and the forces of Islam. This conflict had begun in the eighth century with the invasion of Spain, had revived during the Crusades of the thirteenth century, and was still very much a burning issue in the sixteenth century with the Turkish invasion of Hungary and repeated attacks on Vienna and Italy. Spenser evidently saw how this historical struggle between Christianity and paganism could be symbolically converted into a figure for the conflict between the true religion (Protestantism) and the false one (Roman Catholicism), which was similarly both historical and spiritual. Charlemagne's struggle against the saracens could be represented as a battle between grace (in the person of Arthur and his knights) and the forces of evil, while Godfrey's liberation of Jerusalem could be reworked into a figure for the salvation of the individual Christian from imprisonment in sin, the freeing of England from its subjection to a corrupt papacy, and the release of the true Church from its Babylonian captivity.

Moreover, the teleological design that governs the plots of the *Furioso* and the *Gerusalemme liberata* could be appropriated as a vehicle for asserting the historical inevitability of the formation of the Protestant English state under Elizabeth and her governors, given that it represented a fulfilment of the divine will. In the *Orlando furioso*, despite the apparent randomness of its local actions, events are contained within an ultimate outcome that is divinely predestined. It consists of the victory of Charlemagne over the infidels, and of the marriage between Bradamante and Ruggiero that will make possible the future Italian glory to be achieved by their descendants, the Estensi.[25] In Tasso's epic the outcome is equally certain: Jerusalem will be liberated because God constantly intervenes in the action to support the worthiness of the Christians' endeavour, despite the continuous efforts of Satan to subvert it. At the beginning of the work he sends the angel Gabriel to exhort Goffredo to undertake the crusade; he sends the archangel Michael to chase back to hell the evil spirits, furies and fiends that Satan has unleashed on the earth; and when the fortunes of the Christian army are at their lowest ebb he resolves to put an end to their woes by recovering Rinaldo from his sensual enslavement to Armida so that he might return as the champion who will assist them to secure ultimate victory.[26] The overarching contest between God and Satan generates a distinctive pattern that is imparted to the action. For much of the time, the subversions perpetrated by Satan, his supernatural fiends and his earthly ministers lead to a progressive decline of faith, valour and virtue in the Christian troops, followed by a regenerative recovery following God's providential intervention. All that Spenser needed to do was to combine the providential teleology manifest in both works with the paradigmatic pattern of fall and redemption that Tasso had exemplified, and he had the basis of a myth that could explain the significance of Elizabeth's England, especially once he had blended it with the Calvinist doctrine of God's predestinate will, and the apocalyptic vision of history prophesied in the Book of Revelation. Through conflating these elements, Spenser was able to suggest through the fictive pattern of *The Faerie Queene* that the act of becoming Protestant had been the fulfilment of a divinely ordained, universal, predestinate intention, both for the individual English man or woman at the level of his or her spirituality, and also for the English nation in terms of its historical identity.

Spenser's second major task – to present imaginatively a Protestant interpretation of the meaning of (fallen) human experience – was greatly facilitated by the latent significations which many of the commonplaces that the Italian romantic epics contained. Certain of the archetypal characters appearing in the works of Ariosto and Tasso could readily be turned into personifications of good or evil forces as understood in the light of Protestant doctrine. The wizard with supernatural powers – Atlante, for example –

---

25 See *Orlando furioso*, 3.9.
26 See, respectively, *Gerusalemme liberata*, 1.7–18; *Gerusalemme liberata*, 9.58–66; and *Gerusalemme liberata*, 13.73.

could be adapted variously into a figure for Hypocrisy (Archimago), or the devil (again, Archimago), or male libido (Busyrane). Similarly, the beautiful enchantress – such as Alcina or Armida – could be turned into an embodiment of duplicity (Duessa), or the worldly corruption of the Roman Catholic Church (Duessa again), or the dangerously seductive power of intemperate sensual desire (Acrasia). The many saracens that populate the pages of Ariosto's epic had a special usefulness for Spenser. Being pagans, they could stand for various forms of spiritual infidelity – Sansfoy (lack of faith), Sansjoy (lack of joy) and Sansloy (lawlessness), or for more specific forms of iniquitous behaviour. In Book V of *The Faerie Queene*, for example, Spenser converts the cruel saracen tyrant, Rodomonte, into a figure for unjust fiscal rapacity (Pollente). On the positive side, the good hermit – such as Piero l'Eremita, who exhorts the distraught Tancredi to recover his true Christian commitment after the death of Clorinda, or the 'mago' who instructs Rinaldo on the true path to bliss and reveals the glory of his descendants following his escape from Armida – could be turned into a personification of Contemplation, imaged as the hermit who shows the Red Cross Knight the way to the 'new Hierusalem' that God has built for his saints.[27] Interestingly, however, it is mainly for the purpose of exemplifying various vices that Spenser draws upon the characters in his Italian sources.

Just as Spenser was able to turn Italianate character stereotypes into embodiments of moral qualities, so too was he able to use many of the characteristic episodes, especially in the *Furioso*, as a means for exploring the psychology of sin. Astolfo's metamorphosis into a myrtle by Alcina could be turned into a figure of the imprisoning consequences of doubt (Fradubio), wrought through the agency of duplicity (Duessa).[28] Likewise, episodes such as the vengeful deceit of Polinesso in seeking to ruin Ginevra by making Ariodante believe she is unfaithful could be reworked into an allegory of the role of a disordered imagination in causing one to abandon the truth (the Red Cross Knight's separation from Una), or of the tragic consequences of unbridled emotional intemperance wrought by sexual jealousy (Phedon's killing of Claribell and his capture by Furor and Occasion).[29] Even the supernatural 'marvels' with which Tasso sprinkles his epic could be converted to good use. Spenser turns the moment when Tancredi leaps through a wall of flames in the *Gerusalemme liberata*, for example, into an allegory of the power of Chastity to withstand the flames of sexual desire when he has Britomart pass through the wall of fire surrounding Busyrane's castle to rescue the imprisoned Amoretta from Lust.[30]

[27] See, respectively, *Gerusalemme liberata*, 12.85–9; *Gerusalemme liberata*, 17.59–95; and *Faerie Queene*, I.x.55–7.

[28] *Orlando furioso*, 6.23–53; *Faerie Queene*, I.ii.30–43.

[29] *Orlando furioso*, 5–6; *Faerie Queene*, I.ii.3–6; *Faerie Queene*, II.iv.3–36

[30] *Gerusalemme liberata*, 13.33–6; *Faerie Queene*, III.xi.21–5.

Encompassing all these specific aims was the more general task Spenser had set himself: of writing a work that would answer to the emotional and psychological needs of his compatriots, and for this, too, he found imitation of the Italian romantic epics to be uniquely appropriate.

A glimpse into the reasons for this appropriateness can be found in the circumstances surrounding the first English translation of the *Orlando furioso* by Sir John Harington in the late 1580s. According to Thomas Park, the editor of *Nugae Antiquae*, the enterprise began when Harington circulated around the court of Elizabeth a translation of Canto 28, containing the sexually explicit tale of the exploits of Giocondo and Astolfo, together with the trick played on them by the amorous Fiammetta in order to entertain her lover in the very bed in which they are all sleeping. When the manuscript came to the attention of the Queen and she had discovered that Harington (her god-son) was the author,

> she sent immediately for him, and severely reprimanded him for endangering the morals of her maids of honour, by putting into their hands so indecorous a tale; and, as punishment, ordered him to retire to his country-seat, and not appear again in her presence till he could produce a complete version of the whole poem.[31]

This humorous exchange betrays two things: the Queen's reprimand acknowledges the authority of a severe moral code that seeks to control certain aspects of life – such as sexuality – through shame and repression, while her facetious penance betrays a desire to have at least her curiosity concerning those matters satisfied. That her interest in Ariosto's subject matter was ultimately able to overpower her respect for the code that should have proscribed it is indicative of a real appetite in the court for literature that dealt with such issues.

Harington's own prefatory remarks in defence of the *Furioso* confirm this impression. Like the Queen, he acknowledges the authority of the repressive code, conceding the validity of the puritan view that poetry is 'vaine and superfluous' as far as the health of one's soul is concerned, because 'whatsoever is under the sunne is vanitie of vanities and nothing but vanitie'. Having made this concession to the Elizabethan equivalent of political correctness, however, he quickly adds:

> But sith we live with men and not with saints and because few men can embrace this strict and stoicall divinitie ... therefore we do first read some other authors, making them as it were a looking glasse to the eyes of our minde, and then after we have gathered more strength, we enter into

---

31 *Nugae Antiquae*, ed. Thomas Park (London, 1804), pp. x–xi; quoted in *Orlando furioso*, trans. Harington, ed. McNulty, p. xxv.

profounder studies of higher mysteries, having first as it were enabled our eyes by long beholding the sunne in a bason of water at last to looke upon the sunne it selfe.[32]

The images Harington uses in this passage are revealing for they suggest what it was that he and his contemporaries found in Ariosto's fiction that was missing from their 'strict and stoicall' new Protestant religion. His Italianate fiction supplied 'a looking glasse to the eyes of our minde' – in other words, a representation of experience that mirrored certain of its fundamental realities in a way that enabled men and women to work out imaginatively their deeper feelings concerning them. It also interposed a barrier against the unmitigated intensity of their new religion, as is implied in Harington's image of the sun being viewed by way of its reflection in a basin of water rather than looked on directly. Other images Harington uses in his 'Preface' reinforce this idea. In justifying Ariosto's narrative discontinuities, he writes:

> sure I am, it is both delightfull and verie profitable and an excellent breathing place for the reader, and even as if a man walked in a faire long alley to have a seat or resting place here and there is easie and commodious, but if at the same seat were planted some excellent tree that not onely with the shade should keepe us from the heat but with some pleasant and right wholsom fruit should allay our thirst and comfort our stomacke, we would thinke it for the time a little paradise, so are Ariostos morals and pretie digressions sprinkled through his long worke to the no lesse pleasure then profit of the reader.[33]

The image of Ariosto's narrative as providing the reader with a 'breathing place' in which he or she can rest while being shaded from the scorching 'heat' of the sun implies the importance of its mediating function. Similarly, the images of 'thirst' being allayed and stomachs being 'comforted' with 'right wholsom fruit' suggest that the fiction will satisfy natural needs in a way that is life-sustaining. Most revealing of all is the idea that the experience of the fiction will be like entering a 'little paradice' for a short time – it will allow the reader temporarily to experience the happiness of an unfallen world. In short, for Harington and other readers at the court of Elizabeth, the *Orlando furioso* provided not only recreation but, more importantly, a mediating function that could protect them against the extreme implications of their new religion by which they did not necessarily wish to be bound.

Although Harington does not explain precisely why he thought the Italian romantic epic had this mediating function, the reasons for it can be inferred – not least from his decision to choose the notorious Canto 28 as the first part of the *Orlando furioso* that he would translate. As with the other

---

[32] Ibid., p. 3.
[33] Ibid., p. 13.

Italianate genres discussed in chapters 3 and 4 above, the romantic preoccupations of the Italian epic furnished English readers with an opportunity for
coming to terms imaginatively with issues of desire – precisely those aspects
of human experience that Calvinist theology was seeking to repress. At the
heart of this theology was a conviction that human nature was inescapably
tainted with sin – inherited from Adam and Eve as a result of the Fall, just as
crab-apples inherit their sourness from the parent tree. In Calvin's view,
'everything in man, which is not spiritual, falls under the denomination of
carnal', which means that the 'old man' described by St Paul (Ephesians 4:23)
is inevitably 'corrupt according to the deceitful lusts', not just of the flesh but
also of the mind. The true believer must be born again in the spirit through
regeneration as a consequence of God's grace working on the will of the
elect.[34] Accordingly, he or she must be constantly vigilant in conforming to
the rule of Paul, '"make not provision for the flesh to fulfil the lusts thereof,"
(Rom. xiii. 14)', for which there is no surer way 'than by despising the present
life and aspiring to celestial immortality'.[35] Such was the 'strict and stoicall'
divinity to which Harington alludes, from the heat of which Italianate fiction
provided such welcome relief.

The problem for Elizabethan Protestants was how to reconcile these religious beliefs with their daily experience of the imperatives of desire, whether
in the domain of individual sexuality, of artistic aspirations or of political
ambitions. Because of their combination of heroic chivalry and erotic
romance, and their tendency to generate a conflict between the two, the
Italian romantic epics could offer an imaginative space in which such issues
could be vicariously contemplated. This is, perhaps, what Harington meant
when he claimed that fictive writing provided 'a looking glasse to the eyes of
our minde'. Both the *Orlando furioso* and the *Gerusalemme liberata* are organized primarily around situations that require individuals to determine their
priorities and commitments when confronted with the imperatives of desire.
Ariosto requires Bradamante to choose between her duty to assist her
desperately imperilled Christian peers, or to rescue the man she loves – the
pagan Ruggiero, who has been captured by the sorcerer Atlante – and she
chooses the latter. Ariodante has to choose whether to allow his wounded
egotism to trap him into suicidal despair when he thinks he witnesses
Ginevra's infidelity, or to allow his love for her to inform his faith in her
constancy, and eventually opts for the latter. Similarly, in the *Gerusalemme
liberata* Rinaldo has to decide whether he will remain in Armida's paradise of
sensual delights or allow his sense of honour and duty to overcome his infatuation for her, and chooses the latter.[36] In all these (and many similar) cases

---

[34] Jean Calvin, *Institutes of the Christian Religion*, trans. Henry Beveridge, 3 vols (Edinburgh,
1845), II.iii.1, vol. 1, p. 336.
[35] Ibid., III.x.3, vol. 2, pp. 295–6.
[36] See, respectively, *Orlando furioso*, 2.64–5; *Orlando furioso*, 5.36–6.6; and *Gerusalemme
liberata*, 16.34–5.

the Italian authors show their protagonists in the process of making identity-forming discriminations in response to conflicts arising from desire, and it was this psychological activity, one suspects, that largely accounts for the fervent interest in the Italian epics by their late-sixteenth-century readers.

Spenser chose to prioritize the Italian romantic epics over the classical epics proper, I believe, because he recognized that, in the particular circumstances of the time, they possessed to a greater degree the mediating function to which Harington alludes. He must also have realized that this mediating function could be enhanced if the subject matter of the Italian epics could be realigned to accord with Protestant values. If it could be shown that, through a process of accumulating discriminations based on a distinction between use and abuse, the individual could legitimately engage with life in such a way as to enjoy a fullness of emotional being, then the asceticism and world-renunciation of extreme puritanism could be avoided.

In the event, Spenser opted to present each of the virtues by which a gentleman was to be fashioned through a romance fable constructed out of elements selected from the epics by Ariosto and Tasso. In developing each of these fables, he modified the borrowed material so as to incorporate it into an allegory of the psychological processes inherent in the attainment of the virtue concerned. To do this, he systematically modified the signification inherent in the source material to make it illuminate the world and human nature as understood in the light of Protestant doctrine. In this way, he was able to show that true virtue is developed through a full experience of the world rather than a renunciation of its joys, as the more extreme among the 'godly' were preaching. In the truest sense, then, Spenser was indeed 'over-going' the Italians – by revealing through the act of imitation the existence of unrealized redemptive possibilities inherent in their glorious, though (from a Protestant viewpoint) incomplete Renaissance humanist culture. To demonstrate this, I shall now examine the process of selection, adaptation and creative transformation involved in Spenser's construction of the virtues that were to constitute an Elizabethan Protestant gentleman, focusing on the presentation of Holiness, Temperance and Chastity.

With striking boldness, Spenser chose to represent the virtue of Holiness by creating a character, the Red Cross Knight, who is made to re-enact the experience of Ruggiero in the *Orlando furioso*, and Rinaldo in the *Gerusalemme liberata*, first, by being diverted from his mission through a surrender to eroticism and the lure of the senses, and then of being restored to a nobler self through a process of re-education.[37] Like Ruggiero, Red Cross is separated from his true love through the agency of a sorcerer who delivers

---

[37] For further comment on the material borrowed from the Italian epics by Spenser in Book I, see Hough, *Preface to The Faerie Queene*, pp. 139–40.

him into the power of an enchantress, from which he needs to be set free through the intervention of a good agent with magic powers. Like Ruggiero, too, Red Cross receives corrective instruction from a team of women representing spiritual virtues. Then, like Rinaldo, he undergoes a spiritual illumination in which he attains a fuller sense of his true commitments and destiny. In making the Red Cross Knight pass through this paradigmatic experience of fall and recovery, Spenser turns him into a living exemplar of the larger process by which God's providential intentions – to bring goodness out of evil through regenerating the elect – are realized in the life of the individual, of a nation, and in history at large.

In order to make his Italianate fable carry this full burden of signification, Spenser subtly, but decisively, transforms the material he borrows. The agent of Red Cross's fall, Archimago, is clearly based on Ariosto's necromancer, Atlante, in that both scheme to remove the hero from the protective influence of his mistress, both disguise themselves under the appearance of a knight, and both are defeated in martial combat, and are about to be killed (Atlante by Bradamante, and Archimago by Sansloy) when the removal of their helmets reveals them to be old men.[38] Beyond that, however, the differences that Spenser introduces are more important than the similarities.

Most significantly, Spenser completely transforms the necromancer's motives for separating the hero from his beloved, as well as the mode by which that separation is achieved. Ariosto's Atlante has raised Ruggiero since childhood and loves him more than if he were his own son ('l'amai sempre più che figlio').[39] Having heard the prophecy that Ruggiero will meet his death by a traitor's hand after he has been converted to the Christian faith, Atlante's chief motive for abducting him is to try to protect him against this fate. It is for this reason that he built the castle of steel, and his motive for carrying away knights and ladies on the hippogriff is to supply Ruggiero with company to keep him happy. It is for the same reason that Atlante later has the hippogriff deposit Ruggiero on Alcina's island, and subsequently lures him to his palace of illusions, where he keeps him prisoner by trapping him into an endless pursuit of the simulacrum of what he most desires.[40] Atlante is thus thoroughly humanized and is allowed to elicit considerable reader sympathy, being recognizably human in his emotional vulnerability rather than truly evil. Archimago, on the other hand, is an agent of the devil, being motivated by the most sinister form of malice.

This is apparent when Spenser describes the necromantic incantations he utters after his guests, Una and the Red Cross Knight, have gone to sleep:

---

38 For these episodes, see respectively *Orlando furioso*, 2.37 and *Faerie Queene*, I.ii.10–11; and *Orlando furioso*, 4.27 and *Faerie Queene*, I.iii.38.
39 *Orlando furioso*, 4.38.
40 *Orlando furioso*, 12.20–1.

He to his study goes, and there amiddes
His Magick bookes and artes of sundry kindes,
He seekes out mighty charmes, to trouble sleepy mindes.

Then choosing out few wordes most horrible,
(Let none them read) thereof did verses frame,
With which and other spelles like terrible,
He bad awake black *Plutoes* griesly Dame,
And cursed heauen, and spake reprochfull shame
Of highest God, the Lord of life and light;
A bold bad man, that dar'd to call by name
Great *Gorgon*, Prince of darknesse and dead night,
At which *Cocytus* quakes, and Styx is put to flight.

And forth he cald out of deepe darknesse dred
Legions of Sprights, the which like little flyes
Fluttring about his euer damned hed,
A-waite whereto their seruice he applyes,
To aide his friends, or fray his enimies.
                            (*Faerie Queene*, I.i.36–8)

In Spenser's reconception, the necromancer becomes an embodiment of the primal force of evil in the world that constantly seeks to subvert human beings into surrender to sinful impulses that will lead them to commit destructive acts. At the beginning of Book II he is described as 'That cunning Architect of cancred guile' who ranges forth

... full of malicious mind,
To worken mischiefe and auenging woe,
Where euer he that godly knight [i.e. Red Cross] may find.
                            (*Faerie Queene*, II.i.1–2)

Archimago, therefore, is the eternal enemy of Holiness wherever it is to be found.

Having invested the figure of the sorcerer with a far greater weight of thematic signification, Spenser correspondingly transforms his mode of action. Whereas Ariosto has Atlante overpower his victims through outright conquest, using his hippogriff and magic accoutrements (his shield, lance and book), Spenser abandons the hippogriff altogether and replaces it with a process of psychological subversion that Archimago is able to perpetrate through the manipulation of false appearances. When Una and the Red Cross Knight first meet Archimago, for example, he has the appearance of a holy hermit:

At length they chaunst to meet vpon the way
An aged Sire, in long blacke weedes yclad,
His feete all bare, his beard all hoarie gray,
And by his belt his booke he hanging had;
Sober he seemde, and very sagely sad,
And to the ground his eyes were lowly bent,
Simple in shew, and voyde of malice bad,
And all the way he prayed, as he went,
And often knockt his brest, as one that did repent.
(*Faerie Queene*, I.i.29)

This creates a very different impression from that which Atlante makes as a knight in shining armour wheeling in descending circles on his flying horse, as does the change in the appearance of the sorcerer's dwelling from Atlante's castle of steel into 'a little lowly Hermitage' where Archimago says prayers 'each morne and euentyde'.[41] Both changes disarm the Red Cross Knight of any suspicion, thus preparing for the more insidious spiritual subversion still to come.

Spenser's account of Red Cross's downfall exemplifies a Calvinist understanding of what constitutes temptation: 'depraved conceptions of our minds provoking us to transgress the law – conceptions which our concupiscence suggests or the devil excites'.[42] In this episode Archimago, unlike Atlante, becomes a figure for the devil, whose wiles his subversive strategy illustrates. Instead of simply kidnapping the Red Cross Knight as Ariosto's 'mago' abducts Ruggiero, Archimago subverts him by playing upon his concupiscence in order to distemper his faculties, and through that to lead him into a loss of faith. He does this, first, by undermining the Knight's confidence in his own and his lady's virtue by causing him to have an erotic dream in which he makes love to Una. The effect is to fill Red Cross with a 'great passion of vnwonted lust, / Or wonted feare of doing ought amis' that causes him to start up in a state of anxiety about his own capacity to experience what he takes to be sinful motions. When, upon rising, he sees the False Una whom Archimago has contrived at his bedside, 'Vnder blake stole hyding her bayted hooke', he is completely dismayed and converts his anxiety at his own experience of lust into anger at her.[43] Finally, Archimago, in a tactic that would soon be imitated by Shakespeare's Iago, delivers the *coup de grace* by making the Red Cross Knight believe he is seeing Una and a young squire in the act of infidelity. What Archimago has done, in Spenser's reconception, is to make the Red Cross Knight the victim of sexual jealousy through an abuse of his imagination, with the effect that his reason is impaired by intemperate

---

41 *Faerie Queene*, I.i.34.
42 Calvin, *Institutes*, III.xx.46, vol. 2, pp. 519–20.
43 *Faerie Queene*, I.i.47–55.

passions – or concupiscence. When he thinks he sees the false couple 'in wanton lust and lewd embracement', 'he burnt with gealous fire, / The eye of reason was with rage yblent, / And [he] would haue slaine them in his furious ire'.[44] Once his rational self-control has been destroyed by the release of these distempered emotions, the Red Cross Knight is increasingly vulnerable to faithlessness (symbolized in the encounter with the saracen Sansfoy), duplicity (Duessa) and pride (the giant Orgoglio).

The changes that Spenser made to the figure of the necromancer, therefore, gave him huge advantages as far as imparting a Protestant signification to the Italianate commonplace was concerned. Archimago functions simultaneously as a personification of Hypocrisy, as a figure for the pretence by Roman Catholicism to constitute the true Church (when Archimago presents the False Una to the Red Cross Knight), as a figure for the hypocritical simulation of holiness by the Roman Catholic Church (when Archimago tries to deceive Una into believing he is the Red Cross Knight), as a figure for the devil, and also as an exemplification of the psychological forces arising from original sin that lead men and women to commit sinful acts because of the disordered intemperance of their own passions.

A similar process of transformation takes place when Spenser develops the second stage in the Red Cross Knight's fall – his seduction by the enchantress, Duessa. In broad outline, Spenser follows very closely the sequence in which Ruggiero first falls under the enchantments of Alcina, and is then rescued by a good agent who frees him by reversing the spell. In each case, the seduction is prepared for by an ironic encounter between the hero and one of the enchantress's previous victims (Astolfo in *Orlando furioso*, and Fradubio in *The Faerie Queene*) who has undergone metamorphosis at her hands, and who warns the hero to beware of her treachery. Before they meet the enchantress, both heroes battle with a monster that embodies the vice that will subvert them: Ruggiero's fight with the monster Erifilla, representing cupidity, is mirrored in the Red Cross Knight's battle with Error. The domains into which both the heroes are led share an emblematic similarity: the 'altezza' (height) of the glittering, golden 'muraglia lunga' (great wall) that surrounds Alcina's citadel is repeated in Spenser's description of the walls of the House of Pride, which are overlaid with 'golden foile', with 'many loftie towres' that are 'high lifted vp', and the 'strada … ampla e diritta' that leads into Alcina's city is reproduced in the 'broad high way' that leads into Lucifera's palace.[45] Each hero is rescued because of the solicitous intercession of his abandoned lady (Bradamante, Una), who persuades a good agent with supernatural powers (Melissa, Arthur) to undertake a mission of recovery. Following their release, both heroes realize that their enchantress is old and

[44] *Faerie Queene*, I.ii.5.
[45] *Orlando furioso*, 6.59–60; *Faerie Queene*, I.iv.2–4.

ugly, and they are each directed to a realm which is the antithesis of the corrupting one they have left, to be instructed in the virtues that will lead to their moral recovery (Ruggiero in the kingdom of Logistilla, and the Red Cross Knight in the House of Holiness). Clearly, then, Spenser had Ariosto's treatment of the surrender to idle sensual pleasure very much in mind.

As with his reconception of Archimago, however, Spenser transformed the particular elements that constituted this basic pattern in order to deepen its significance. His first change is to alter dramatically the conception of the enchantress. Alcina, representing the allure of the senses, is unequivocally beautiful; indeed, the extended blazon that Ariosto creates of her ravishing physical charms became the basis for the similar top-to-toe description that Spenser would give of Belphoebe in Book II of *The Faerie Queene*.[46] Duessa, on the other hand, is given no physical description at all; instead, she is described entirely in terms of her outward trappings and behaviour, as when the Red Cross Knight first sees her in the company of Sansfoy:

> He had a faire companion of his way,
>   A goodly Lady clad in scarlot red,
>   Purfled with gold and pearle of rich assay,
>   And like a *Persian* mitre on her head
>   She wore, with crownes and owches garnished,
>   The which her lauish louers to her gaue;
>   Her wanton palfrey all was ouerspred
>   With tinsell trappings, wouen like a waue,
> Whose bridle rung with golden bels and bosses braue.
>
> With faire disport and courting dalliaunce
>   She intertainde her louer all the way.
>   (*Faerie Queene*, I.ii.13–14)

The emphasis here is not on her beauty but rather on the worldliness and vanity that her ostentatious accoutrements imply, and on her lascivious behaviour – appropriate for a figure who is meant to suggest not merely Falsehood but also the Whore of Babylon, and through her, the Roman Catholic Church and the papacy.

Just as her appearance is changed, so too is her mode of seduction. Alcina's method is relatively crude: in Astolfo's case, she simply kidnaps him on the back of a whale; in Ruggiero's case, she physically blocks his way to Logistilla's kingdom with her brutish horde of border guards, and sends two of her lady attendants to lead him into her earthly paradise. Finally, having aroused Ruggiero to a fever of erotic expectation, she makes a direct sexual advance to him to which he readily accedes. This is consistent with her role, which is

[46] *Faerie Queene*, II.iii.22–30.

to precipitate in Ruggiero an abandonment to the gratification of the senses. Duessa is much more subtle, and insidious. Like Archimago, she manipulates appearances so as to work a spiritual subversion from within the mind of the hero himself. Her strategy is to play upon the male ego so as to arouse pride. When she and Sansfoy approach the Red Cross Knight, she manages to get Sansfoy to attack him out of 'hope to winne his Ladies heart that day', which in turn excites the Red Cross Knight to emulous rivalry, as is indicated by the simile Spenser uses to describe their dazed state following their first charge:

> As when two rams stird with ambitious pride,
>   Fight for the rule of the rich fleeced flocke,
>   Their horned fronts so fierce on either side
>   Do meete, that with the terrour of the shocke
>   Astonied both, stand sencelesse as a blocke,
>   Forgetfull of the hanging victory:
>   So stood these twaine, vnmoued as a rocke,
>   Both staring fierce ...
>   (*Faerie Queene*, I.ii.16)

The reference to 'pride', and the comparison with rams who are fighting to decide which one will have the right to service a flock of ewes, shows that it is not simply lust which motivates the combatants but also the more serious spiritual vice of pride – in this case exacerbated by the sexual jealousy that Duessa has been able to arouse in the two combatants. Once the Red Cross Knight has defeated Sansfoy, she furthers her strategy of psychological subversion by affecting feminine vulnerability and helplessness in order to appeal to his masculine vanity as someone who has the 'mighty will' to decide her fate. Having succeeded in flattering him, Duessa is then able – by telling him a hard-luck story to arouse his pity – to manipulate him into volunteering to assume the role of her protector. Once that happens, she is easily able to guide him into the House of Pride which symbolizes the sinful spiritual vice that she and Archimago, between them, have been able to unleash in him. The purpose of Spenser's reconception of the enchantress, then, has been to show that the real evil involved in the seduction of the hero is not so much the surrender to the pleasures of the flesh as the spiritual corruption that attends it, which, in turn, is the greatest enemy to holiness.

Spenser's fundamental reconception of the process and significance of the hero's seduction is inevitably accompanied by an equally radical reworking of the stages by which he is redeemed. The actions required relate directly to the condition from which the hero has to be recovered, and here, too, Spenser made some startling changes to his source. After Ruggiero has been seduced by Alcina, he lapses into a state of pampered, effeminized decadence, as Melissa discovers when, disguised as Atlante, she arrives to free him from Alcina's spell:

Il suo vestir delizioso e molle
tutto era d'ozio e di lascivia pieno,
che de sua man gli avea di seta e d'oro
tessuto Alcina con sottil lavoro.

Di ricche gemme un splendido monile
gli discendea dal collo in mezzo il petto;
e ne l'uno e ne l'altro già virile
braccio girava un lucido cerchietto.
Gli avea forato un fil d'oro sottile
ambe l'orecchie, in forma d'annelletto;
e due gran perle pendevano quindi,
qua' mai non ebbon gli Arabi né gl'Indi.

Umide avea l'innanellate chiome
de' più suavi odor che sieno in prezzo:
tutto ne' gesti era amoroso, come
fosse in Valenza a servir donne avezzo:
non era in lui di sano altro che 'l nome;
corrotto tutto il resto, e più che mézzo.
Così Ruggier fu ritrovato, tanto
da l'esser suo mutato per incanto.

(The exquisite attire which he had on
Was soft and sensuous, an idler's wear,
Woven in silk and gold with subtle touch
By her who held him in her evil clutch.

A splendid chain he wears about his neck;
Glittering with gems, it reaches to his breast.
Two shining bracelets now his arms bedeck
(Alas! once of all arms the manliest!)
Two little threads of gold his ear-lobes prick,
Forming two rings from which the loveliest
Of pearls are hung, one dangling at each ear,
Finer than Indians or Arabs wear.

From curling tresses, scented with pomade,
A costly and delicious fragrance came.
So amorous was every move he made,
It was as though, to his undying shame,
A servile courtship all his life he'd paid
To women of Valencia. His name
Alone remains unaltered, nothing else,
So greatly is he changed by magic spells.)
(*Orlando furioso*, 7.53–5)

The decadent condition in which Melissa finds Ruggiero reflects the irresponsible surrender to self-gratification that has unmanned him. All that Melissa has to do to get him out of it is to arouse his shame by reminding him of the noble deeds that he is destined to perform and the glorious offspring that will descend from his union with Bradamante, and then to break Alcina's spell by placing a magic ring on Ruggiero's finger that enables him to see Alcina as the aged and hideous crone that she really is.[47]

The contrast between Ruggiero and the Red Cross Knight at this point could not be greater. Rather than enjoying a life of pampered luxury, the Red Cross Knight is immediately overpowered by the giant Orgoglio (Pride) when he fornicates with Duessa, and is thrown into a dungeon in the giant's castle until Arthur arrives with Una to rescue him. By making this change, Spenser is signifying that spiritual bankruptcy through surrender to pride, rather than unmanning enslavement to the senses, is the real danger to be feared from the kind of experience that Ruggiero and the Red Cross Knight undergo. That state of spiritual inanition is symbolized in the desperately enfeebled physical state of the Red Cross Knight when Arthur releases him from the dungeon:

> He found the meanes that Prisoner vp to reare;
> Whose feeble thighes, vnhable to vphold
> His pined corse, him scarse to light could beare,
> A ruefull spectacle of death and ghastly drere.
>
> His sad dull eyes deepe sunck in hollow pits,
> Could not endure th'vnwonted sunne to view;
> His bare thin cheekes for want of better bits,
> And empty sides deceiued of their dew,
> Could make a stony hart his hap to rew;
> His rawbone armes, whose mighty brawned bowrs
> Were wont to riue steele plates, and helmets hew,
> Were cleane consum'd, and all his vitall powres
> Decayd, and all his flesh shronk vp like withered flowres.
> (*Faerie Queene*, I.viii.40–1)

Spenser presents the Red Cross Knight's physical condition as the metaphorical equivalent of the spiritual condition into which human beings are imprisoned by the interior corruption that is worked when they are led through distempered passions to surrender to spiritual vices. Once in this state, a man or woman, in Spenser's Protestant conception, is unable to get out of it of their own volition, as is represented by the Red Cross Knight's encounter with Despair soon after he is released from Orgoglio's castle.

---

[47] *Orlando furioso*, 7.72–3

Not surprisingly, the process of recovery that the Red Cross Knight has to undergo is very different from that experienced by Ruggiero. Ruggiero is able to make his own way to Logistilla's kingdom (signifying reason), where he is received by four ladies who represent the cardinal virtues – Andronica (fortitude), Fronesia (prudence), Dicilla (justice) and Sofrosina (temperance) – and where he is taught by Logistilla how to control the hippogriff (his passions).[48] The Red Cross Knight, on the other hand, must be taken by Una (religious truth) to the House of Holiness, where he must undergo a far more thorough-going process of purification and regeneration. At this point in his narrative, Spenser had difficulties with the entirely secular nature of Ariosto's vision and found it expedient to draw upon Tasso's more theologically oriented account of the comparable regeneration that Rinaldo undergoes in the *Gerusalemme liberata*. But here, too, the difference between the Protestant assumptions underpinning Spenser's vision and the Counter-Reformation Catholic assumptions underlying Tasso's one are striking.

At the heart of the differences is a different conception of the will. When Rinaldo and his companions arrive back in Palestine from Armida's enchanted isle, the 'mago' who has orchestrated Rinaldo's escape offers him an entirely natural choice: between indulging in dishonourable sloth 'tra fonti e fior, tra ninfe e tra sirene' ('among fountains and flowers, nymphs and sirens'), or lifting his forehead to the skies to perform heroic deeds against Christ's foes. Nature has given Rinaldo ireful force and valour, the 'mago' declares, so that he might restrain his wicked internal enemies, cupidinous desires ('sian con maggior forza indi ripresse / le cupidigie, empi nemici interni'). The 'mago's' instruments for rousing Rinaldo to make this choice are, first, his shame, which he provokes by showing him how far behind the glory of his ancestors he trails, and then his pride, which he activates by giving him an intimation of the valiant posterity that will descend from him.[49]

Once Rinaldo has chosen – through his own agency – to rejoin Goffredo's Christian forces, only then is he cleansed from the pollution of his sin. This occurs when he climbs to the top of Mount Olivet, at the instigation of the holy hermit Pietro, to repent of his sins and pray to God for forgiveness, in answer to which, heavenly dew falls upon his garments, transfiguring their whiteness, which is a sign to Rinaldo that his sins have been purged and that he is now ready to resume his role as a champion of the Christian forces.[50]

Although Spenser decided to follow Tasso in putting the Red Cross Knight through a process of spiritual repentance and regeneration, rather than simply of moral instruction, the theology underpinning Tasso's account of Rinaldo's purgation was entirely incompatible with the Protestant

[48]　*Orlando furioso*, 10.52–67.
[49]　*Gerusalemme liberata*, 17.61–95.
[50]　*Gerusalemme liberata*, 18.6–17.

underpinnings of his own beliefs. Spenser's version of this episode, therefore, significantly modifies both Ariosto and Tasso. Unlike Rinaldo or Ruggiero, the Red Cross Knight cannot find the place of recovery by himself. Dame Caelia, the governor of the House of Holiness, says that most knights miss it, through keeping on the 'broad high way',[51] and Una has to lead the Red Cross Knight there, which reflects Spenser's belief in the essential agency of the true Church. When he gets there, the Red Cross Knight is greeted not by the four cardinal virtues as Ruggiero had been, but by the three Christian virtues: Fidelia (faith), Speranza (hope) and Charissa (charity).

Once his re-education actually begins, the order of the Red Cross Knight's instruction is reversed. Before anything else can happen, Fidelia has to teach him 'celestiall discipline' from her 'sacred Booke', reflecting Spenser's Protestant belief in the prime need for faith to reveal God's will towards humanity through his Word enshrined in Scripture. The effect on the Knight is to fill him with an exaggerated sense of *contemptus mundi*:

> That wretched world he gan for to abhore,
> And mortall life gan loath, as thing forlore,
> Greeu'd with remembrance of his wicked wayes,
> And prickt with anguish of his sinnes so sore,
> That he desirde, to end his wretched dayes:
> So much the dart of sinfull guilt the soule dismayes.
> (*Faerie Queene*, I.x.21)

Spenser presents this state of mind as one from which the Red Cross Knight needs to be cured by Hope, but even that is not enough:

> ... yet the cause and root of all his ill,
> Inward corruption, and infected sin,
> Not purg'd nor heald, behind remained still,
> And festring sore did rankle yet within,
> Close creeping twixt the marrow and the skin.
> (*Faerie Queene*, I.x.25)

Unlike Rinaldo, the Red Cross Knight is not merely 'profane' ('profano'), being tainted by the world and the flesh ('ché sei de la caligine del mondo / e de la carne asperso'),[52] but 'soule-diseased', reflecting Spenser's deeper Calvinist sense of sin as a depravity diffused throughout the body and soul. Consequently, the cure is far more painful than anything that Rinaldo has to endure. All that Rinaldo has to do is kneel and pray that God will look with pity on his former life and sins, and bestow grace so that the old Adam in him

---

[51] *Faerie Queene*, I.x.10.
[52] *Gerusalemme liberata*, 18.7–8.

can be purged and renewed ('in me tua grazia piovi, / sì che il mio vecchio Adam purghi e rinovi').[53] The Red Cross Knight, in contrast, has to experience a spiritual penitence involving suffering that is not dissimilar to the very pains of hell:

> And euer as superfluous flesh did rot
> *Amendment* readie still at hand did wayt,
> To pluck it out with pincers firie whot,
> That soone in him was left no one corrupted iot.
>
> And bitter *Penance* with an yron whip,
> Was wont him once to disple euery day:
> And sharpe *Remorse* his hart did pricke and nip,
> That drops of bloud thence like a well did play;
> And sad *Repentance* vsed to embay,
> His bodie in salt water smarting sore,
> The filthy blots of sinne to wash away.
> So in short space they did to health restore
> The man that would not liue, but earst lay at deathes dore.
>
> In which his torment often was so great,
> That like a Lyon he would cry and rore,
> And rend his flesh, and his owne synewes eat.
> His owne deare *Vna* hearing euermore
> His ruefull shriekes and gronings, often tore
> Her guiltlesse garments, and her golden heare,
> For pitty of his paine and anguish sore.
>
> (*Faerie Queene*, I.x.26–8)

As might be expected, the representation of these more severe agonies of conscience reflects Spenser's deeply Protestant sense that regeneration depends upon a penitential transformation that must take place in the heart and mind of the individual.

Not only does Spenser prioritize faith and present a much more fully conceptualized vision of the process of regeneration, but he also depicts a different outcome. Repentance, in Calvinist doctrine, must issue forth in the fruits of repentance, and Spenser affirms this when he has Mercy, at the behest of Charissa, instruct the Red Cross Knight in the seven corporal works of mercy: to provide lodging for those in need of shelter, to feed the hungry, to cloth the naked, to provide relief for poor prisoners, to care for the sick, to bury the dead, and to look after the widows and orphans of the deceased. There is no hint of this in Tasso; rather, Rinaldo is enjoined to exact revenge on the pagans for the death of the Prince of Danes.[54]

[53] *Gerusalemme liberata*, 18.14.
[54] See, respectively, *Faerie Queene*, I.x.37–43 and *Gerusalemme liberata*, 17.83.

One final significant change Spenser makes to his source occurs in his use of the holy hermit figure and the hero's ascent up Mount Olivet, which he imitates from the *Gerusalemme liberata*. Rinaldo meets Piero l'Eremita before he undergoes regeneration; the Red Cross Knight meets the Hermit Contemplation only after he has become regenerate, which means that he is in a state to be shown a vision of the New Jerusalem – that is, the heavenly city of God's saints. This reflects the fact that Spenser has given the Red Cross Knight a much larger quest than Tasso had given Rinaldo: whereas Rinaldo is enjoined to put his chivalric prowess in the service of Goffredo's struggle against the pagans, the Red Cross Knight is enjoined to look beyond his chivalric quest (to slay the dragon) to the more important spiritual quest that will lead him to fulfil his destiny as the future Saint George – the saint who, in his regenerate holiness, will define the values of Elizabeth's English Protestant nation.

In developing his exemplar of holiness, then, Spenser has imitated the Italian romantic epic archetype in order to reveal a deeper significance in the experience it depicts. He has shown that the implications of this experience are fully revealed only when it is reinterpreted in the light of Protestant understandings about the innate susceptibility of human nature to sinfulness, and of the interior reformation of spirit, activated as a consequence of faith made possible by the intervention of God's grace. I have dwelt upon Spenser's exemplification of holiness at some length because it demonstrates most clearly why he found the romance material of the Italian epics so useful, and also the fundamental doctrinal assumptions that shape his adaptation of them.

In presenting his second virtue, Temperance, Spenser was equally creative in transforming his Italian sources. Even though the basic design of Book II results from a marriage of Aristotle's conception of the irascible and concupiscible passions with Protestant notions about original sin and the necessary agency of grace (symbolized in Arthur's rescue of Sir Guyon from Pyrochles and Cymochles, and his defence of the Castle of Alma against Maleger and his forces), Spenser nonetheless relies upon imitation of key episodes from the *Furioso* and the *Liberata* for his exemplification of irascible and concupiscible forms of intemperance and the way they are to be restrained.

The influence of Ariosto is visible from the outset, with the knight who must overcome the enemies of temperance, Sir Guyon, being loosely based on Rinaldo in the *Orlando furioso*. Both are forced to pursue their quests on foot as a result of having lost their horses, Rinaldo when he dismounted from Baiardo to fight Ruggiero, and Guyon when he dismounts to attend to the dying Amavia with her blood-stained babe, Ruddymane.[55] This may seem a

---

[55] *Orlando furioso*, 2.21; *Faerie Queene*, I.i.39.

trivial detail, but the significance is important. Rinaldo dismounts so that he can fight his pagan enemy on equal terms. Spenser replicates this idea by requiring Guyon to combat intemperance through the exercise of his reason, thus demonstrating the level of temperance that ordinary individuals can expect to attain through making judicious rational discriminations. This can only take place, however, once grace (Arthur – who, in contrast to Guyon, is significantly mounted on a fierce horse, Spumador) has destroyed the effects of original sin on the body (Maleger), in a battle that is itself suggested by the fight between Astolfo and the monster-robber, Orrilo, with his supernatural powers of reconstitution.[56]

Spenser's first extended use of Ariosto occurs when he has Sir Guyon witness the destructive consequences of unbridled irascibility in preparation for his own encounter with the embodiment of that intemperate passion in the form of Pyrochles. For this purpose, Spenser drew upon the story of Ginevra and Ariodante in the *Orlando furioso*, turning it into the episode in which Phedon tells his story after being saved from Furor and Occasion by Sir Guyon. In order to fortify Guyon with an understanding of why the irascible impulse must be restrained, he converts the literal action of the source-fable into a representation of the psychological forces that can subvert and corrupt a person from within once rational control has been impaired by anger.

In broad outline, Spenser follows Ariosto fairly closely. Both episodes use the same basic story of a lover deceived into believing his beloved is unfaithful when her maid, at the instigation of a jealous rival, dresses up in the clothes of her mistress to entertain a lover.[57] As far as specifics are concerned, however, Spenser thoroughly reworks Ariosto's conception of the story.

His first major change is to redistribute the roles of the main characters in order to make the deceived lover, Phedon, the author of crime rather than simply its victim, as Ariodante is. When the sequence opens, it is Phedon himself whom Guyon sees being assaulted 'with great crueltee', by Furor and Occasion, not Dalinda the maid, whom Rinaldo sees about to be killed by two ruffians at the behest of Polinesso. Similarly, the central betrayal of trust is not that of Dalinda betraying her mistress, Ginevra, but of Philemon, Phedon's childhood companion and confidant, betraying his friend.

The motive for the deception is also different. In the *Furioso*, Polinesso orchestrates it as a means of gaining revenge on Ginevra for her refusal to requite his love. Philemon, on the other hand, acts out of envy at Phedon's good fortune in winning the love of Claribell, 'a Ladie faire of great degree', and acts out of a malice directed at Phedon himself. These substitutions completely alter the behaviour and status of the hero, and hence the signification

---

[56] *Orlando furioso*, 15.79–89.
[57] *Faerie Queene*, II.iv.17–33; *Orlando furioso*, 5.5–6.16.

of the whole story. Whereas Ariodante suffers extreme grief at Ginevra's supposed infidelity, leading him to attempt suicide, Phedon, like the Red Cross Knight in Book I, is filled with a vindictive sexual jealousy, which, once unleashed, leads him to heap 'crime on crime, and griefe on griefe / To losse of loue adioyning losse of frend', first by killing his innocent beloved, Claribell, and then by poisoning his former friend, Philemon. At the time when Furor and Occasion take Phedon captive, he is pursuing Claribell's maid, Pryene, to exact revenge on her, too, for having been complicit in the deception. The effect of this is to change what had been essentially a tragicomic romance (Dalinda, the sexually liberal maid, ends up becoming a nun in Denmark!) into an unequivocal tragedy, of which Phedon is not merely the spectator but also the prime actor.

What Spenser has done, in fact, has been to rework the Ariostean original into a fiction that represents the psychopathology of sinful anger together with its destructive spiritual consequences. As the narrator observes at the beginning of the next canto, there is no greater enemy to temperance than 'stubborne perturbation', 'For it the goodly peace of stayed minds / Does ouerthrow, and troublous warre proclame'.[58] The Phedon episode, in Spenser's treatment, indicates the stages by which the victim of perturbation becomes 'His owne woes authour'. Once Philemon has been able to unsettle the peace of Phedon's mind with his allegation that Claribell is unchaste, Phedon's perturbation quickly converts into sexual jealousy:

> The gnawing anguish and sharpe gelosy,
>   Which his sad speech infixed in my brest,
>   Ranckled so sore, and festred inwardly,
>   That my engreeued mind could find no rest
>   Till that the truth thereof I did outwrest.
>   (*Faerie Queene*, II.iv.23)

The images of disease in this passage suggest the terms in which Spenser elsewhere describes the effects of original sin, as when he ponders whether the indelible stain on Ruddymane's hands might result from 'the charme and venim' which his parents had drunk, which

> Their bloud with secret filth infected hath,
>   Being diffused through the senselesse truncke,
>   That through the great contagion direfull deadly stunck.
>   (*Faerie Queene*, II.ii.4)

The real tragedy of Phedon's reaction to Philemon's malicious manipulation of appearances is that the perturbation it arouses also paves the way for the

[58] *Faerie Queene*, II.v.1.

activation of other manifestations of original sin. Phedon's anger is aggravated by his wounded pride, which Philemon is able to play on by telling him 'that it was a groome of base degree, / Which of my loue was partner and Paramoure', just as he is able to trick Pryene into being his accomplice by making her 'proud through praise' of her beauty.[59] Thus, Spenser has fundamentally relocated the meaning of the story away from Ariosto's focus on the injustice of the sexual double standard that men often invoke in their treatment of women, together with the idea that crimes are ultimately impossible to conceal, to a new emphasis on the interior degeneration that is liable to be set in motion by a failure to bridle intemperate emotions. In characteristic fashion, therefore, he has been able to harness the representational possibilities inherent in the Italian original to the realization of a new signification that is weighted with the insights of Protestant doctrine.

As important as Spenser's use of Ariosto was for his demonstration of the dangers of irascible intemperance, it is dwarfed by the use he made of Tasso's *Gerusalemme liberata* to present his view of concupiscible intemperance. Indeed, Guyon's encounter with the concupiscible passions is entirely shaped by the episode in the *Liberata* in which Rinaldo is first captured by Armida, and then rescued through the intervention of the Christian knights, Carlo and Ubaldo.

One indication of how important the Rinaldo/Armida episode was to Spenser is his decision to replicate elements from it in five discrete, though closely related, episodes. The first occurs near the beginning of Book II when Sir Guyon hears from the dying Amavia the story of the sensual entrapment of her lord, Sir Mortdant, in Acrasia's Bower of Bliss and of the enchantress's dreadful revenge when he tried to escape from her.[60] The second occurs when Atin arrives at the Bower of Bliss to rouse Cymochles to avenge his brother, Pyrochles, who has been defeated by Guyon, which imitates the moment when Carlo and Ubaldo confront Rinaldo in Armida's arbour and shame him into abandoning the life of voluptuous pleasure he has been leading.[61] The third consists of the episode in which Cymochles is distracted from his mission by Phaedria (Immodest Mirth), who transports him to her floating island in the Idle Lake and lulls him into a state of enervated sensual delight,[62] which imitates the moment when Armida has Rinaldo transported to an island in the middle of the River Orontes where he is similarly lulled into an unmanning sensual captivity. This is closely followed by the fourth episode, in which Phaedria attempts to repeat the action of the second, except that Sir Guyon, the intended victim, is able to resist her blandishments.[63] The final episode, which constitutes the climactic and most

[59] *Faerie Queene*, II.iv.24, II.iv.25–7.
[60] *Faerie Queene*, II.i.49–56.
[61] *Faerie Queene*, II.v.25–37; *Gerusalemme liberata*, 16.29–34.
[62] *Faerie Queene*, II.vi.2–18.   [63] *Faerie Queene*, II.vi.19–38.

important sequence in the whole work, replicates the first (but at much greater length), and consists of the voyage of Guyon and the Palmer to Acrasia's Bower of Bliss, together with her capture, the destruction of the Bower, and the release of Acrasia's former victims from their metamorphosed imprisonment, all of which again imitates the rescue of Rinaldo from Armida's power by Carlo and Ubaldo. Spenser's insistent reiteration, with variations, of this central action – a surrender to, and a recovery from, a life of sensual pleasure – attests to his recognition of the imaginative power inherent in Tasso's version of this Italianate thematic commonplace.

The question arises as to why Spenser should have given the Armida/Rinaldo episode such extraordinary prominence by reiterating it so insistently in Book II of *The Faerie Queene*. One reason is that, by its very nature, a story showing the chivalric hero diverted from his duty through sexual seduction provided Spenser with a fictive vehicle for addressing head-on one of the most problematical issues for contemporary Protestants: how to reconcile the Calvinist belief that all desires are sinful with the powerful human urge to take delight in art, beauty, sex and all those aspects of life that involve an appeal to the senses – deemed to be corrupted since the advent of original sin at the fall of Adam and Eve. A second reason is that Tasso's extended account of the stages of seduction, which is much more elaborately developed than Ariosto's account of Alcina's seduction of Ruggiero, sets the stage for Guyon to make a series of rational discriminations which, in Spenser's vision, could resolve the issue. A third reason is that the narrative strategy that Tasso adopts in presenting the rescue of Rinaldo offered Spenser a hint as to how he could depict Guyon in the act of making these discriminations. Nevertheless, in order to realize these potential advantages, Spenser needed to reshape and modify Tasso's account of the Armida/Rinaldo episode even more radically than he had adapted Ariosto's comparable account of Alcina's seduction of Ruggiero in constructing his legend of holiness.

Spenser had one particular thematic problem he needed to resolve. Tasso's version of the archetype, like that of Ariosto upon which it is modelled, showed the hero actually succumbing to seduction, following which he is led to reject the life of sensual pleasure by which he had been captivated. The problem with this pattern of action was that it manifested intemperance in two respects: first, in the hero's surrender to the senses, and, second, in the absolute repudiation of the senses that his restoration required. Spenser, on the other hand, had decided to present the notion of temperance by showing a hero, Sir Guyon, who is able to demonstrate the qualities of that virtue in the nature of his reactions to various manifestations of intemperance, and in his ability to resist the temptation to become intemperate. It would, therefore, be entirely inappropriate for Spenser to show him re-enacting the experiential pattern undergone by Ruggiero and Rinaldo. Besides, he had already made use of that pattern in presenting the Red Cross Knight in the process of attaining holiness in Book I. Tasso's narrative gave Spenser a cue as to how he might preserve the effectiveness of the Armida/Rinaldo archetype as a cautionary exemplum without destroying the integrity of his conception of Guyon as the exemplar of temperance.

He did this by redistributing the roles of the main actors in his Italian model. The experience of Rinaldo is re-enacted not by Guyon himself but by three separate warriors, who are unmanned (symbolized in the shedding of their weapons and armour) when they surrender to the seduction of sensual pleasure: Mortdant, Cymochles and Verdant. Guyon, on the other hand, instead of being the victim of concupiscible intemperance as Rinaldo is, is allowed to remain a discriminating observer capable of discerning why and how he should avoid it. Spenser preserves this function by giving him the role performed in the source by Carlo and Ubaldo – that is, he becomes the agent whose mission it is to recover the fallen champion by resisting the temptations to which the latter has succumbed. This, indeed, is why Spenser divided the source story into a number of distinct episodes. In his conception, the concupiscible passions divide themselves into two categories: those having their origins in the desires of the mind, and those which have their origins in the desires of the body. In order to exemplify each category, Spenser created two versions of the enchantress – Phaedria, representing 'immodest Merth' and 'vaine iolliment' (II.v.3), and Acrasia, representing 'vaine delightes' and 'idle pleasures' (II.v.27). To emphasize the difference between the two temptresses, he places them in two different locations: Phaedria on an island in the middle of the Idle Lake, and Acrasia in the Bower of Bliss, situated on a wandering island in the Perilous Gulf. Spenser then assigns two episodes to each of these categories of intemperate concupiscence. In the first of each pair we are shown Cymochles – the embodiment of the concupiscible passions – corrupted by surrender to them. In the second episode of each pair, we are shown Guyon refusing to surrender to the same temptation. Thus, whereas Phaedria's 'light behauiour and losse dalliaunce' give 'wondrous great contentment' to Cymochles as she transports him across the lake in her 'litle frigot' (echoing the 'picciol batello' with which Rinaldo is transported to Armida's isle),[64] Guyon's response is very different:

> The knight was courteous, and did not forbeare
> Her honest merth and pleasaunce to partake;
> But when he saw her toy, and gibe, and geare,
> And passe the bonds of modest merimake,
> Her dalliance he despisd, and follies did forsake.
> (*Faerie Queene*, II.vi.21)

---

[64] *Faerie Queene*, II.v.8; *Gerusalemme liberata*, 14.57.

Indeed, it is not long before Guyon realizes that Phaedria has misled him from his 'right way' and requests her to convey him back to the shore of the lake so that he can resume his quest. Similarly, while Cymochles is 'giuen all to lust and loose liuing' to 'serue his Lemans loue' in Acrasia's Bower of Bliss (II.v.28), Guyon, under the instruction of the Palmer, is able to restrain the motions of 'kindled lust' that are aroused in him by the sexual temptations he encounters in the Bower and proceed to the successful accomplishment of his mission.

Because Spenser wanted his hero to perform this exemplary role, he also found it necessary to implant more sinister signifiers in his reworking of the Armida/Rinaldo story so as to identify more clearly the fallacies and abuses that Sir Guyon needs to discern.

The erotic allure with which Tasso had invested Armida provided him with his first problem. Imitating Virgil, Tasso had decided to ennoble Armida (something that Ariosto had not dared attempt with Alcina), just as Dido had been ennobled in the *Aeneid*.[65] When Armida first lures Rinaldo to the island in the middle of the Orontes she means to kill him in revenge for having slain her knights and having freed her prisoners. Once she has him in her power, however, she falls in love with him as she gazes on his sleeping form, binds him in a chain of flowers and carries him off to her earthly paradise in the Fortunate Isles, 'ove in perpetuo april molle amorosa / vita seco ne mena il suo diletto' ('[W]here in perpetuall, sweet and flowring spring / She liues at ease, and ioies her Lord at will').[66] There is no doubt, either, that Rinaldo loves her unreservedly in return.

The effect of this depiction of mutual romantic love is to turn Armida into a romantic heroine who elicits reader sympathy when the hero decides to abandon her. Rinaldo himself, once he has realized that he must reject love in order, like Aeneas, to fulfil a nobler duty, tries to reassure her that in choosing this course he is not rejecting her:

Poi le risponde: – Armida, assai mi pesa
di te; sì potess'io, come il farei,
del mal concetto ardor l'anima accesa
sgombrarti: odii non son, né sdegni i miei,
né vuo' vendetta, né rammento offesa;
né serva tu, né tu nemica sei.
Errasti, è vero, e trapassasti i modi,
ora gli amori essercitando, or gli odi:

[65] See A. Bartlett Giamatti, *The Earthly Paradise and the Renaissance Epic* (Princeton, 1966), pp. 207–8.
[66] *Gerusalemme liberata*, 14.65–71.

ma che? son colpe umane e colpe usate:
scuso la natia legge, il sesso e gli anni.
Anch'io parte fallii: s'a me pietate
negar non vuo', non fia ch'io te condanni.
Fra le care memorie ed onorate
mi sarai ne le gioie e ne gli affanni,
sarò tuo cavalier quanto concede
La guerra d'Asia e con l'onor la fede.

(Gerusalemme liberata, 16.53–4)

('Madame (quoth he) for your distresse I grieue,
And would amend it, if I might or could,
From your wise hart that fond affection driue:
I cannot hate nor scorne you though I would,
I seeke no veng'aunce, wrongs I all forgiue,
Nor you my seruant, nor my foe I hould,
    Truth is, you err'de, and your estate forgot,
    Too great your hate was, and your loue too hot.

'But those are common faultes, and faults of kind,
Excus'd by nature, by your sexe and yeares;
I erred likewise, if I pardon find,
None can condemne you, that our trespasse heares,
Your dear remembrance will I keepe in minde,
In ioies, in woes, in comforts, hopes and feares,
    Call me your souldiour and your knight, as farre
    As Christian faith permits, and Asias warre.')[67]

In effect, Rinaldo not merely excuses and forgives Armida, but also declares his ongoing loyalty to her, which renders dubious the possibility that sinfulness, rather than simply a dishonourable prioritizing of love over honour, has been involved in their relationship. The result, inevitably, was moral confusion.

Spenser could not countenance this portrayal of the enchantress as a fully humanized, neo-classical, tragically romantic heroine as it cut right across his Protestant conviction that unbridled concupiscence was sinful. Consequently, he reworked the material he borrowed from Tasso in order to make it perfectly clear that a surrender to the pleasures of sensuality was to be avoided not merely because it was dishonourable, but also because it was spiritually harmful and corrupting.

Signs of this thematic readjustment appear in the images which Spenser uses to describe the 'delights' encountered on Phaedria's isle and in Acrasia's

---

[67] In Fairfax's translation these stanzas are numbered 52 and 53, as a result of his omission of Tasso's stanza 41 ('Dissegli Ubaldo allor ...').

bower. The 'flocke of Damzels' that attend the 'carelesly displayd' Cymochles when Atin finds him in the Bower of Bliss are striving to arouse him by competing with one another to flaunt their naked beauty:

> One *boastes* her beautie, and does yeeld to vew
> Her daintie limbes aboue her tender hips;
> Another her *out boastes*, and all for *tryall* strips.
> (*Faerie Queene*, II.v.33; emphases added)

The reiteration of the notion of boasting, together with the idea of rivalry, suggest that the offer of pleasure is tainted by the presence of narcissistic pride. These hints are reinforced in the scene where Guyon and the Palmer watch two naked damsels disporting themselves in a fountain within the Bower of Bliss. Spenser lifts this sequence practically word for word from his source, but subtly reorientates the meaning, even when he is following Tasso closely. For example, Tasso describes how one of the nymphs titillates the onlookers by exposing her naked breasts above the waters of the lake:

> Una in tanto drizzossi e le mammelle
> e tutto ciò che più la vista alletti
> mostrò, dal seno in suso, aperto al cielo:
> e 'l lago a l'altre membra era un bel velo.
>
> (And one of them aboue the waters quite,
> Lift vp her head, her brests, and higher partes,
> And all that might weake eies subdew and take,
> Her lower beauties vaild the gentle lake.)
> (*Gerusalemme liberata*, 15.59)

In imitating this moment, Spenser adds some cautionary signifiers in his customary manner:

> Sometimes the one would lift the other quight
> Aboue the waters, and then downe againe
> Her plong, as ouer maistered by might,
> Where both awhile would couered remaine,
> And each the other from to rise restraine;
> The whiles their snowy limbes, as through a vele,
> So through the Christall waues appeared plaine:
> Then suddeinly both would themselues vnhele,
> And the'amarous sweet spoiles to greedy eyes reuele.
> (*Faerie Queene*, II.xii.64)

By having both damsels, not just one of them, involved in this exposure, Spenser is able to introduce the familiar element of competition, which intimates the desire to gain 'mastery' at the expense of another that Spenser believes lies at the heart of any erotic experience that is egotistically motivated. His reworking of the episode thus makes it simultaneously more pornographically titillating – in subtly insinuating a fantasy of rape – and also more spiritually dangerous, as it invites the onlookers who observe it to gratify sexual desire through 'theft' (suggested by the image of 'spoiles') in response to an impulse that is 'greedy' – that is, inordinate – which the scene itself is designed to arouse.

There are countless descriptive details in Spenser's reworking of Tasso, in fact, that reiterate the idea that the pleasures offered by Phaedria and Acrasia are liable to excite sinful impulses. When Spenser imitates the song with which Rinaldo is invited to abandon the search for glory in order to accept a life of pleasure and joy ('O giovenetti, mentre aprile e maggio'), he adds details that turn it into a parody of Christ's sermon on the mount (Matthew 6:25–34), thus emphasizing the sinful presumption in God's providence that is implicit in the view that Nature will take care of all human needs without effort or pain.[68] Similarly, when Spenser imitates Tasso's account of the journey that Carlo and Ubaldo undertake to reach Armida's earthly paradise, he converts it into an allegory of the spiritual dangers that threaten anyone who is tempted to lead a life of inordinate pleasure. Thus, instead of passing by literal geographical locations in the Mediterranean as Carlo and Ubaldo do, Guyon and the Palmer have to successfully traverse or avoid the Gulf of Greediness, the Rock of Reproach, the Wandering Islands, the Quicksand of Unthriftyhead, the Whirlpool of Decay, not to mention an assortment of monsters, sirens and wild beasts that signify the dangers and deforming consequences of a surrender to sensuality. Finally, when they reach the Bower itself, the scene that greets them gives ample testimony to the spiritual corruption that awaits anyone who succumbs to its pleasures. Whereas the doors leading into Armida's palace depict the story of Antony and Cleopatra, which illustrates the theme of 'all for love', the gates leading into Acrasia's Bower of Bliss portray the much more sinister story of Jason and Medea, with its tragic demonstration of the false faith, inconstancy, homicidal vengefulness and despair that can attend surrender to inordinate sexual passion.

Every detail of the Bower, in fact, is made to suggest the attributes of sin. For example, when Guyon and the Palmer first enter the Bower, they see a 'pleasaunce' beautified

> With all the ornaments of *Floraes* pride,
> Wherewith her mother Art, as halfe in scorne
> Of niggard Nature, like a pompous bride
> Did decke her, and too lauishly adorne,
> When forth from virgin bowre she comes in th'early morne.
> (*Faerie Queene*, II.xii.50)

---

[68] *Gerusalemme liberata*, 14.62–4; *Faerie Queene*, II.vi.15–17.

The figurative language here makes it clear that the beauty of the place derives from an artifice that is undesirable not merely because it is tasteless in its lavish excess, but more importantly because it is designed to gratify pride. Similarly, when they view the porch of 'rare deuice' constructed out of 'boughes and braunches, which did broad dilate / Their clasping armes, in wanton wreathings intricate', Spenser makes sure that the reader notices that the bunches of grapes are not natural, but made variously of precious jewels and burnished gold that oppress 'the weake bowes', causing them to bow down 'as ouer-burdened'.[69] This suggests the debasing effect that delight in such excessive artifice is likely to have on an individual's moral being.

Without doubt, however, the greatest change that Spenser makes to his source was in the conception of the enchantress herself. Far from being a romantic heroine, Spenser turns her unequivocally into a witch who is repeatedly labelled 'vile'. Moreover, he takes great pains to show what constitutes her vileness.

This can perhaps best be seen in the strategic substitutions he makes in adapting Tasso's description of Armida into the description of Acrasia. For the ease of the reader who does not know Italian, I shall quote Fairfax's translation of the original text describing the moment when Carlo and Ubaldo first see Armida and Rinaldo, and then Spenser's adaptation of it. Tasso writes:

> Her breasts were naked, for the day was hot,
> Her lockes vnbound, wau'd in the wanton winde;
> Somedeale she swet (tir'd with the game you wot)
> Her sweat-drops bright, white, round, like pearles of Inde,
> Her humide eies a firie smile foorth shot,
> That like sunne-beames in siluer fountaines shinde,
>   Ore him her lookes she hung, and her soft breast
>   The pillow was, where he and loue tooke rest.
>
> His hungrie eies vpon her face he fed,
> And feeding them so, pinde himselfe away;
> And she, declining often downe her hed,
> His lippes, his cheekes, his eies kist, as he lay,
> Wherewith he sigh'd as if his soule had fled
> From his fraile breast to hers, and there would stay
>   With her beloued sprite, the armed pare
>   These follies all beheld and this hot fare.
>   (*Gerusalemme liberata*, 16.18–19)[70]

---

[69] *Faerie Queene*, II.xii.55.

[70] Tasso's original reads:

Ella dinanzi al petto ha il vel divisio,
e 'l crin sparge incomposto al vento estivo;

Spenser spreads the details from this passage across several stanzas, treating the second of Tasso's descriptive stanzas first. When Guyon and the Palmer first see Acrasia, she, like Armida, is 'solacing' herself with a lover 'after long wanton ioyes':

> And all that while, right ouer him she hong,
>   With her false eyes fast fixed in his sight,
> As seeking medicine, when she was stong,
> Or greedily depasturing delight:
> And oft inclining downe with kisses light,
> For feare of waking him, his lips bedewed,
> And through his humid eyes did sucke his spright,
> Quite molten into lust and pleasure lewd;
> Wherewith she sighed soft as if his case she rewd.
>   (*Faerie Queene*, II.xii.73)

Significantly, Spenser has entirely altered the nature of the transaction between the lovers. Whereas Tasso shows Rinaldo and Armida in a reciprocal exchange of emotional adoration, Spenser turns Acrasia into a self-gratifying predator, which is indicated by some important new details. It is no longer the male lover who is feeding hungrily on the sight of her, but rather she who is 'greedily depasturing delight', an expression that not only indicates intemperate excess but also – in the implied image of a cow cropping grass – the bovine animality of her sexual appetite. In contrast to Armida, there is nothing lovable about Acrasia. Her eyes are no longer 'humid' ('umidi') but 'false', and they no longer shoot forth a smile 'like sunne-beames in siluer fountaines' ('qual raggio in onda'). Instead, it is the eyes of the lover, Verdant, that are described as 'humid', thus serving to indicate the enervated state of his post-coital languor, and it is through them that Acrasia, like a vampire, sucks

---

langue per vezzo e 'l suo infiammato viso
fan biancheggiando i bei sudor più vivo:
qual raggio in onda, le scintilla un riso
ne gli umidi occhi trimulo e lascivo.
Sovra lui pende: ed ei nel grembo molle
le posa il capo, e 'l volto al volto attolle,

e i famelici sguardi avidamente
in lei pascendo si consuma e strugge.
S'inchina, e i dolci baci ella sovente
liba or da gli occhi e da le labra or sugge,
ed in quel punto ei sospirar si sente
profondo sì che pensi: "Or l'alma fugge
e 'n lei trapassa peregrina." Ascosi
mirano i duo guerrier gli atti amorosi.

Typically, Fairfax, with his sterner Protestant morality, editorially labels 'atti amorosi' as 'follies'.

out the vitality of his spirit. With a deft stroke, Spenser also implies the sinful nature of what she is doing in the image of the 'medicine' that she is seeking. Implicitly, this is a cure for the disease that rankles within and creeps like close fire into the heart – that is, sin, manifest in the lust that springs from an inordinate surrender to sexual concupiscence.

Spenser refrains from giving his version of Tasso's description of the enchantress's physical appearance until after he has delivered a *carpe diem* song (also closely imitated from Tasso) that makes it clear that to gather the rose of love in the way that the song invites is to engage in 'louing ... with equall crime'.[71] It is only once the sinfulness of sexual intemperance has been firmly established that he gives his description of the enchantress's ravishing beauty, and even then he intrudes details that highlight the dangers she represents. Acrasia is laid upon a bed of roses 'As faint through heat, or dight to pleasant sin'. The veil of silk through which her alabaster skin can be seen is as subtle as any web that *Arachne* can spin, an image which implicitly reinforces the idea that Acrasia is a dangerous predator who snares her victims like a spider traps a fly. Her 'snowy brest' is 'bare to readie spoyle', thus tempting the victim to acquiesce to desire for something to which he is not properly entitled.[72] As beautiful and seductive as she is, Spenser leaves no room for anyone to doubt that she is thoroughly evil.

Spenser acknowledges this intrinsic evil in his recasting of her fate. Unlike Armida, there is no possible redemption for her. We know from the opening Canto of Book II that whereas Armida seeks to avenge herself against the lover who abandons her, Acrasia actually does it, with mortal consequences for both Mortdant and Amavia. Because the nature of her intemperance makes her quintessentially corrupt, Spenser allows Acrasia no conversion; she is simply tied in adamantine chains and her Bower destroyed with 'rigour pittilesse', along with all the perverted values that it represents.[73] Spenser does conceive of the possibility of a legitimate fulfilment of desire, but it finds expression in the procreative love of Venus and Adonis, the union of Cupid and Psyche, and the fertility of the Garden and Adonis that he would depict in Book III of *The Faerie Queene*, not in the solipsistic narcissism and sterility of the intemperate lust that Acrasia embodies.

Having shown a sinfully corrupt response to desire in Book II, Spenser needed to depict its corrective opposite in his legend of Chastity. In contrast to the tendency in both medieval Catholicism and extreme puritanism to equate chastity with abstinence, or virginity, Spenser conceived of chastity as a branch of temperance involving the right uses of sexuality.[74] His task was

---

[71] *Faerie Queene*, II.xii.75.   [72] *Faerie Queene*, II.xii.77–8.   [73] *Faerie Queene*, II.xii.82–3.
[74] I am indebted here to suggestions made by Thomas Roche, Jr, in his comments on Book III of *The Faerie Queene* in A.C. Hamilton, ed., *The Spenser Encyclopedia* (Toronto and Buffalo, 1990), pp. 270–3.

to create a fable that could effectively exemplify such a conception, and for this purpose, predictably, he drew once again upon his two main Italian sources.

The legend of Chastity, which is pursued from Book III of *The Faerie Queene* right through into Book V, being left incomplete at Spenser's death in 1596, is modelled in broad conception on Bradamante's quest to be united with Ruggiero in Ariosto's *Orlando furioso*. Spenser turns this into the quest of his own female warrior, Britomart, to be united with Artegall, the exemplar of Justice, whose image she has seen in a magical crystal globe created by Merlin. In the course of pursuing her quest, Britomart is made to interact with exemplifications of the attributes of womanhood that she needs to develop in order to attain her destiny, and also with the aspects of womanhood that could inhibit the fulfilment of that destiny.

The first danger that Britomart must overcome is the temptation to be unchaste, which Spenser exemplifies in her encounter with Malecasta (Unchasteness) and her six knights that represent various forms of flirtatious behaviour: Gardante (looking), Parlante (speaking), Iocante (joking), Basciante (kissing), Bacchante (revelling) and Noctante (nocturnal activity). In constructing Britomart's encounter with Malecasta, Spenser draws together elements from a number of episodes in the *Orlando furioso*. Malecasta's mistaken passion for Britomart, whom she thinks is a man, imitates the passion of Fiordispina for Bradamante, whom, with her short hair and being fully clad in armour, she also takes for a man.[75] Malecasta's incursion into Bradamante's bedchamber when the rest of the company have fallen asleep duplicates the action of Alcina when she similarly goes to Ruggiero's bedchamber, while her approach to the bed and her groping for Bradamante's sleeping form is reminiscent of Greco's approach to Fiammetta in Canto 28 of the *Furioso*.[76] This eclectic collage shows just how reliant Spenser was on the Italianate representation of human behaviour to lend reality to the kind of experiences he was trying to depict.

At the other extreme, Britomart witnesses feminine vulnerability to the pain and danger of love in the form of Florimell, whom Spenser bases on Ariosto's Angelica. Angelica, in Ariosto's conception, is the object of male desire. She is loved by both Rinaldo and Orlando; she escapes from imprisonment by Namo; Sacripante attempts to rape her, as does an aged hermit, as well as Ruggiero; men recurrently fight over her and pursue her; the Ebudans even want to sacrifice her to the Orc. Angelica, however, is not entirely innocent. She is heartless and calculating, and her arrogance and pride are eventually punished by Cupid, who makes her fall in love with a

---

[75] *Faerie Queene*, III.i.47; *Orlando furioso*, 25.28–9.
[76] See, respectively, *Faerie Queene*, II.i.59–60 and *Orlando furioso*, 7.26; and *Orlando furioso*, 28.63.

social inferior, the common soldier, Medoro, whom she has to woo, in an ironic reversal of her former role. It was her status as victim that interested Spenser in Angelica, and in translating her into Florimell, he removed the traces of moral flaws, making her even more helpless and vulnerable. The underlying similarity, nevertheless, is very close: she is pursued successively by a 'griesly forester', a witch's son and a hyena-like monster, and then she, too, is subject to attempted rape by an aged mariner, then to the intimidations of Proteus, who wishes her to surrender her chastity to him.

Having removed the flawed aspects of Angelica from Florimell, Spenser transferred them to a male equivalent, Marinell, whose self-absorption, pride and arrogance prevent him from reciprocating Florimell's love, just as Angelica refused to requite the passion of her various smitten lovers. The importance of Florimell to Britomart is that she represents the passive fear of men that Britomart repudiates by conquering men on their own terms through her own active prowess.

While she does not suffer the helpless victimization of Florimell, Britomart nevertheless has to overcome a fear of male sexuality in order to realize the full potential of her chastity. To exemplify this idea, Spenser created the episode in which Britomart frees Amoret, the embodiment of 'godly womanhood' – the female potential that realizes itself in sexual fulfilment within marriage – from imprisonment in the castle of the evil magician, Busyrane. In constructing this fable, Spenser repeated his habit of assembling motifs from a number of sources to create an action that can reveal their hidden significance from a new perspective.

The main outline for the climactic episode in Book III involving Amoret, Scudamour and Busyrane is drawn from the earlier chivalric romance, *Rinaldo*, that Tasso wrote in 1562 as a preparatory exercise for his *Gerusalemme liberata*. In Canto 5 of the *Rinaldo*, the hero discovers a grieving shepherd, Florindo, who describes how he fell in love with Olinda, the daughter of his king, who, inevitably, has spurned him. Rinaldo, too, is suffering grief, because his own beloved, Clarice, has been carried off by a magician, Malagigi. Having decided to seek a remedy for their ills, the pair find an enchanted cave created by Merlin in which a golden statue of the God of Love proclaims that they will each attain their desired ends if they dedicate themselves to chivalry.[77]

Spenser adopts many elements from this story, characteristically reworking them in his accustomed manner. Britomart's discovery of the prostrated, grieving Scudamour is closely based on Rinaldo's discovery of Florindo, except that in translating Florindo into Scudamour, Spenser changes him from a shepherd into a knight, and alters his complaint from one reproaching

---

[77] All references to the *Rinaldo* are to the edition published in Torquato Tasso, *Opere di Torquato Tasso*, ed. Bortolo Tommaso Sozzi, 3rd edn, vol. 2 (Turin, 1974).

Amor for his perfidiousness into one questioning God as to why he allows injustice in the world.[78] Spenser also conflates Florindo's grief with Rinaldo's own dilemma, in that he bases Amoret on Clarice, who has been abducted by the enchanter from Rinaldo after granting him her love, rather than on Olinda, who has rejected Florindo. His final debt to the *Rinaldo* is for the wall of flames ('un foco ardente') that guards the entry to the enchanted cave,[79] and certain details of the sanctuary of the God of Love, such as the golden statue that stands on the altar and the display of Love's triumphs, which form the basis of Spenser's description of the contents of the rooms into which Britomart enters once she has gained access to the castle.

The motif of the wall of fire particularly arrested Spenser's imagination, for he reproduces it in his description of the entry to Busyrane's castle and combines it with further elements drawn from Tasso's later re-use of the motif in the *Gerusalemme liberata*. When Britomart and Scudamour arrive at the castle gate,

> ... no gate they found, them to withhold,
> Nor ward to wait at morne and euening late,
> But in the porch, that did them sore amate,
> A flaming fire, ymixt with smouldry smoke,
> And stinking Sulphure, that with griesly hate
> And dreadfull horrour did all entraunce choke,
> Enforced them their forward footing to reuoke.
> (*Faerie Queene*, III.xi.21)

At this point Spenser switches from the *Rinaldo* to the *Liberata* as his main source, for whereas Florindo and Rinaldo are both able to pass with impunity through the wall of fire, only Britomart is able to repeat that action, while Scudamour is forced to retire back, 'all scorcht and pitifully brent'.[80] In allowing Britomart to pass through the flames, Spenser is imitating the moment when Tancredi leaps into the roaring pallisade of flames that the evil wizard Ismeno has placed around the enchanted forest outside Jerusalem and discovers that he can pass through them unharmed.[81] For the latter part of the Amoret/Busyrane episode, indeed, Spenser relies heavily on the *Gerusalemme liberata*. Tasso's wicked Ismeno gave him hints for converting the 'good' ('buon') wizard Malagigi, who abducts Clarice from Rinaldo in order to rescue her from his wilful desire, into the 'vile Enchauntour' Busyrane, who carries off Amoret following her wedding to Scudamour before their marriage can be consummated.[82]

---

[78] *Rinaldo*, 5.16–18; *Faerie Queene*, III.xi.9–10.
[79] *Rinaldo*, 5.58.
[80] *Faerie Queene*, III.xi.26.
[81] *Gerusalemme liberata*, 13.35–6.
[82] *Faerie Queene*, IV, I.2–4.

All of these strategic changes are governed by Spenser's allegorical intention, which derives from his imaginative reinterpretation of the attitudes and actions he found depicted in Tasso's twin fictions. Busyrane represents the aggressive male sexual urge that Amoret fears in Scudamour, which is why Scudamour cannot pass through the fire that guards the entrance to the castle, being filled 'With greedy will, and envious desire', and being prone to 'augment his mighty rage' when his 'threatfull pride' meets the resistance of the fire.[83] Amoret, who is significantly chained to a phallic pillar with a torturing dagger implanted in her heart (emblems of lust and sinful desire), can only be released from her fear of being made the object of this lust by Britomart, who represents the power of chastity – that is, the right ordering of virtuous and temperate sexuality. Once Britomart has forced Busyrane to reverse the spell, the chains constraining Amoret drop away, 'the great brasen pillour' breaks into pieces, Amoret's wounds close up and she is made 'perfect [w]hole', the rooms in the castle with their emblems of lust have vanished, and the wall of fire that prevented Scudamour from gaining entrance has disappeared. Only then (in the 1590 version) is she able to yield sexually to Scudamour, melting 'in pleasure' and pouring out her spirit 'in sweete ravishment' within the hermaphroditic embrace of her husband.[84]

In releasing Amoret from the tyranny of Busyrane, Britomart is really releasing her ability to love Artegall sexually, as is implied in the envy that she experiences in seeing the two lovers embrace:

> So seemd those two, as growne together quite,
> that *Britomart* halfe enuying their blesse,
> Was much empassiond in her gentle sprite,
> And to herselfe oft wisht like happinesse,
> In vaine she wisht, that fate n'ould let her yet possesse.
> (*Faerie Queene*, III.xii.46a)

Significantly, when Busyrane wounds Britomart with his dagger (indicating the incursion of sexual desire), and she, enraged, is about to kill him, Amoret restrains her, 'For else her paine / Should be remedilesse'.[85] This shows that the fulfilment of godly womanhood does not require the complete repression of sexual desire in Spenser's vision, but rather its disciplined containment. Desire is necessary to harmonize God's creativity with the fact of mutability, as Spenser shows in depicting the Garden of Adonis, where 'Franckly each paramour his leman knowes', where Adonis lives in eternal bliss, 'Joying his goddesse, and of her enjoyed', and where Psyche (soul) and Cupid (love), being reconciled, have given birth to a child, Pleasure.[86] For Britomart to

---

83 *Faerie Queene*, III.xi.26.
84 *Faerie Queene*, III.xii.31–42; *Faerie Queene* [1590], III.xii.45a–46a.
85 *Faerie Queene*, III.xii.34.
86 *Faerie Queene*, III.vii.41–50.

fulfil her predestined union with Artegall, she must aspire to the condition depicted in the Garden, and the episode in which she frees Amoret marks one important stage in the process whereby she does so.

The final episode in which Spenser makes extended use of his Italian sources in developing the relationship between Britomart and Artegall occurs in Book V when she rescues him from his effeminized enslavement by the Amazon queen, Radigund. Allegorically, this episode represents Britomart's need to resist usurping the natural sovereignty owing to men if she is to realize the potential of her erotic union with Artegall.

To present this idea, Spenser assembled a collage of various incidents from the *Orlando furioso*. Radigund and her band of warlike women who humiliate and degrade knights to avenge Radigund's unrequited love for Bellodant are based on Orontea and her women followers who have similarly founded a state ruled by women, Alessandretta, with the aim of degrading men in order to avenge their betrayal by Phalanthus and his band of Grecian youths.[87] Radigund herself takes on the virago-like attributes of the pagan Marfisa in her rage and ferocity, and having made this association, Spenser develops Ariosto's contrast between the two types of warrior women, Marfisa (the terrifying *guerriera*) and Bradamante (the lovely maiden who combines the attributes of Venus and Mars) into a comparable contrast between the emasculating Radigund and Britomart, whose role is to restore Artegall's masculine pride and dignity.[88] Spenser also replicated the love-sick jealousy that Bradamante feels when she believes Ruggiero has fallen in love with Marfisa in the jealousy that Britomart experiences when Artegall does not return, which provides a convincing psychological motivation for Britomart's pitiless fight with Radigund.[89] In assembling this collage of creatively reworked suggestions from Ariosto, Spenser once again demonstrates his uncanny ability to recognize the potential of the humane experiences depicted in his Italianate sources to yield material which could help him to realize a radically different vision of life. Without them, his conception of Chastity in its fullest expression as a legitimized satisfaction of desire encompassing both body and spirit simply would not have been possible.

It should be clear by now that Spenser's imitation of the Italian romantic epics was neither casual nor inconsequential. Rather, it provided the material

---

[87] *Faerie Queene*, V.iv.21–33; *Orlando furioso*, 20.11–64.

[88] For an excellent account of these female-warrior types, see Margaret Tomalin, *The Fortunes of the Warrior Heroine in Italian Literature: An Index of Emancipation* (Ravenna, 1982).

[89] See, respectively, *Orlando furioso*, 30.88–9; *Faerie Queene*, V.vi.3–4; and *Faerie Queene*, V.vii.29–34. In contrast to Bradamante, who has to suffer disappointed rage when she does not succeed in killing Marfisa (*Orlando furioso*, 36.19–30), Britomart actually beheads Radigund, which illustrates the greater importance that Spenser attaches to her role as an enforcer of Protestant values.

that allowed him to construct the three most important pillars supporting his ideal vision of how a virtuous English gentleman – or woman – should be fashioned: chiefly, his conception of the virtues of Holiness, Temperance and Chastity. Moreover, imitation of these sources did not merely provide him with the raw material for the creation of his own fables of exemplification, but the need to harmonize the significations of his sources with basic Protestant doctrinal assumptions led him to develop, through the process of creative imitation, the essential values of the vision that had been espoused by the Elizabethan political establishment.

What does the vision itself amount to? As we have seen, it did not presuppose an outright rejection of Latinate (that is, proto-Catholic) culture. Rather, it assimilates what is legitimate through a process of constructive and transformative differentiation. The result was a synthesis that enabled Spenser to proclaim England's triumphant cultural independence from the Continental European value system from which it was separating, at the same time as it allowed Protestant English men and women to enjoy its best features. Spenser's practice betrays his recognition – founded on sincere personal belief, one supposes – that the extreme 'puritan' implications of Calvinist doctrine would not be tolerated by the ruling political elite. Aesthetically and doctrinally, in his view, this extreme life-denying asceticism was unnecessary anyhow, given that there is a right use of Nature's gifts to be distinguished from their abuse. All of his creative modifications of elements drawn from Italianate source material are designed to illustrate the distinction between use and abuse of natural gifts, which is, of course, what would later appeal to the puritan sensibility of John Milton, who judged Spenser to be a better teacher than Scotus or Aquinas.[90]

At a political level, Spenser's imitative performance confirms that, in the minds of England's governing elite, the individuation of Protestant England as a nation should be decisive in religious terms, but eclectic in the way in which that religious break reflected itself in attitudes and actions relating to the conduct of practical worldly affairs. It would fall to the imaginative genius of William Shakespeare, England's foremost playwright, to test the validity of all that was implicit in such suppositions concerning both the cultural system that was being enforced by Elizabeth's government, and that which it was seeking to displace. The manner in which Shakespeare invited the mass audience for whom he wrote to evaluate the relative merits of each system will form the subject of the chapter to follow.

---

[90] John Milton, *Areopagitica*, in *Milton's Prose Writings*, ed. K.M. Burton (London, 1958), p. 158.

6

Appraising 'the Seeming Truths' of the Times: the Italianate Plays of Shakespeare

As I have been arguing, the extraordinary Elizabethan appetite for Italianate literature coincided with the entrenchment of Protestantism and was partly motivated by it. Both readers and writers found that Italianate fiction served as a means for vicariously addressing the issues that concerned them. At an individual level, a lyricist like Sir Philip Sidney could seek through imitation of Petrarch to resolve personal issues arising from an experience of desire that his religion denounced as sinful. On the other hand, Edmund Spenser, who was aspiring to achieve a more public voice, could, by strategically modifying the romantic epics of Ariosto and Tasso, articulate a vision of the virtues that he hoped would define the new Elizabethan social and political order itself. In turning to the drama of the period, one finds that there was yet another function for Italianate literary imitation – that of questioning the validity not only of the old order from which England was separating, but also of the new order with which Elizabeth's Protestant subjects were looking to replace it. The most striking examples of this interrogatory function are to be found in the plays of the greatest dramatist in the period, William Shakespeare. The ones which he based on Italian-derived sources retain their fascination precisely because they engage the playgoer or reader imaginatively in the necessity of responding to the limitations that are shown to be inherent in rival value systems when their values are brought into play with one another. Because this interrogatory function was activated to address the most compelling concerns of a mass audience of Elizabethan English men and women, the Italianate plays of Shakespeare open to us one of the best possible windows into the minds of the vast majority who remained sceptical or perplexed about the implications for daily living of the new religion to which they were being enjoined, not only by patriotic feeling but also by the coercive power of the state.

The extent of Shakespeare's use of Italian literary source material was remarkable even by the standards of the day. The nature of his debt, however, is frequently overlooked and has been less than well understood. Of his thirty-seven extant plays no fewer than ten depend on Italian narrative or dramatic sources for their primary plot material, while less direct Italian influences have been traced in at least four others. Moreover, Shakespeare drew upon Italian sources across the entire span of his career as a dramatist, from the period of his early comedies, with *The Taming of the Shrew* (1593–4) – based on Ariosto's *I suppositi* (1509) – to the late romance, *Cymbeline* (1609–10), which, like *The Merry Wives of Windsor* (1600–1) and *All's Well that Ends Well* (1602–4(?)) before it, is constructed around a story derived from Boccaccio's *Decameron*.

As well as plundering Italian literature for source material, Shakespeare was also highly aware of developments in Italian drama during the sixteenth century, as is evident in his ongoing efforts to imitate them. How he gained this knowledge is uncertain, but it is possible that he heard the reports of travellers and witnessed performances by Italian dramatic troupes that toured England in the later part of the sixteenth century. Drusiano Martinelli, an Italian comedian, is known to have appeared in England in 1577–8, and an Italian troupe including one Flaminio Curtesse is known to have performed at the English court in 1602.[1] Certainly, Shakespeare's earliest known play, *The Comedy of Errors* (written some time between 1588 and 1593) – based on Plautus' *Menaechmi* – reflects the influence of the revival of Roman new comedy that had taken place in the late fifteenth and early sixteenth centuries in Rome, Florence and Ferrara. It also betrays the influence of the *commedia erudita* that had arisen as a result of the efforts of Italian dramatists like Ariosto, Niccolò Machiavelli and Bernardo Bibbiena to imitate their classical forebears.[2]

Subsequent plays show him equally determined to keep up with, and where possible surpass, contemporary Italian theatrical fashions. The earlier comedies are liberally sprinkled with references to the stereotype characters of the *commedia dell'arte* such as the Zanni, the Pedant, the Pantaloon and the Magnifico, and Shakespeare created his own Pantaloon for *The Taming of the Shrew* (1593–4) in the form of Gremio, as well as several Pedants, the most colourful of whom is Holofernes in *Love's Labours Lost* (1588–94).[3] Later in

[1] *The Oxford Companion to the Theatre*, ed. Phyllis Hartnoll, 4th edn (Oxford, New York, Toronto, Melbourne, 1983), p. 172, under 'Commedia dell'arte'.
[2] See Ernest Hatch Wilkins, *A History of Italian Literature*, revised by Thomas G. Bergin (Cambridge, Massachusetts, 1974), p. 237.
[3] See ibid., p. 291; also Ninian Mellamphy, 'Pantaloons and Zanies: Shakespeare's "Apprenticeship" to Italian Professional Comedy Troupes', in *Shakespearean Comedy*, ed. Maurice Charney (New York, 1980), pp. 141–51. References to the Zanni may be found in

his career, Shakespeare experimented with different types of Italianate mixed genres, most notably in *Romeo and Juliet*, which has been described as a comedy that is made to swerve aside from its generic destination under the influence of ill fortune, and in *Measure for Measure* (1604–5), which is a *tragedia di fin lieto* (tragedy with a happy ending) modelled on Giraldi Cinthio's story of Juriste and Epitia, which appeared in *Gli ecatommiti* (1565) and subsequently in a dramatized version. In the closing years of his career, Shakespeare demonstrated his continuing receptivity to new theatrical fashions imported from Italy by creating in *Cymbeline* his own tragi-comic pastoral romance in response to the taste for pastoral drama that had developed after the appearance in English of Battista Guarini's *Il pastor fido* in 1602, and a number of plays that were influenced by it, such as Samuel Daniel's *The Queenes Arcadia* (1605) and John Fletcher's *The Faithful Shepherdess* (1608–9).

The manner in which Shakespeare gained access to his Italian sources gives further evidence of the profundity of his interest. It is sometimes assumed that his knowledge of these works was limited to a second-hand acquaintance through English translations and adaptations to be found in collections like Geoffrey Fenton's *Certain Tragical Discourses written out of French and Latin* (1567), William Painter's *The Palace of Pleasure* (1567), Barnabe Rich's *Riche His Farewell to Militarie Profession* (1581), George Whetstone's *The Rocke of Regard* (1576) and *An Heptameron of Ciuill Discourses* (1582), and George Turbervile's *Tragicall Tales Translated by Turbervile in Time of His Troubles out of Sundrie Italians* (1587). While Shakespeare certainly made use of these translations – possibly as a crib – his knowledge of Italian was sufficient for him to refer also to the source stories as they appeared in the original Italian. Several sources, indeed, were available only in Italian; specifically, the story of Othello that Shakespeare found in Cinthio's *Gli ecatommiti* (1565), and the two *novelle* in *Il pecorone* by Ser Giovanni Fiorentino that provided the main plots for *The Merchant of Venice* (1596–7) and *The Merry Wives of Windsor* (1600–1). On occasions when he did use intermediary English or French versions of source stories, he seems also to have cross-checked the differences in signification between the translation and the source by going back to the original Italian. This is clearly the case in *Measure for Measure*, the content of which confirms that Shakespeare read Cinthio's tragi-comedy, *Epitia* (written before 1573 and published in 1583), as well as George Whetstone's English play, *Promos and Cassandra* (1578), which is itself based on Cinthio's story.[4]

Love's Labours Lost, V.ii.463 and *Twelfth Night*, I.v.89; to the Pedant in *Love's Labours Lost*, V.ii.539 and *The Taming of the Shrew*, IV.ii.63; to the Pantaloon in *The Taming of the Shrew*, III.i.36 and *As You Like It*, II.vii.157; and to the Magnifico in *The Merchant of Venice*, III.ii.280 and *Othello*, I.ii.11.

[4] For arguments that Shakespeare knew both of Cinthio's versions in Italian as well as George Whetstone's play based on them, *Promos and Cassandra* (1578), see Madeleine Doran, *Endeavours of Art* (Madison, 1954), pp. 385–9; and Kenneth Muir, *The Sources of Shakespeare's Plays* (London, 1977), pp. 175–7.

Certain key details in *Cymbeline*, too, show that Shakespeare consulted not only the English translation of a German version of the tale by Boccaccio that furnished the basis for the wager plot, *Frederyke of Jennen* (published in 1560), but also Boccaccio's original Italian version as it appeared in the *Decameron*.[5] This dual approach through the original as well as the translated versions of Italian sources indicates that Shakespeare was not simply interested in the stories as stories, but also in the way that they had been culturally inflected during the process of re-telling. By going back to the originals, he was able to apprehend the cultural alterity of his sources without the distorting editorial interference that had been introduced by the English translators. As I shall demonstrate, his sense of the different mores, values and assumptions that distinguished Italian from English culture was all important in determining the use he made of Italianate sources in constructing his own drama.

Shakespeare's purpose in imitating the Italians differed from that of Spenser in that he was concerned to entertain a mass audience of playgoers rather than appeal to the inclinations of a select aristocratic elite. His instincts were also to proceed heuristically rather than to be proselytizing or corrective. To these ends Italianate source material suited him ideally. Its subject matter, especially that which was drawn from the *novelle*, appealed to the Elizabethans because it tended to deal either with the exercise of human self-agency in the pursuit of desired ends (usually erotic ones), or else with 'the extremes produced by the human mind ... especially in its moments of perversity', as Francesco Boncioni theorized when analysing the nature of the genre in his *Lezioni sopra il comporre delle novelle* (1574).[6] Both categories of subject matter were bound to appeal to Protestant English writers for the same reasons I have identified in earlier chapters: Protestant morality had identified the impulses of desire and the experience of intemperate passions as confirmation of the deep sinfulness of human nature, yet ordinary English men and women knew that they were a daily reality in their lives. Any works which presented men and women in the pursuit of desire or displaying the perversity of human intellect would attract playgoers by holding up a mirror in which they could see images of their own hopes, fears and capacities, especially as interpreted by the officially prescribed religion of the Elizabethan state and its more radical puritan offshoots. Shakespeare knew, too, that these subjects would be particularly arresting when presented with the highly charged emotional effects attainable through imitation of the new Italian dramatic forms. At one level, therefore, he engaged in Italianate imitation because it would be a sure-fire hit at the box office.

[5] See Geoffrey Bullough, ed., *Narrative and Dramatic Sources of Shakespeare*, 8 vols (London and New York, 1957–75), vol. 8, pp. 16–19.
[6] I quote from the translation of a passage from Boncioni's work by Robin Kirkpatrick in his *English and Italian Literature from Dante to Shakespeare: A Study of Sources, Analogy, and Divergence* (London, 1995), p. 232.

Nevertheless, Shakespeare was equally aware that this theatrical entertainment needed to be produced in the context of a society that had committed itself to a state religion founded in a deeply embedded Calvinist theology. Indeed, Calvinist discourse was ubiquitous. At least once a year each of Queen Elizabeth's Protestant subjects had to repeat the Thirty-nine Articles of Religion that had been formulated in the Settlement of 1559, affirming the helplessness of Man to 'turn and prepare himself, by his own natural strength and good works, to faith, and calling upon God', and his inability 'to do good works pleasant and acceptable to God, without the grace of God by Christ preventing us that we may have a good will'.[7] Preachers constantly reiterated these assumptions about the natural depravity of humanity, and their message was reinforced by the Homilies which had been appointed to be read in any service in which a sermon was lacking. In 1593, Parliament passed severe legislation that bound the Queen's subjects to attend Church, thereby affirming their submission to the Acts of Supremacy and Uniformity, or else face the equivalent of what amounted to house arrest.[8] No English subject in the reign of Elizabeth could, in fact, escape being affected by the doctrines of the reformed religion. As the new ideology came to be progressively entrenched, puritan extremists began to attack the stage itself as irreligious. Phillip Stubbes' denunciations in *The Anatomie of Abuses* (1583) epitomize the puritan mistrust of the theatre: 'Oh blasphemy intolerable! Are filthy plays and bawdy enterludes comparable to the word of God, the food of life, and life itself?'[9] Impelled on one hand by an impulse to dramatize Italian stories because of their humane relevance and box-office appeal, Shakespeare nevertheless had to reconcile this endeavour with the realities of a dominant ideological system whose values were seriously at odds with those inherent in his source materials. In the rest of this chapter I shall demonstrate how he responded to the inherent clash between rival value systems, identifying the strategies he employed to explore the relationship between the two, and the thematic consequences of those strategies.

Shakespeare's characteristic method of appraisal, especially in the early and middle phases of his career, was to imitate Italian source material so as to activate an interrogatory process, usually involving the triangulation of opposing values or belief systems. Italianate source material assisted him in doing this, as it usually contained moral or metaphysical issues latent in the behaviour or attitudes of its characters that were unrealized in the source but apparent to the gaze of anyone accustomed to – as Shakespeare was – the

---

[7] Article X, in *The Thirty-nine Articles*, ed. B.J. Kidd (London, 1900), p. 128.
[8] 35 Elizabeth I, caps 1–2; reprinted in Henry Bettenson, ed., *Documents of the Christian Church*, 2nd edn (Oxford, New York and Toronto, 1963), pp. 340–4.
[9] Phillip Stubbes, *The Anatomie of Abuses*, ed. Frederick J. Furnivall (London, 1877–9), I, pp. 143–4.

preoccupations of Protestant discourse. All he needed to do was adapt it in such a way as to expose to view the latent issues.

The method itself he learnt, in the first instance, from the practice of Italian dramatists earlier in the sixteenth century. At some point early in his career he became aware of the art of *contaminatio* as practised by the likes of Ariosto in *I suppositi* (1509), or Bernardo Bibbiena in *La Calandria* (1513), both of which are built around motifs from Plautus combined with materials from Boccaccio's *Decameron*, according to principles that Terence had justified in the prologue to his *Andria*.[10] Shakespeare's earliest known play, *The Comedy of Errors*, shows him attempting to use *contaminatio* in the Italian manner by merging material drawn deliberately from disparate sources. Not only does he combine a classical Plautine intrigue plot with a framing medieval romance narrative derived from Gower's story of Apollonius of Tyre in the *Confessio Amantis*, but he also creates a second set of identical twins in the main plot as servants to the first, creates a sister for the wife of one of the first set of twins with whom the second brother falls in love, and adds a living (and loving) set of parents to replace the dead father in Plautus' play. As a result, the possibilities for confusion are compounded to create an elaborateness of action and theatrical effect that seems designed to outdo the Italian comedic writers at their own game. More than this, however, the merging of the disparate elements has a thematic advantage. The effect of combining a classical intrigue plot, the norms of which are fairly cynical and amoral, with elements of a medieval romance narrative that involves religious symbolism associated with nativity, rebirth, restoration and miracles, is to activate a new perspective on the meaning of the confusions in the main plot. Instead of representing simply the comic predicament of characters whose pursuit of their ends is frustrated by coincidences that they cannot foresee or control, the play now intimates the possibility that the ironies it depicts may attest to the workings of a beneficent providence: the actualization of the 'beneficial hap' by which the Duke hopes that Egeon's life will be saved at the outset of the play.[11] Through experimenting with the device of *contaminatio* in *The Comedy of Errors*, Shakespeare had learnt, in effect, the advantage of triangulating disparate or contrasting values into an arrangement whereby the values

---

[10] See Kirkpatrick, *English and Italian Literature*, pp. 201–15; and Louise George Clubb, 'Shakespeare's Comedy and Late Cinquecento Mixed Genres', in *Shakespearean Comedy*, ed. Maurice Charney (New York, 1980), pp. 129–39, esp. p. 130.

[11] *The Comedy of Errors*, I.i.151, in William Shakespeare, *Complete Pelican Shakespeare*, ed. Alfred Harbage and others, 3 vols (Harmondsworth, 1969). All references to Shakespeare's plays are taken from this edition. The line from *The Comedy of Errors* that I have quoted is a contentious one. The Folio version of 1623 has the Duke urge Egeon 'To seek thy help by beneficial help', which the Penguin editor emends to 'To seek thy life by beneficial help', and the editors of *The Oxford Shakespeare* to 'To seek thy health by beneficial help'. I have adopted the reading of 'hap' for the second occurrence of 'help', as presented in the televised performance

of one category could interrogate or provide a commentary on the values of the other, in order to imply the existence of a third order of possibilities that might not be located discretely in either of the two sets of originary values.

Having mastered the basic technique of merging two disparate plots in *The Comedy of Errors*, Shakespeare proceeded to apply it again in *The Taming of the Shrew* (1593 or 1594), this time working with an actual Italian exemplar, Ariosto's *I suppositi*, which had been translated into English by George Gascoigne as *Supposes* in 1566. The Italian source play exemplifies prototypical features of the neo-classical *commedia erudita*. Young lovers, aided by good fortune, triumph over impediments to the fulfilment of their love through a series of deceits that induce false suppositions. As Gascoigne puts it in the 'Prologue' to his translation: 'you shall see the master supposed for the servant, the servant for the master: the freeman for a slave, and the bond-slave for a freeman: the stranger for a well known friend, and the familiar for a stranger'.[12] To a Protestant mind the plot must have seemed scandalously immoral. Aided by a 'scabbed old queane', Psiteria, the heroine, Polynesta, has already been sleeping with her seducer, Erostrato, when the play begins, and Erostrato tries to secure her as his wife by attempting to cheat her father, Damon, of the large dowry he is hoping to get from a rival suitor, the aged Cleander, who also hopes to marry Polynesta. When the plot goes awry and Erostrato (as the feigned Dulipo) is thrown into prison, the situation is only retrieved by an extraordinary sequence of fortunate coincidences: Cleander is placated by the happy discovery that the real Dulipo (who has been masquerading as Erostrato) is his long-lost son, and Damon is appeased by the discovery that his daughter's seducer is actually the son of a very wealthy and respectable Sicilian who is willing to proffer all his lands in dower as recompense for the injury his son has committed. At the comparable moment of discovery in Shakespeare's adaptation of this plot, Lucentio, Shakespeare's version of Erostrato, excuses the duplicitous way he has acted on the grounds that 'Love wrought these miracles'.[13] In adapting Ariosto's play into the Lucentio/Bianca plot of *The Taming of the Shrew*, it was precisely this assumption that Shakespeare decided to put under critical scrutiny.

To do so, he merged the Ariostean plot with one derived from an English source that was its dialectical opposite. For all its rather sordid immorality, Ariosto's *I suppositi* nevertheless retained the appearance of a romantic wish-fulfilment fantasy in which the gratification of erotic desires was presented as

---

of *The Comedy of Errors* in the BBC Shakespeare series, on the assumption that the correct reading of the line is: 'To seek thy help with beneficial hap', which is entirely consistent with the reiterated wordplay throughout the opening scene of Act I on 'hap' (ll. 38, 113), 'happy' (l. 138) and 'mishap' (l. 141) that foregrounds the main thematic preoccupation of the play.

[12] George Gascoigne, *Supposes*, in Bullough, *Narrative and Dramatic Sources of Shakespeare*, vol. 1, p. 112.

[13] *The Taming of the Shrew*, V.i.112.

the triumph of love. For his second main source Shakespeare turned to the lively tradition of anti-feminist satire that had reached its apotheosis in literature depicting shrewish women and their taming, or – in the case of Chaucer's Wife of Bath – the opposite.[14]

Although the precise shrew-story that Shakespeare may have used has not been identified with certainty, the most likely one is *A Merry Jest of a Shrewd and Curst Wife Lapped in Morel's Skin, for her Good Behaviour* (*c.*1550–60).[15] The basic details are the same as in the Petruchio-Katherina story in *The Taming of the Shrew*. A father has two daughters, the younger of whom is 'meeke, and gentle' (like Bianca), the other 'franticke, and sometime mad' (like Kate). The father favours the younger (just as Baptista favours Bianca), and would fain be rid of the elder, but despairs of marrying her off because of her cursed shrewishness – that is, until a young man turns up as a suitor whose motive is primarily mercenary (as Petruchio's is, at least initially). While Shakespeare substitutes a process of psychological subjugation for the brutal marital rape, battery and flaying by which (with an obscenity that has disgusted critics) the young man breaks his wife's froward will and secures her obedience, in other respects the outlines of the story are recognizably similar and amount to an extremely de-romanticized view of marital relationships and how harmony is to be attained within them.

Why did Shakespeare conflate plots drawn from two such disparate genres? His reasons may be inferred from the chiastic inversions of behaviour and sympathy that he promulgates within the course of the play. In the Lucentio/Bianca plot the 'good' girl, Bianca, turns into the 'bad' girl by the end, while the 'bad' girl, Katherina, displaces her as the 'good' girl. Similarly, the romantic love that appears to govern the relationship between Lucentio and Bianca ends up with a display of disrespectful wilfulness which does not augur well for a stable or long-lasting marriage, while the calculatedly anti-romantic manner in which Petruchio and Kate conduct their personal interchanges paradoxically produces a love that is characterized by true romance (signalled when Kate kisses Petruchio in the street) and a genuine loyalty and commitment that Kate proclaims in her final admonition to the two other errant wives. In effecting these paradoxical transpositionings of role and status, Shakespeare seems to have been concerned to expose the factitiousness of 'suppositions', including not only those that he found in his Italian and English sources, but also larger suppositions concerning the nature of our very identities as we subjectively perceive them. Indeed, it was for this reason that he added a third plot – in the form of the Sly induction – in which a

[14] For a summary of exemplars of the shrew theme, see Bullough, *Narrative and Dramatic Sources of Shakespeare*, vol. 1, pp. 61–2.
[15] The text of *A Merry Jest* is reprinted in W.C. Hazlitt, ed., *Shakespeare's Library: A Collection of the Plays, Romances, Novels, Poems, and Histories Employed by Shakespeare in the Composition of His Works*, 2nd edn, 4 vols (London, 1875), vol. 4, pp. 415–48.

beggar is persuaded to believe that he is a Lord when he awakes from a drunken stupor to find himself dressed in sumptuous apparel and attended upon hand and foot. In so far as Sly's belief that he is a Lord is as insubstantial 'as a flatt'ring dream or worthless fancy' (Induction.i.42), it foreshadows Lucentio's similarly unfounded belief that the beauty in Bianca's face is identical to her true qualities (I.i.163–4). On the other hand, the transformative influence on Sly's behaviour of the assumed aristocratic identity that is thrust on him anticipates the similar changes that will occur in Kate when Petruchio attributes to her the demeanour of a gentle, modest, well-conducted young woman, and then proceeds to 'kill' her with 'kindness' by affecting a solicitude that deprives her of food and sleep, and to 'kill' her 'in her own humour' by manifesting her own shrewish behaviour towards others (in IV.i, for example). The overall effect of Shakespeare's playful variations on the motif of feigned identity and the illusions it can produce – with their positive and negative effects – is to focus attention back on to the motives of those who perpetrate the various forms of deceit, and the consequences of those deceits. In Lucentio's case, the deceit is self-serving and dishonourable, in so far as it seeks to defraud his mistress's father of his rights over his daughter, and abrogates the filial loyalty he owes to his own father. In Petruchio's case, the deceit is equally self-serving but differently motivated, being designed 'out of reverent care' of Kate (IV.i.191) to activate in her a sense of compassion and an ability to discriminate between true and false values as the basis for a marital relationship in which both he and she can be happy – as he observes when commenting on Kate's obedience at the end of the play:

> Marry, peace it bodes, and love, and quiet life,
> An awful rule and right supremacy,
> And, to be short, what not that's sweet and happy.
> (V.ii.113–15)

By placing the two plots together and prefacing them with a third, therefore, Shakespeare was seeking to raise questions in the minds of his audience concerning the very status of their being and conduct in relation to the rival sets of codes that might govern them (a liberal, 'romantic', indulgent Italianate one versus a restrictive, patriarchal and rigidly authoritarian English one). The chiastic ironies he depicts in the relations between the two main plots reveal that there are deficiencies inherent in each system. The illusion of romance suffusing the action in the Italianate plot is shown to obscure a self-indulgent moral ugliness that is prefigured in the image of Sly as a 'monstrous beast' as he lies 'like a swine' in his drunken stupor before being dressed in rich apparel at the outset of the play (Induction.i.32). Equally, the roughness with which Petruchio 'woos' and then subjugates Kate in attempting to enforce his patriarchal authority carries with it an element of cruelty which the audience feels at the sight of Katherina's grief when he fails to arrive for their wedding (III.ii), or when she queries whether he means to 'make a puppet' of her (IV.iii.103).

It is only when the positive values of one system are allowed to cross over and ameliorate the deficiencies of the rival system that the existence of a third order of possibilities is intimated. This occurs when Lucentio chooses to submit to patriarchal authority when he realizes that to perpetuate his deceit would require him to deny and forswear his own father, which he refuses to do, in spite of Biondello's urging (V.i.99). In the other plot, it occurs as the actions of Petruchio and Kate become conditioned by the genuinely romantic attraction that develops between them – in short, they fall in love. This essential fact ensures that the patriarchal 'taming' will have a creative rather than a merely repressive outcome.

Viewed as a comment on the condition of the times, *The Taming of the Shrew* reveals a concern with the relative desirability of liberty or licence with respect to the authoritarian moral codes being preached from every pulpit in England during the 1590s. One infers that Shakespeare was disquieted at the Italianate licence and self-indulgence displayed in his Ariostean source, while nevertheless remaining ambiguous about the rigidities of English patriarchal authoritarianism as reinforced by contemporary Calvinist discourse. In typical fashion, the play allows, through Shakespeare's skill in using *contaminatio*, for the possibility that a more creative outcome might arise from a cross-fertilization of the values of the two systems.

After these initial forays into using Italianate imitation as an interrogatory instrument, Shakespeare progressively extended the range of his exploratory techniques, especially in the mature comedies written after 1595. While continuing to use *contaminatio*, he also increasingly experimented with devices that enabled him to create categories of values arranged almost paradigmatically, against which the characters and actions of his plays could be judged. These devices included the multiplication of plots, the multiplication of characters within a certain category, the reiteration of significant units of action, and the creation of symbolic image structures. Almost invariably, the mainspring for this innovative activity was imitation of an Italian source, and even when Shakespeare was not imitating an Italian source directly, as in the case of *As You Like It* (1599–1600), he simply transferred the methods of construction to it that he had learnt from his exercises in creative imitation.

One can see the maturing process at work in *The Merchant of Venice* (1596–7), for which he drew mainly upon Day 4, Story 1 of *Il pecorone*, a collection of *novelle* written by Ser Giovanni Fiorentino in the late fourteenth century (first published in 1558), and Christopher Marlowe's *The Jew of Malta* (performed about 1592). In addition, he amplified the main storylines derived from these two sources by turning to other works from which he drew a number of specific details.[16]

Ser Giovanni's *novella* is a typically Italianate fable showing resourcefulness and trickery overcoming impediments to the triumph of love. The richest Christian merchant in Venice, Ansaldo, so loves his penniless godson, Giannetto, that he finances him for three voyages to win a rich widow, 'la donna del Belmonte', the condition of which, imposed by the lady, is that he pass a test of sexual virility or else surrender his possessions to her.[17] When Giannetto fails on the first two occasions (because his wine has been drugged), leading in each case to the confiscation of his goods, Ansaldo, in order to equip him for a third, final attempt, sells everything he has and borrows 10,000 ducats from a Jew at Mestri on the surety that his creditor might take a pound of flesh from any part of his body should he default. On his third attempt, Giannetto (being warned not to drink the drugged wine by a sympathetic maid) succeeds in making love to the widow of Belmonte, marries her, and is proclaimed sovereign of the country – upon which he forgets all about Ansaldo and his plight until the day comes for the bond to be repaid. It is only through the intervention of his lady, disguised as a lawyer, that Ansaldo's life is saved. She ensures that the Jew is caught in the snare of his own legalism and ends up with nothing. After subjecting Giannetto to a mortifying proof of his dubious constancy by asking him to return a ring she had given him (which he believes he has given to the 'lawyer' as payment), the lady forgives him, Ansaldo is married to the damsel who had warned Giannetto about the drugged wine, 'et così stettero lungo tempo in allegrezza et festa, mentre che durò la lor vita' ('and thus they lived for a long time in happiness and festivity for the rest of their lives').[18]

For his second main plot Shakespeare turned to a source of a very different order, Christopher Marlowe's *The Jew of Malta*, a lurid melodrama in which a vengeful Jew procures the death of his enemies through a series of treacherous double-dealings until he is finally hoist with his own petard. The motive for revenge occurs when Barabas has his goods and property confiscated for refusing to comply with an unjust determination by the Christian governors of Malta that a tribute being demanded by the Turks is to be collected only from Jews, each of whom is to pay half of his estate, under pain of forced conversion to Christianity and the loss of all his possessions.

---

[16] These, including Anthony Munday's *Zelauto* (1580), Alexander Silvayn's *The Orator* (1581, translated into English in 1596), Robert Wilson's *The Three Ladies of London* (printed 1594) and a story in *Il novellino*, a fifteenth-century *novella* collection by Masuccio Salernitato, are surveyed by Bullough, *Narrative and Dramatic Sources of Shakespeare*, vol. 2, pp. 445–62; and Muir, *Sources of Shakespeare's Plays*, pp. 86–90.

[17] The Italian text is conveniently reprinted in Hazlitt, *Shakespeare's Library*, vol. 1, pp. 319–53. Bullough prints only an English translation.

[18] Hazlitt, *Shakespeare's Library*, vol. 1, p. 353; translation altered.

Believing that the Christians are motivated by 'malice, falsehood, and excessive pride, / Which methinks fits not their profession',[19] Barabas' bitterness
deepens when his daughter, Abigail, turns apostate out of love for a Christian,
Lodowick, and joins a nunnery. To requite the wrongs done to him, Barabas
poisons his daughter along with the rest of the nuns in her convent, contrives
for her two Christian suitors to kill each other, and is only prevented from
murdering the rulers of Malta by accidentally falling into the pot of boiling
oil he has prepared for them.

From the Italian *novella* Shakespeare took most of the essential ingredients
of his main plot, which revolves around the attainment of felicity through an
exercise of human ingenuity. From the English play he derived the deeper
motivation that animates Shylock's search for revenge – a sense of injustice
that is crystallized in, and aggravated by, the defection of his daughter and
her conversion to Christianity. The idea of combining these very disparate
elements probably occurred to Shakespeare in the first instance because each
of the sources contained a Jew who seeks the death of one or more Christian
enemies. There was also a theatrical advantage in integrating material from
works of two such diametrically opposed modes, as it allowed him to deepen
the tragic aspects of his play and thus secure more powerful emotive effects.
The most compelling reason for the *contaminatio*, however, was that
Shakespeare recognized that the two sources, in spite of their ostensible differences, shared much in common – at least implicitly. He saw that they were
linked by questions concerning the justice that should animate transactions
between human beings, especially those expressed in 'bonds', whether
natural, social or legal. He was particularly interested in identifying values
that could enhance the attainment of felicity, as well as the values which,
when affronted, could compound infelicity. It was to bring these issues into
a collocation which could allow the exploration of their interrelationships
that Shakespeare decided to combine elements from his two very disparate
main sources.

The focus of his concerns is very clearly reflected in the alterations he
made to his first source, and the selectivity with which he drew material from
the second. In adapting the narrative of Ser Giovanni's tale from *Il pecorone*,
Shakespeare made several major changes to the chief characters. First, in converting Ansaldo into Antonio, Shakespeare makes him not so much a father
figure as an older lover/friend – reminiscent, in fact, of the 'poet' in
Shakespeare's own *Sonnets* – whose sadness springs from his awareness that he
might lose his beloved to another (marital) relationship that is likely to
exclude him. Similarly, in converting 'la donna del Belmonte' into Portia,
Shakespeare changes Ser Giovanni's widowed and predatory *femme fatale* into

[19] *The Jew of Malta*, I.i.119–20, in Christopher Marlowe, *The Complete Plays*, ed. J.B. Steane
(Harmondsworth, 1969).

an unmarried, orphaned heiress, and rather than giving her the untram-
melled power that the widow has, he makes Portia bound by the will of a
dead father concerning the choice of her future husband. Finally, he changed
the sexual virility test into a moral test involving a choice between the values
signified in the metals of three caskets.

The effect of these changes is to present the main characters in the play
with a range of moral dilemmas that require them to exercise their powers of
choice with a degree of responsibility that is entirely absent from the Italian
source. The homoerotic self-interest that underlies Antonio's generosity
towards Bassanio turns him into a real threat to Portia, in that he is a serious
competitor for the emotional loyalty that Bassanio, as her husband, should
owe his wife – at least in her opinion. Antonio himself focuses the issue for
Bassanio when he urges him to give the supposed Balthasar (alias Portia) his
wife's ring:

ANTONIO
   My Lord Bassanio, let him have the ring.
   Let his deservings, and my love withal,
   Be valued 'gainst your wife's commandèment.
                  (IV.i.447–9)

Bassanio must choose which of these three competing obligations he is going
to prioritize, and the ease with which he surrenders the ring makes us wonder
whether Portia is right in supposing that should he ever part from it, its loss
would 'presage the ruin of ... [his] love' (III.ii.173).

Similarly, the transformation of Portia from a sexually experienced *femme
fatale* into an innocent maiden places her in the position of having to choose
whether to assert her own will concerning the choice of her future husband,
or affirm her obedience to her dead father's will out of filial respect for his
wisdom. All of the characters, indeed, are placed in situations that challenge
them to demonstrate their ability to discern the nature of the higher values,
principles and loyalties that may assist them to attain the felicity they are
seeking.

Having identified the issues at stake in the main Italianate plot,
Shakespeare proceeded to put them in dialogue with the issues he discerned
in the Marlovian revenge plot. To do this he stripped Marlowe's Jew of his
most villainous excesses and focused on the most painful epitomization of the
injustice that Barabas believes he suffers: the defection and apostasy of his
daughter, whom (with double-edged irony) he holds 'as dear / As
Agamemnon did his Iphigen' (I.i.140). The purpose of this narrowed focus
was to humanize the Jew so that the injustice Shylock feels is experienced as
an affront to the most precious personal bonds he has. The first is his pater-
nal bond with his daughter, which she betrays by stealing his casket of jewels

and ducats and eloping with the Christian Lorenzo. The second is his marital bond with his dead wife, Leah, whose pledge of love, a turquoise ring, we learn (in one of the most poignant moments of the play) Jessica has sold in exchange for a monkey (III.i.105–9). The third is his bond with his religion, which Christians like Antonio affront by calling him 'misbeliever', 'cutthroat dog', and by spitting upon his 'Jewish gaberdine' (I.iii.107–8), and by enforcing his conversion at the conclusion of the trial (IV.i.385).

Because the affronts that Shylock suffers all relate to 'bonds' that recur in the Italian-derived plot, a structure of relationships is established that creates a prismatic ambivalence concerning the moral issues in the play. Specifically, a series of parallels and contrasts are set up that become multi-directional in such a way as to break down the ostensible opposition between the moral positions of the Jew on one hand, and the Christians on the other. Shylock's mercenariness can be seen shadowed in Bassanio's hopes for a wealthy marriage, and Antonio's 'hazard' in venturing his argosies to make a profit. There are parallel treasures to be gained (Portia's dowry, Antonio's fortune and Shylock's fortune), parallel risks to be taken, and parallel bonds symbolized in rings that are variously kept, given away or stolen. Other parallels transmute into contrasts. That existing between the two daughters, Portia and Jessica, each of whom has a father who seeks to confine her, turns into a contrast as Portia remains dutiful while Jessica becomes undutiful. Jessica's defection from Shylock is paralleled in that of Launcelot Gobbo, the Clown, but Launcelot differs from her in being troubled by scruples of conscience over running away from his master (II.ii.1–29). In the end, even justice and mercy threaten to turn inside-out into their opposites as Christian 'mercy' comes to seem as arbitrary as the rigid legalism that it purports to be redressing. Consequently, the audience's sympathy and condemnation threaten to exchange their objects. Indeed, the triangulation that Shakespeare has achieved through integrating his two sources has served to activate a multivalent perspectivism that becomes so insistent and pervasive that it problematizes every interpretative issue contemplated in the play.

Why did Shakespeare contrive *The Merchant of Venice* to have this effect? His intent is probably reflected in the words that Bassanio utters when he is about to make his choice of the three caskets, and warns himself against 'The seeming truth which cunning times put on / To entrap the wisest' (III.ii.100–1). By extension, the whole age could be interpreted in these terms, and Shakespeare seems to have been concerned to make it impossible for his audience to be beguiled by the 'seeming truths' that appeared to animate the revolutionary society in which they lived. As he looked back into his own times Shakespeare may have seen on one hand a proclivity among his playgoing audience towards the indulgent and irresponsible licence he found in his Italian source, while on the other hand an inclination fostered by contemporary puritanism to invoke an excessively harsh and restrictive spiritual and moral order. The first, his play implies, needs to be fortified by a heightened awareness of the moral choices that inhere in personal and social relationships; the second, it also implies, needs to be mitigated by an expansion of imaginative compassion and charity. The contrived ambivalence of the play seems to be designed to make a determinate resolution of the issues impossible. Instead, Shakespeare leads his audience to experience the problematical nature of the issues to be decided, with a view to activating in them a willingness to seek an answer, whatever that might prove to be.

From about 1595 onwards, Shakespeare seems to have become increasingly interested in the building of symbolic paradigms in which contrary values were structurally opposed to one another. His purpose was to provide a set of bearings by which his characters and their actions could be judged, and his inclination can be related to a deepening preoccupation with the nature of human nature and the forces in the external world that have the power to influence behaviour and shape events. Notably, he became increasingly concerned with exploring the corruptibility of human nature, its capacity for goodness, and above all the susceptibility of men and women to self-deception as a result of limitations imposed by their own subjectivity. The more preoccupied Shakespeare became with these themes, the more varied became the methods by which he sought to turn his Italianate sources into vehicles for exploring them.

His next play based on an Italian work, *Much Ado About Nothing* (1598–1600), shows him making significant changes to both the characters and action of his source in order to create out of it the paradigmatic arrangement of contrasting values that he wanted. The play is based primarily on Novella XXII of Matteo Bandello's *Novelle* (1554), amplified with details from Ariosto's *Orlando furioso*, and, possibly, Spenser's *The Faerie Queene*.[20]

Bandello's *novella* is a typical Italian tale of amorous intrigue in which a Sicilian nobleman, Timbreo di Cardona, is tricked by his friend, Girondo Olerio Valenziano, into repudiating the woman he is going to marry, Fenicia, so that Girondo can have her for himself. Overcome with grief and remorse when he hears a report that Fenicia has died, Girondo confesses his deceit to Timbreo, who discovers that the woman he has accepted as his wife is actually Fenicia. Finally, in an excess of sensibility and compassion, Fenicia forgives Girondo and Timbreo, Timbreo forgives Girondo, reaffirming their friendship, and Girondo is rewarded with Fenicia's beautiful younger sister, Belfiore, as his wife.

[20] See the discussions in Bullough, *Narrative and Dramatic Sources of Shakespeare*, vol. 2, pp. 61–81; and Muir, *Sources of Shakespeare's Plays*, pp. 113–16.

Shakespeare evidently saw more in this story than simply the consequences of a 'frenzy of amorous desire' as Bandello had done, and he was sceptical about the effusions of magnanimity and forgiveness with which the tale concludes. Instead, he interpreted the fable as illustrating the negative and positive outcomes that can be produced by the workings of malice and good will, respectively, and to convey this perception, he made some important modifications to it. The instigator of the plot to discredit Hero is no longer a love-sick rival, who wants her for himself, but a malcontent, Don John, a bastard brother to the Duke, who 'had rather be a canker in a hedge than a rose in his grace' (I.iii.24). Like Iago in a later play, Don John wishes to spoil the joy of others out of sheer envy of their good fortune, and Shakespeare, unlike Bandello, allows him no redemption or forgiveness at the end of the play.

The deceived hero, Claudio, is also presented with much less sympathy than Timbreo, his prototype. Claudio is not unmindful that Hero is her father Leonato's only heir, which taints his motives in wooing her, and there is more than a little self-love in him that helps to explain the contemptible vehemence and vengefulness with which he condemns her at their interrupted wedding. By making these changes, in fact, Shakespeare establishes a polarity between those characters who are motivated by ill will, or vulnerable to its effects because of weaknesses in their nature, and those who are motivated by good will, such as Beatrice and Benedick, who never doubt that Hero has been wronged, or Leonato, whose challenge to Claudio in defence of his innocent child throws into shameful contrast the readiness with which the younger man discards the faith in her that the others are able to sustain.

The invention of the second plot involving Beatrice and Benedick, indeed, is largely designed to reinforce the audience's sense of the contrast between ill will and its effects, as against good will and its effects. This central contrast is further reinforced by the addition of a comic underplot (Dogberry and his Watch), and the multiplication of parallels (for example, between all those who 'overhear') and contrasts (for example, between those who conspire to promote love-relationships and those who plot to destroy them). Linking all the various activities in the play is the motif of 'noting', with its extension into the concept of perceiving through the (mis)constructions that are fabricated as a result of subjective preconceptions – as when Claudio is predisposed to believe that he sees his future bride receiving a lover into her chamber on the eve of their wedding, or when Benedick is persuaded that Beatrice loves him. On each occasion, the subjective assumption has an overwhelmingly transformative influence on the person who possesses it, and the point that Shakespeare is making is that whether the transformation is for better or for ill depends upon the condition of good will, or the lack of it, that animates the possessor.

If we ask ourselves what Shakespeare is causing the play to interrogate in social terms, the answer has to be that the object of critique is the excessively indulgent assumption in the source that the world is a place in which benevolence and charity can easily resolve such 'misunderstandings'. Shakespeare's view of the world is much sterner than Bandello's: it is a place in which forces for good and forces for evil contend for possession of the human soul, and given the human propensity to self-deception, Shakespeare believed that the men and women who comprised his audience had better be feelingly aware of that fact.

Most of the strategies of interrogation identified so far recur in the rest of Shakespeare's mature comedies, all of which, with the exception of *A Midsummer Night's Dream* (1594–6) and *As You Like It*, are based on Italian sources, usually *novelle*. For the most part, he seems to have been drawn to stories that suggested issues of sexual morality, and then adapted them in such a way as to place their implicit sexual licence under serious critical scrutiny.

In *The Merry Wives of Windsor* (1597–1601) changes he makes to the source *novella* show this licence up for what he believed it was – lust, associated with venality and corruption of spirit. The play is based very largely on the second *novella* of Day One in Ser Giovanni Fiorentino's *Il pecorone*, the same collection from which Shakespeare had drawn *The Merchant of Venice*. Bucciuolo, a young student at Bologna, is in love with a woman, Madonna Giovana, who, unknown to him, is the wife of his professor. When he seeks advice on how to advance his suit, the professor unwittingly assists in bringing about the seduction of his own wife, and has to suffer listening to Bucciuolo's account of how he accomplished it. Through the cunning of Madonna Giovana, the professor ends up being beaten by her two brothers who think he has gone mad ('impazzato') when, in a jealous fury, he runs his sword through the linen in which he realizes Bucciuolo had hidden the night before. The moral of the story is summed up in the professor's final words to Bucciuolo as he lies bruised and bound on his bed: 'Bucciuolo Bucciuolo vatti con Dio che tu hai bene apparato alle mie spese' ('Bucciuolo, Bucciuolo, go away in God's name, for you have learned all too well at my expense').[21]

To Shakespeare, this *significatio* was all too easy, and he makes strategic changes that allow the episode to be revealed in a different light. Instead of an untutored youth, the seducer becomes Falstaff, an aged lecher and glutton who describes himself as being 'in the waist two yards about' (I.iii.38), and whom the wives regard as a 'whale' with 'so many tuns of oil in his belly' that he is to be left 'till the wicked fire of lust have melted him in his own grease'

---

[21] Hazlitt, *Shakespeare's Library*, vol. 3, p. 25; cf. Bullough, *Narrative and Dramatic Sources of Shakespeare*, vol. 2, p. 26.

(II.i.58–62). Unlike Bucciuolo, who gets away scot free, Falstaff is not allowed to escape punishment. Whereas Bucciuolo hides in a heap of freshly washed laundry that is not yet dry ('sotto un monte di panni di bucato, i quali non erano ancora rasciutti'),[22] Shakespeare places Falstaff in a basket filled with stinking, dirty laundry that symbolically suggests his own moral condition:

> FALSTAFF By the Lord, a buck-basket! – Rammed me in with foul shirts
> and smocks, socks, foul stockings, greasy napkins, that, Master Brook,
> there was the rankest compound of villainous smell that ever offended
> nostril.
>
> (III.v.79–83)

Similarly, the beating meted out to the husband-victim in the source is transferred to Falstaff himself as the would-be seducer, when the plotters – disguised as fairies, satyrs and hobgoblins – surround him at night in Windsor Park, pinching him and burning him with their tapers as 'Corrupt, corrupt, and tainted in desire'. The words of the song they sing blazon his crime:

> Fie on sinful fantasy!
> Fie on lust and luxury!
> Lust is but a bloody fire,
> Kindled with unchaste desire,
> Fed in heart, whose flames aspire,
> As thoughts do blow them, higher and higher.
>
> (V.v.91–6)

If there were ever any doubt that Shakespeare was responsive to the injunctions of Calvinist discourse, this song should dispel it. More explicitly than is usual with Shakespeare, it reveals an intention to adapt his Italian source in such a way as to underline the need for a corrective perspective on what might otherwise appear as an unconscionable amorality.

Twelfth Night (1599–1600) presents an interesting variation on Shakespeare's usual practice, in that it generates the play's most important thematic issues by relying more heavily on the presence of a central character who articulates a counter-discourse than on the manipulation of contrary plots. Possibly this is owing to the close interrelationship between the two main sources of *Twelfth Night*. The first is a neo-Plautine Italian farce, *Gl' ingannati*, a play written by the literary society called the Intronati da Siena in 1531 (published in 1537). The second is the story of 'Apolonius and Silla' in Barnabe Rich's *Riche His Farewell to Militarie Profession* (1581), which is

---

[22] Hazlitt, *Shakespeare's Library*, vol. 3, p. 21.

itself one of several prose narratives that derived from *Gl' ingannati*.[23] In both sources a young woman, who becomes separated from a twin brother, disguises herself as a man to serve the man whom she loves, and ends up wooing a woman on his behalf who falls in love with her as the disguised go-between. Eventually, the mistresses in each of these sources end up marrying the identical brothers of the girls-disguised-as-boys with whom they have fallen in love. The burden of the story, like that of countless other Italian romantic intrigue plots, is summed up in Barnabe Rich's concluding observation that the lovers 'passed the residue of their daies with suche delight as those that have accomplished the perfection of their felicities'.[24]

Characteristically, Shakespeare presents a parodic perspective on the main romantic action by developing a highly unromantic underplot, the characters of which (Sir Toby Belch, Sir Andrew Aguecheek, Maria and Feste) display qualities that raise questions about the protagonists themselves. In Sir Toby's 'quaffing and drinking' one detects a baser sensual version of the self-indulgence and excess that characterize the emotional intemperance of Orsino and Olivia at the beginning of the play, while the plot proposed by Maria to make an ass of Malvolio shadows the deception-through-disguise by which Viola seeks to further her own romantic interests. Uncharacteristically, however, Shakespeare invents a major new figure for whom there is no hint in either source: Malvolio (whose name signifies 'Ill Will'). Not only is Malvolio 'sick of self-love' to the point where he believes 'that all that look on him love him' but, more specifically, he is characterized as 'a kind of Puritan' who tastes 'with a distempered appetite' and aspires to be a kill-joy, particularly where revelry is concerned (I.v.85–6; II.iii.128–39). As Patrick Collinson has pointed-ed out, Malvolio represents the 'Stage Puritan', a familiar stereotypical character of the Elizabethan theatre who arose out of the anti-Martinist backlash following the appearance of the Marprelate Tracts in 1588–9.[25]

Given Malvolio's origins in popular anti-puritan sentiment, it is interesting to see the use that Shakespeare makes of him in the context of this particular play. On one level Malvolio represents the kind of person who, in Rich's words, is 'led by the apetite of his owne affections ... groundyng them on the folishnesse of his owne fancies'.[26] In portraying him as such,

[23] See Bullough, *Narrative and Dramatic Sources of Shakespeare*, vol. 2, pp. 270–85. A number of similar plays based on Plautus' *Menaechmi*, such as *Gl' inganni* (1562) by Nicolò Secchi or *Gl' inganni* (1592) by Curzio Gonzaga, have been suggested as Shakespeare's source, but given that none of them resembles *Twelfth Night* as closely as the play by the Intronati, it seems perverse to prefer them over the more obvious choice.

[24] Ibid., p. 363.

[25] See Patrick Collinson, 'Ecclesiastical Vitriol: Religious Satire in the 1590s and the Invention of Puritanism', in *The Reign of Elizabeth I: Court and Culture in the Last Decade*, ed. John Guy (Cambridge, 1995), pp. 150–70.

[26] Bullough, *Narrative and Dramatic Sources of Shakespeare*, vol. 2, p. 345.

Shakespeare is not only commenting (negatively) on the motivation of contemporary puritans, but also providing a mirror in which a comparable condition of egotistical self-indulgence can be detected in Orsino, Olivia, Sir Toby and Sir Andrew, each in their respective domains. On another level, his presence generates questions concerning the validity not only of his own puritan moral sobriety, but also of the erotic and sensual/comedic licence that Shakespeare found in his Italianate sources. The issue is summed up in Sir Toby's rejoinder to Malvolio:

> TOBY Dost thou think, because thou art virtuous, there shall be no more cakes and ale?
>
> (II.iii.105–6)

The audience's spontaneous impulse is to side with Sir Toby in rejecting this proposition. However, the grossness of Sir Toby's sensual intemperance, and the inhumane treatment to which Maria and her crew subject Malvolio (however well deserved it may appear to be), raise questions as to the extent to which the licence displayed by these characters is to be condoned. What had been unproblematical in both of the sources thus becomes problematized through the simple expedient of introducing a character who questions the basis upon which the whole comedic enterprise proceeds, and while Shakespeare does not allow his viewpoint to prevail, he does not allow it to be deprived of all justification either. Indeed, the Clown's song which closes the play reminds the audience of a real world outside the theatre marked by natural vicissitudes and human corruption, in which it is wise for the prudent to take precaution against the tribulations of life, 'For the rain it raineth every day' (V.i.378ff.). Paradoxically, even while delighting in the festive revelry it begets, *Twelfth Night* simultaneously gives cause for its audience to wonder whether there might not be some justice underpinning Malvolio's viewpoint, even though he himself may not thereby be justified.

From about 1602 a discernible shift of practice occurred in the plays written during Shakespeare's tragic period. The interrogatory function that we have seen him securing through creative adaptation of Italianate source material tended to be replaced by a more demonstrative one. Indeed, Shakespeare appears to have moved far closer to the method that Spenser had adopted in *The Faerie Queene*, according to which the purpose of imitation is to present a corrective vision rather than to raise questions. Possibly this change of procedure resulted from his deepening sense of human fallibility and corruptibility, as displayed in a play like *Julius Caesar* (1599–1600), and his sense of the power of evil to shape human affairs, as manifest in a play like *Hamlet* (1600–1). Whatever the cause, he seems to have wanted increasingly to leave his audiences in little doubt as to what values they should espouse, and which ones they should reject.

All's Well that Ends Well (1602–4) reflects the consequences of Shakespeare's shift of perspective. Based on the ninth Novella of the third Day in Boccaccio's *Decameron* (translated by William Painter in *The Palace of Pleasure*), the play follows the source closely, reproducing the essential details of the narrative in which a physician's daughter, Giletta, cures the French king of a fistula in order to gain Beltramo, son of the Count of Roussillon, as her husband, and then succeeds through trickery to fulfil the apparently impossible conditions he stipulates before he will bed her: that she may call him husband only when she has got the ring off his finger and borne a son begotten by him. In converting Beltramo and Giletta into Bertram and Helena, Shakespeare simply exposes Bertram's behaviour for what it is: a combination of social snobbery, untrustworthiness and dishonour that shows him to be little more than a deceitful liar who cannot discern the worth of the woman who loves him, and who seeks to 'flesh his will' in the 'spoil' of another woman's honour whom he has 'perverted' (IV.iii.13–15). To make this condemnation of Bertram quite unequivocal, Shakespeare develops the French King and a new character, the Countess (Bertram's mother), into normative choric figures who approve of Helena for her virtue and condemn Bertram for his unworthy behaviour. He also creates a comic subplot in which the actions of a pompous *miles gloriosus*, Parolles, provide a parodic commentary on the false values underpinning Bertram's actions in the main plot, with his lack of honour in failing to fight Lafew shadowing Bertram's lack of honour in refusing to bed Helena; his belief that he has been captured by the enemy reflecting Bertram's belief that he has been trapped by someone who is not worthy of him, and so on. Finally, Shakespeare introduces a new discourse, voiced by characters like Lavatch, the Clown, that foregrounds awareness of the lusts of the flesh in the context of good and evil, and a lot of talk about death, the devil, burning, hell and damnation (for example, in IV.v.38–51). The total effect is to leave the audience aware of a system of values that have been affronted and then reaffirmed in the course of the play, with nothing in doubt but (ironically) the ultimate outcome – expressed in the conditionals of the King's final words: 'All yet *seems* well, and *if* it end so meet, / The bitter past, more welcome is the sweet' (V.iii.329–30; emphases added).

Just as Shakespeare's consolidating value system is apparent in *All's Well that Ends Well*, so too is his deepening insight into the corruptibility of human nature evident in *Othello* (1603–4), the domestic tragedy based on an Italian *novella* that he wrote during this period. The source, the seventh Novella of the third Decade of Giambattista Giraldi Cinthio's *Gli ecatommiti*, presents the story of a valiant Moor of Venice who is deceived by a wicked Ensign – 'di bellissima presenza, ma della più scelerata natura, che mai fosse uomo del mondo' ('of a very agreeable outward appearance, but with the most wicked nature of any man who ever lived') – into murdering his beloved wife, a virtuous woman of great beauty called Disdemona.[27] For Cinthio, the moral of the story is summed up in Disdemona's realization that her example 'will teach young women never to marry against the wish of their parents, and Italian women in particular not to connect themselves with men from whom they are separated by nature, Heaven, and manner of life'.[28] The Moor is also blamed for believing too foolishly, and the group to whom the story is narrated in the fictional context of *Gli ecatommiti* marvel that such malignity as that displayed by the Ensign could have been discovered in a human heart. All join in praising God, however, for inflicting on the criminals a suitable punishment.[29]

Shakespeare saw in Cinthio's tale an opportunity for examining the very well-springs of the capacity for evil in human nature. In the source, the Ensign's motivation is quite simple: having fallen in love with Disdemona, he concludes, when she fails to requite his passion, that it is because she is burning with passion for a corporal whom the Moor also favours. His love then converts into the most bitter hatred ('in acerbissimo odio'), and he determines that he will kill the corporal in revenge, after which, if he could not enjoy the lady, then neither would the Moor ('se non potesse goder della donna, il Moro anco non ne godesse').[30] The Ensign's motivation, therefore, consists simply of a malignant desire for revenge that springs from wounded self-love and envy.

In reconceiving the Ensign as Iago, Shakespeare invested him with a psychological complexity that shows just how deeply the dramatist had assimilated Calvinist discourse concerning the power of tainted desires to corrupt the will. The broad outline of Iago's characterization remains similar, in that he is motivated by a deep-seated envy to seek the destruction of Cassio, Desdemona and Othello, but Shakespeare goes way beyond Cinthio in explaining how this malignant predisposition might have come about. There is no hint in the source for the disillusioned view of the world in which Iago is imprisoned. Most strikingly, he has come to view with disgust 'the blood and baseness of our natures', which he associates with impulses of sexual desire that he labels 'our raging motions, our carnal stings, our unbitted lusts'. Indeed, Iago has come to experience such a recoil against sensuality that he fears love as 'merely a lust of the blood and a permission of the will' (I.iii.327–34), having replaced it with an exaggerated belief in the power of

---

[27] Cinthio's *novella* is reprinted in Hazlitt, *Shakespeare's Library*, vol. 2, pp. 285–308, from whence the quotation is taken (p. 288, translation altered).

[28] '… e temo molto di non essere io quella, che dia essempio alle giovani di non maritarsi contra il voler de' suoi; che da me le donne Italiane imparino, di non si accompagnare con uomo, cui la natura, e il Cielo, e il modo della vita disgiunge da noi' (ibid., p. 300, translation altered).

[29] Bullough, *Narrative and Dramatic Sources of Shakespeare*, vol. 7, p. 252.

[30] Hazlitt, *Shakespeare's Library*, vol. 2, pp. 289–90.

will and reason to control the terms and conditions by which humans live, as well as the outcome of events.

In this respect, however, Iago protests too much, as is confirmed by the obsessive sexual jealousy he displays. Not only does he believe that Othello has cuckolded him, but Cassio as well, even though he has no objective evidence to support his supposition:

> ... I know not if 't be true;
> But I, for mere suspicion in that kind,
> Will do as if for surety.
> (I.iii.382–4)

The effect of his suspicion is to fill him with a corrosive emotional perturbation that can find relief only in the idea of requiting Othello like for like:

> ... I do suspect the lusty Moor
> Hath leaped into my seat; the thought whereof
> Doth, like a poisonous mineral, gnaw my inwards;
> And nothing can or shall content my sould
> Till I am evened with him, wife for wife;
> Or failing so, yet that I put the Moor
> At least into a jealousy so strong
> That judgement cannot cure.
> (II.i.289–96)

Ironically, the most powerful form of revenge that Iago can think of is to reduce Othello into the same self-tormenting condition of irrational sexual jealousy that he suffers. From words spoken by Emilia we can surmise, in fact, that Shakespeare imagines Iago as once having been very like Othello himself. When Othello in a jealous rage denounces Desdemona as a whore, Emilia instantly guesses that 'Some busy and insinuating rogue, / Some cogging, cozening slave has devised this slander'. She is able to make this assumption because she herself was once slandered in the same way, producing a similar reaction in Iago to that which Othello displays:

> EMILIA
> O, fie upon them! Some such squire he was
> That turned your wit the seamy side without
> And made you to suspect me with the Moor.
> (IV.ii.131–47)

Having had his intellectual being turned 'the seamy side without', Iago can find respite only by 'poisoning the delight' of others who enjoy a felicity from which he feels excluded, by inducing them to repeat the experience of disillusionment that has led to his own emotional dysfunction.

Just as Shakespeare reveals the deeper causes of malignity in the villain, so too does he expose the psychological processes that lead to the subversion of the victim. Iago is able to destroy Othello because of the latter's imaginative and emotional intemperance. Othello's romantic excessiveness – which Desdemona shares – is first evident in his account to the Senate of how he wooed and won her, which Iago later debunks as merely 'bragging' and 'telling fantastical lies' (II.i.221). His emotional intemperance is starkly apparent in his loss of rational composure when he comes across the drunken Cassio at the conclusion of the fight Iago has been able to instigate:

> OTHELLO   Now, by heaven,
>   My blood begins my safer guides to rule,
>   And passion, having my best judgment collied,
>   Assays to lead the way.
>   (II.iii.194–7)

Similarly, his imagination easily escapes from the control of his reason once Iago has planted the seeds of suspicion in his mind. This is what Iago counts upon in insinuating suggestions of Desdemona's infidelity:

> IAGO
>   Dangerous conceits are in their natures poisons,
>   Which at the first are scarce found to distaste,
>   But with a little act upon the blood
>   Burn like the mines of sulphur.
>   (III.iii.326–9)

He only has to imply an image of Cassio and Desdemona in the act of love for Othello's imagination to invest it with the force of a material reality.

The process by which Othello is subverted from without and within is remarkably similar, in psychological terms, to that depicted by Spenser in *The Faerie Queene*, first, when Archimago separates the Red Cross Knight from Una by distempering his faculties through an abuse of his 'fantasy' and, second, when the malicious Philemon causes Phedon to murder his lady by arousing his jealous fury. For Shakespeare, as for Spenser, the underlying cause of the tragic experiences they depict is the vulnerability of human beings to a distempering of their faculties through an arousal of concupiscent passions. According to the Protestant discourse of the times, such a process constituted the very means through which the devil seeks to subvert humankind. Shakespeare implies as much at the end of the play when he has Othello confront the magnitude of his ruin:

OTHELLO
Will you, I pray, demand that demi-devil
Why he hath thus ensnared my soul and body?
(V.ii.301–2)

Even if Shakespeare did not intend Iago to be viewed literally as a demi-devil, he nevertheless presented the process over which he presides as exemplifying the nature, workings and ultimately the psychology of human sinfulness. Consequently, his play offers a far more profound and universalized comment on the nature of the human situation than Cinthio's account of a rather sordid *crime passionnel.* For Cinthio, the story merely illustrated wickedness and error; for Shakespeare, it showed evil as originating in the emotional vulnerabilities that reside in the human condition itself.

About the same time that Shakespeare selected Cinthio's tale of the Moor of Venice as a vehicle for examining the workings of evil in and on human nature, another *novella* in *Gli ecatommiti* must have caught his attention – the story of Juriste and Epitia (Novella 5, Decade 8) – for he chose it as the source of *Measure for Measure* (1604–5), written either shortly before or shortly after *Othello.* While Shakespeare also used an intermediary version of Cinthio's story, George Whetstone's English play, *Promos and Cassandra*, verbal parallels with Cinthio's dramatic tragedy, *Epitia*, show that he also knew that play, along with the narrative version in prose that Cinthio printed in *Gli ecatommiti.* All the evidence suggests, therefore, that he prepared for the composition of *Measure for Measure* with great care, which indicates the importance of its subject matter to him.

Cinthio's novella tells of a good ruler, the Emperor Massimiano (Maximillian), who charges a deputy, Juriste, with upholding justice in Innsbruck. One of Juriste's first acts is to condemn a young man, Vico, who has raped a virgin, to be beheaded. When his sister, Epitia, intercedes with Juriste to have justice tempered with mercy, the deputy, whose own lustful desire has been excited by her loveliness, proposes that Epitia should trade her virginity for Vico's life. At first Epitia refuses, but eventually submits out of love for her brother, who entreats her not to let him die. After Juriste has sexually enjoyed her, he treacherously orders Vico to be beheaded and then sends the head to Epitia. When Massimiano learns what has happened he forces Juriste to marry Epitia to honour his promise in that regard, and then orders him to be executed, upon which Epitia begs the ruler to exercise clemency for the man who is now her husband. The story ends with the observation that 'Juriste, realizing the extent of Epitia's generosity to him, held her ever dear; so that she lived happily with him for the rest of her days' ('Iuriste, considerata quanta verso lui fosse stata la cortesia de Epitia, l' hebbe sempre carissima; onde ella con lui fellicissimamente visse il rimanente de gli anni suoi').[31]

---

[31] Bullough, *Narrative and Dramatic Sources of Shakespeare*, vol. 2, p. 430; Hazlitt, *Shakespeare's Library*, vol. 3, p. 184.

Cinthio's dramatized version differs slightly in that Vico is secretly preserved alive – through the expedient of having another felon's head substituted for his own – and in the intensification of the justice/mercy theme with the introduction of two new characters, the Podestà (Mayor) who wants the severity of the law to be upheld, and the Secretary, who believes that its rigours need to be tempered and softened to equity once the cirumstances surrounding the crime have been taken into consideration.[32] Whetstone, in turn, generally follows *Epitia* very closely, except that he omits the Podestà, foregrounds 'might' versus 'right' as the main theme (rather than 'justice' versus 'mercy'), gives the deputy, Promos, an unscrupulous underling, Phallax, who mirrors his fault by consorting with Lamia, a prostitute, and adds a comic subplot involving characters whose actions parodically reflect those of the protagonists in the main plot.

Out of this raw material, Shakespeare constructed a play concerned not only with 'might versus right' and 'justice versus mercy', but also the larger question of what constitutes 'charity' in relation to various forms of responsibility – personal, social, moral, political and spiritual. In effecting this change of emphasis, Shakespeare seems to have wanted to challenge any manifestation of absolutism in the codes being invoked in his own society relating to the regulation and enforcement of social order. At the same time, he sought to expose the potential for abuse inherent in all power systems, owing to the inevitable fallibilities of the human beings who are charged with operating them.

The signs of these intents are instantly apparent in the major alterations he made to the source. He changes Epitia (Cassandra in Whetstone's play) into Isabella, an ascetically pious and puritanical character who, when the play begins, is about to enter a nunnery in search of 'a more strict restraint' (I.iv.4). Unlike Epitia, she does *not* relent and sleep with Angelo, the deputy, choosing instead to preserve her virtue at the cost of Claudio's life. In her puritanical rigidity, Isabella is thus turned into a mirror of Angelo himself, whom Lucio, a 'fantastic', describes as

> ... a man whose blood
> Is very snow-broth; one who never feels
> The wanton stings and motions of the sense,
> But doth rebate and blunt his natural edge
> With profits of the mind, study and fast.
>   (I.iv.57–61)

Both Isabella and Angelo seek to subordinate their natural instincts to a repressive morality which, ironically, leaves them both equally responsible for

---

[32] Relevant extracts from Cinthio's *Epitia* are printed in English translation in Bullough, *Narrative and Dramatic Sources of Shakespeare*, vol. 2, pp. 431–42.

the impending death of the same man, and for much the same reasons: the one because he is prepared to enforce a harshly restrictive code aimed at restraining sexual licence by an even harsher juridical one, and the other because she is prepared to adhere to a restrictive religious code governing sexuality at the cost of her own brother's life: 'More than our brother is our chastity' (II.iv.185). The irony of this parallelism is pointed out by Angelo himself; should Isabella not accede to his bargain, he suggests, 'Were not you then as cruel as the sentence / That you have slandered so?' (II.iv.109–10).

Other changes Shakespeare makes serve to render the outcome of those codes – Angelo's rigid juridical one, and Isabella's rigid moral and religious one – acutely problematical. He introduces two wise and kindly characters, Escalus and the Provost, whose compassion for Claudio and attempts to save him help to reinforce the audience sympathy that Shakespeare solicits. Similarly, whereas in the source Vico has sex with the virgin against her will ('fe forza ad vna Giouane cittadina di Ispruchi'),[33] Claudio gains possession of Julietta's bed 'upon a true contract', so that 'she is fast my wife / Save that we do the denunciation lack / Of outward order' (I.ii.140–4). Moreover, he does not simply deflower her but makes her pregnant, which implies the birth of a child to the couple in the future that makes the inhumanity of the beheading Claudio is to suffer even more intolerable.

At the heart of Shakespeare's reconception of Cinthio's story lies his awareness of the two main experiential realities that make it necessary to put the rigidities of the repressive juridical and religious codes under critical scrutiny: sex and death. His other main modification of the source consists mostly of a massive elaboration of both these themes.

The most important function of the new comic subplot, indeed, is to provide a realistic perspective on the actualities of human sexual behaviour. Mistress Overdone is a bawd who runs a brothel, whose function as 'Madame Mitigation' in relieving sexual desire parodies – as the legal associations in her nickname imply – the equitable mitigation of the legal sentence that the audience comes to feel should be dispensed to Claudio. Her side-kicks, Lucio and Pompey, equally remind the audience of the ubiquitous power of the sexual urge. Commenting on lechery, Lucio notes that 'it is impossible to extirp it quite ... till eating and drinking be put down' (III.ii.96–7) – in other words, never, since eating and drinking are necessary to sustain life itself. When Escalus announces to Pompey that the law will not allow prostitution to continue in Vienna, Pompey sums up the unlikelihood of this intention in his cynical reply: 'Does your worship mean to geld and splay all the youth of the city?' (II.i.217–18). The scepticism voiced by these characters serves to remind the audience that sexual desire is an inescapable reality of life, and in their simplicity they can see that the 'biting laws' being used as 'needful bits

[33] Hazlitt, *Shakespeare's Library*, vol. 3, p. 171.

and curbs to headstrong jades' – as the Duke calls the measures of enforcement that he is allowing Angelo to apply (I.ii.19–20) – are in danger of producing injustices that outweigh the benefits of the moral order they are designed to uphold:

> LUCIO Why, what a ruthless thing is this in him, for the rebellion of a
>   cod-piece to take away the life of a man!
>
> (III.ii.107–8)

The fact that Angelo himself, who, in the Duke's words, 'scarce confesses / That his blood flows, or that his appetite / is more to bread than stone' (I.iii.51–3), succumbs to sexual desire merely underlines the common sense of what these clowns express.

Death is the other experiential reality that Shakespeare foregrounds in this play, chiefly through the contrast he develops between Claudio and another new character, Barnadine, a prisoner whose imagination is so limited that he has no fear of death at all, and hence lacks any capacity to be touched by remorse:

> DUKE Hath he borne himself penitently in prison? How seems he
>   to be touched?
> PROVOST A man that apprehends death no more dreadfully but as
>   a drunken sleep: careless, reckless, and fearless of what's past, present,
>   or to come; insensible of mortality, and desperately mortal.
>
> (IV.ii.136–41)

Barnadine's attitude contrasts starkly with that of Claudio, whose resolution to die with fortitude out of respect for his sister's honour cracks under the pressure of his imaginative awareness of what death actually means:

> CLAUDIO
>   Ay, but to die, and go we know not where,
>   To lie in cold obstruction and to rot,
>   This sensible warm motion to become
>   A kneaded clod; and the delighted spirit
>   To bathe in fiery floods, or to reside
>   In thrilling region of thick-ribbed ice,
>   To be imprisoned in the viewless winds
>   And blown with restless violence round about
>   The pendent world; or to be worse than worst
>   Of those that lawless and incertain thought
>   Imagine howling, 'tis too horrible.
>   The weariest and most loathèd worldly life
>   That age, ache, penury, and imprisonment

Can lay on nature is a paradise
To what we fear of death.

...

Sweet sister, let me live.

(III.i.118–33)

Although Claudio quickly recovers his resolve in response to Isabella's fierce denunciation of him as a 'faithless coward' who had best die quickly, Shakespeare's point has been made: death, with all that might lie beyond it, is the ultimate reality in worldly human experience against which the justice of all human procedures must be judged. This fact enforces the central question of the play: in a context in which human behaviour is ubiquitously influenced by desire – especially sexual desire – and terminated by death, what constitutes justice, or the 'measure' by which the justness of the codes that regulate human conduct may be 'measured'? Certainly, in Shakespeare's view, the rigid absolutes of both the moral code supported by the religion of his compatriots, and also the kind of juridical code into which it might conceivably be translated, were highly susceptible to questioning.

In order to focus his audience's minds upon the possible answers to this question, Shakespeare fundamentally reconceived the role of the Duke. Cinthio's Massimiano appoints Juriste as his governor in Innsbruck simply because of the good opinion he has formed of the latter's ability to keep justice inviolate. He does not intervene again until Epitia travels to Villaco to seek justice from him. Shakespeare's Duke, on the other hand, has a much more complex motivation. In the first place he wants to rectify a situation in which respect for the law has diminished because of slackness in enforcement: 'so our decrees, / Dead to infliction, to themselves are dead, / And Liberty plucks Justice by the nose' (I.iii.27–9). He appoints Angelo as his deputy as someone who can 'in th' ambush of my name, strike home' without his own justness being called into question (I.iii.41–3). Second, he aims to test Angelo's mettle: 'Hence shall we see, / If power change purpose, what our seemers be' (I.iii.53–4). In other words, the Duke means to conduct an experiment in which he will observe the effects of unleashing a sternly moralistic law enforcer on a society that has become morally permissive, while at the same time examining whether power has the ability to corrupt the probity of the human agent who exercises it. To do this, he adopts a friar's disguise and remains present throughout, superintending events with a shaping oversight that Angelo, for one, comes to recognize as being 'like power divine' (V.i.364).

By having the Duke remain present in disguise throughout the action, Shakespeare is able to make him perform three functions. His first role is to undergo an educative experience in which he realizes that the retributive legal enforcement he has unleashed is too severe to serve the ends of true justice, as is indicated by his decision to spare the lives not only of Claudio, but also of Angelo and even, eventually, of Barnadine. His second role is to act with charity to mitigate the affliction that the various characters are suffering. Before ministering to Julietta and Claudio, he announces to the Provost that, 'Bound by my charity and my blest order, / I come to visit the afflicted spirits / Here in the prison' (II.iii.3–5).[34] The charitable ministry he provides is first to bring Julietta to repent and 'try' her penitence, and then to bring Claudio to mortification (in the spiritual sense) by leading him to understand that 'To sue to live, I find I seek to die, / And, seeking death, find life' (III.i.42–3). Likewise, he brings Isabella to an acceptance of a need for spiritual 'patience', keeping her ignorant of her good (the outwitting of Angelo and the rescue of Claudio), 'To make her heavenly comforts of despair / When it is least expected' (IV.iii.107–8). The Duke's third role (as Angelo intuits) may be to figure forth the 'power divine' of God himself to govern the affairs of his creatures with a beneficent providence. Belief in such a divine providence was deeply imbued in Calvinism, and hence in Elizabethan Protestantism generally. Shakespeare had demonstrated an interest in Calvinist notions of providence a couple of years earlier in *Hamlet*, in which the prince's reference to a 'special providence in the fall of a sparrow' (V.ii.208–9) directly echoes – with, as it turns out, considerable irony – Calvin's *Institutes*.[35] In *Measure for Measure* the Duke's role as a dispenser of providence similarly appears to exemplify Calvin's thesis that

> After learning that there is a Creator, it [i.e. faith] must forthwith infer that he is also a Governor and Preserver, and that, not by producing a kind of general motion in the machine of the globe as well as in each of its parts, but by a special Providence sustaining, cherishing, superintending, all the things which he has made, to the very minutest, even to a sparrow.[36]

Whereas the sustaining and cherishing functions of the Duke as a dispenser of providence are seen in his pastoral role, the superintending function is manifest in the way that he shapes and determines the outcome of events.

[34] The Duke is here echoing 1 Peter 3:19; see Richmond Noble, *Shakespeare's Biblical Knowledge* (London, 1935), p. 224.
[35] 'The Christian, then, being most fully persuaded, that all things come to pass by the dispensation of God, and that nothing happens fortuitously, will always direct his eye to him as the principal cause of events, at the same time paying due regard to inferior causes in their own place. Next, he will have no doubt that a special providence is awake for his preservation, and will not suffer anything to happen that will not turn to his good and safety … Hence, our Saviour, after declaring that even a sparrow falls not to the ground without the will of his Father, immediately makes the application, that being more valuable than many sparrows, we ought to consider that God provides more carefully for us' (*Institutes*, I.17.6, in Jean Calvin, *Institutes of the Christian Religion*, trans. Henry Beveridge, 3 vols (Edinburgh, 1845), vol. 1, pp. 255–6).
[36] Calvin, *Institutes*, I.16.1, trans. Beveridge, vol. 1, p. 231. For a discussion on the relevance of these passages from the *Institutes* to Shakespearean drama, see Alan Sinfield, *Faultlines: Cultural Materialism and the Politics of Dissident Reading* (Berkeley and Los Angeles, 1992), pp. 222–30.

The most striking example of this occurs in another major change to the source, when the Duke decides upon the bed-trick, in which Angelo's jilted betrothed, Mariana, will be substituted for Isabella to sleep with Angelo in fulfilment of his bargain. A second specific instance occurs when the Duke arranges for the head of Ragozine, a notorious pirate who has died of a fever, to be substituted for that of Claudio, on the grounds that ''tis an accident that heaven provides' (IV.iii.74). Generally, however, the Duke manipulates events, especially through the withholding of knowledge of his beneficent intentions, in order to induce the characters in the play into a condition of spiritual health: loss of the fear of death through *contemptus mundi* in Claudio, repentance in Julietta for surrendering to her concupiscence, patience and merciful compassion in Isabella, remorse and a 'penitent heart' in Angelo. In the attitudes and activities of the Duke, one feels, in spite of the unease that a modern audience may feel at the cruelty of his emotional manipulation of the suffering protagonists, we see figured the providence of a beneficent 'Governor' who is concerned to reconcile compassionately the exigencies of divine justice with the realities of the human condition.

After writing *Measure for Measure*, Shakespeare's preoccupation with exploring life in its tragic aspect through the experience of men and women of heroic stature left little scope for Italianate imitation. Whereas Italian *novelle* could supply material suitable for a domestic tragedy like *Othello*, or a tragedy of situation like *Romeo and Juliet*, there was little they could offer to furnish Shakespeare with the imaginative stimulation he needed for tracing the workings of evil in political contexts in which kingdoms were to be lost and won, nor for investigating the tragic interface between political philosophies and the personality traits of greatly flawed leaders. For that he went to English chronicles and the works of the classical historians, and plays such as *King Lear*, *Macbeth*, *Antony and Cleopatra* and *Coriolanus* were the result. At the conclusion of this effort, however, he returned to Italianate imitation one more time to write the second of his four late romances, *Cymbeline* (1609–10). This is a fitting play with which to end this discussion, as it shows Shakespeare engaged in a grand summation of all his earlier imitative strategies as he sought to give final expression to his matured vision of the world and its humane processes.

Cymbeline picks up where *Measure for Measure* left off in that it depicts an action in which the main characters' experience of tribulation leads them into a felicity they could not have predicted, under the influence of a benign providence they have no power to control. To construct a fictive vehicle capable of realizing this vision Shakespeare exploited the technique of *contaminatio* on a more massive scale than he had ever attempted before, combining elements from a wide variety of disparate sources to create a mixed-genre, tragi-comic pastoral romance of extraordinary complexity.

For the outline of the main story, and for several of the chief characters, he turned to an earlier English romantic play, *The Rare Triumphes of Love and Fortune* (printed in 1589), dealing with a king's daughter, Fidelia, who falls in love with a social inferior, Hermione, a supposed orphan who has been brought up at her father's court, is separated from him after he is banished by her father, and is reunited with him after adventures which centre upon a mountain cave inhabited by a banished nobleman, Bomelio.[37] Shakespeare gave this basic story an extra dimension of epic seriousness by fusing it with pseudo-historical British and Roman material drawn mainly from the 1587 edition of Holinshed's *Chronicles* (King Phizantius becomes Cymbeline, a British king who refused to pay tribute to the Emperor Augustus, while Hermione becomes Posthumus Leonatus, the son of a dead Roman hero). He further enhances the pastoral element in the play by imitating the episode in Tasso's *Gerusalemme liberata* in which Erminia encounters an old man and his two sons living a virtuous life in a pastoral setting, transforming these into Belarius (loosely based on Bomelio from *The Rare Triumphes of Love and Fortune*) and his valiant sons Cadwal (alias Guiderius) and Polydore (alias Arviragus), who are really the lost sons of Cymbeline himself. Shakespeare's greatest stroke of brilliance, however, was to combine this romantic epic-pastoral plot with an Italianate intrigue plot drawn from Boccaccio's *Decameron*.

The story Shakespeare chose was Novella 9 from the second Day of the *Decameron*, dealing with the wager between a husband, Bernabò Lomellin of Genoa, and a young merchant from Piacenza, Ambrogiuolo, concerning the constancy of Bernabò's beautiful young wife, Zinevra. In order to win the wager, Ambrogiuolo hides himself in a chest which is carried into Zinevra's bedchamber, from whence he emerges to note details of the room and her body, and also steals items belonging to her, including a ring and her girdle. Persuaded of Zinevra's infidelity, Bernabò orders one of his servants to kill her, but the servant spares her out of compassion, after which she adopts a male disguise and enters the service of the Sultan of Alexandria, rising to great favour with him. Eventually, the disguised Zinevra is able to contrive a situation in which Ambrogiuolo is forced to confess how he came by her possessions, which leads to his brutal and degrading death by impalement, followed by Zinevra's restoration to her husband when she reveals her true identity. The moral of the story, for Boccaccio, was the truth of the proverb that 'a dupe will outwit his deceiver' ('che lo ingannatore rimane a piè dello ingannato').[38]

---

37 Relevant extracts from *The Rare Triumphes of Love and Fortune* are reprinted in Bullough, *Narrative and Dramatic Sources of Shakespeare*, vol. 8, pp. 90–103.
38 Giovanni Boccaccio, *The Decameron*, trans. and ed. G.H. William (London, 1972), p. 208; for the Italian text see Giovanni Boccaccio, *Decameron; Filocolo; Ameto; Fiammetta*, ed. Carlo Salinari, Enrico Bianchi and Natalino Sapegno, vol. 8, La Letteratura Italiana: Storia e Testi (Milan and Naples, 1952), p. 162.

While Shakespeare indubitably knew the original Italian version of Boccaccio's story, he also knew a German version called *Frederyke of Jennen* [i.e. Genoa], which had been translated into English in 1518 and republished in 1560.[39] Apart from a few minor changes of detail (the wife goes not to Alexandria but to Cairo where, disguised as Frederick, she becomes a distinguished military leader), the story remains essentially the same as in the Boccaccesque original. The moral, however, is quite dramatically altered. Whereas the Italian version is secular in its orientation, focusing on the ironies inherent in human processes and the ability of men and women through their own powers of ingenuity to overcome adversity, the German version Christianizes the signification in order to affirm the existence of a moral universe:

> Our lord god sayeth in the gospel, 'what measure ye mete withal, ther with shall ye be mete agayn'. And do your besynes ryghtfully and justly ye shal have a blessyd and a good ende to your rewarde; and occupye your besynes unryghtfully, and ye shall have an yl rewarde therfore, as this story maketh mencion.[40]

To a playwright who had recently written *Measure for Measure*, such sentiments were undoubtedly of more than a passing interest, especially since he was choosing as his other main source a play in which the happy outcome is ascribed to the power of Jupiter, whose intervention as a *deus ex machina* Shakespeare would literally reproduce in his own *Cymbeline* (V.iv.92, stage direction).

The advantage to Shakespeare of combining an Italian intrigue plot with a romantic fable in which separated lovers are reunited through the beneficent agency of the gods was that it enabled him to multiply the number of ironic coincidences that lead to the happy outcome, compounding in the process the number of tribulations that the main characters have to endure before they recover their happiness. Posthumus, for example, summons Imogen to the cave not simply so that he can be reunited with her as Hermione intends in summoning Fidelia, but so that he can, imitating Bernabò in the other source, have her killed by his servant, Pisanio. The effect is to intensify vastly the tragic predicament and suffering of the heroine. By then having Pisanio show Cloten, Imogen's degenerate suitor, the letter in which Posthumus asks Imogen to meet him at Milford Haven, Shakespeare is able to contrive it so that Cloten, dressed in Posthumus' clothes, will pursue Imogen with the intent of raping her, which leads to his beheading by Guiderius. This in turn prepares for Imogen's further suffering when she awakens from the sleeping potion she has taken – ironically given to her by the wicked Queen who believes it to be a poison that will kill her – next to a

---

[39] See Bullough, *Narrative and Dramatic Sources of Shakespeare*, vol. 8, pp. 16–19.
[40] Ibid., p. 63.

headless body dressed in Posthumus' clothes. Recognizing the clothes, she instantly jumps to the conclusion that Pisanio has killed her husband at the instigation of his jealous rival, Cloten, the Queen's son. Irony upon irony thus compounds because of the conflation of the two plots, creating an action of such intricate complexity that it evades any ability on the part of the main players to shape the outcome of events according to their own will. Further complications arise when Lucius invades Britain, taking Imogen/Fidele (believed by all to be dead) into his train, and when Posthumus, who has been drafted into Lucius' Roman army, deserts in order to fight upon the side of the Britons as a means of atoning for his betrayal of Imogen. The helplessness of human beings to determine their own fate is graphically illustrated in Posthumus' futile attempts to procure his own death, first at the hands of the Romans and then at the hands of the Britons when, in despair, he throws away his Briton disguise. Shakespeare's point in elaborating the plot so fantastically is to place the fates of the protagonists well beyond their own control.

The effect is to throw the characters into reliance on a mysterious providence that is shown to work towards their good. In the later parts of the play this theme is recurrently insisted upon. Lucius, when he receives Imogen/Fidele into his service, urges her to be cheerful for 'Some falls are means the happier to arise' (IV.ii.403). Pisanio, too, who is 'perplexed in all' at hearing no news of either his master, Imogen or Cloten, realizes that in these matters 'The heavens still must work':

> PISANIO
> All other doubts, by time let them be cleared;
> Fortune brings in some boats that are not steered.
> (IV.iii.41–6)

Pisanio's image of a boat being brought into harbour by (good) Fortune despite the absence of controlling human agents captures the vision of human affairs that Shakespeare is seeking to represent through his amazing reshaping of his two main sources. It is perhaps best summed up in the words of Jupiter, during the dumb show that occurs in the final Act, when he intervenes to silence the ghosts of Posthumus' dead family who are repining at his apparent injustice in allowing the misfortunes that have afflicted Posthumus to occur. Accusing them of effrontery, he makes the following affirmation:

> Be not with mortal accidents opprest.
>   No care of yours it is; you know 'tis ours.
> Whom best I love I cross; to make my gift,
>   The more delayed, delighted. Be content.
> Your low-laid son our godhead will uplift;

His comforts thrive, his trials well are spent.
...
He shall be lord of Lady Imogen,
And happier much by his affliction made.
(V.iv.99–108)

The view that Jupiter expresses here is not too distant from that which Milton would voice in *Paradise Lost* half a century later, and it is deeply imbued with the same Calvinist sense of a 'special providence' that ensures that goodness will be brought out of events in excess of human desert. As the rest of *Cymbeline* reveals – and as *Measure for Measure* had shown before it – the gift to which Jupiter alludes does not consist simply of a happy outcome but of the ameliorated interior condition which results from the affliction that the characters have had to endure. Penitential shame and remorse in turn lead to a healing of vexations and distempers in the body politic itself, which is figured forth in the universal pardons and reaffirmation of obligations that mark the end of the play. It is difficult to detect any irony in the oracular words Shakespeare gives to the Soothsayer when he says that 'The fingers of the pow'rs above do tune / The harmony of this peace' (V.v.465–6), which leads one to believe that in *Cymbeline*, as in the other late romances, we have an attempt on Shakespeare's part to give expression – through the contrived artifice of their generically mixed forms – to his maturest understanding of the meaning of things.

It is time now to stand back and establish the larger implications of Shakespeare's engagement in Italianate imitation for the theatre. When one contemplates the nature of the material he selected, and the nature of the changes he made to it, it becomes clear that he used Italian sources as a means of constructing a drama that could stimulate his audience into participating through the arousal of their emotional and intellectual energies in a critical appraisal of issues that were of central concern to the society of his day. He did this by using the divergence between the mores and value systems inherent in English and Italianate culture to problematize the issues he addressed, so as to create an effect that would arouse members of his audience to question certain tendencies evident in the codes that various factions were attempting to enforce in contemporary Elizabethan society.

All of Shakespeare's plays that make use of Italian material focus upon issues that had been made problematical for Elizabethan Protestants by the Calvinist underpinnings of the religious Settlement of 1559. Chief among them was sexual morality, especially in relation to the obligations attendant upon marriage. What is required to make men conduct themselves responsibly, Shakespeare asks, in a world in which natural concupiscence and the fallibility of the faculties are liable to render them victims to the mistaken perceptions, perverse desires or corruption of will that he reveals in the likes of Claudio, Bertram or Othello? Likewise, to what extent, and for what reasons, should women like Katherina or Portia be bound by restrictions imposed by patriarchal expectations when the men who profit by them are shown to be motivated by venality, as in the case of Petruchio, or to be both venal and unreliable, as in the case of Bassanio? How can men and women determine with certainty what their obligations are, or how they should act, in a world characterized by the circumstances that an anonymous observer of events in *All's Well that Ends Well* describes:

> 2. LORD The web of our life is of a mingled yarn, good and ill together; our virtues would be proud if our faults whipped them not, and our crimes would despair if they were not cherished by our virtues.
>
> (IV.iii.66–9)

Shakespeare's main intent seems to be to make it impossible for the members of his audience to remain adherents of an easy bigotry on these matters. An apparently rapacious and vindictive Jew, such as Shylock, may turn out to be just as sinned against by those who believe they are dispensing the chastisement he merits, as the Christians who believe that right is on their side.

Another focus of Shakespeare's concern is the nature of human nature generally. The fact that he invariably removes the more ostentatious instances of pornographic lubricity from the Italian sources he uses – such as the furtive sexual couplings between Fabrizio and Isabella, and between Flaminio and Lelia in *Gl'ingannati*, or Brucciuolo's successful seduction of his professor's wife in the source of *The Merry Wives of Windsor* – shows that Shakespeare was far from happy with the easy sexual amorality to be found in Italian literary culture. Indeed, he was sufficiently impressed by Calvinist dogma on natural human depravity to make sure that he introduced figures of exemplary innate evil into all Italianate sources in which none had existed previously. Don John, for whom there is no hint in Boccaccio, appears in *Much Ado About Nothing*, while there is equally no hint in any of the sources for the evil Queen in *Cymbeline*, whose malice is responsible for much of the grief that the characters in that play suffer. As Shakespeare shifted his perspective away from comedy towards tragedy, his Calvinist sense of the corruptibility of human nature deepened still further. In *Measure for Measure*, Angelo, to his horror, finds he has a 'cunning enemy [the devil] that, to catch a saint, / With saints dost bait thy hook' (II.ii.180–1), and quickly surrenders to a corrupting concupiscence whose existence neither he, nor anyone else, had expected. In *Othello*, the great tragedy – which Cinthio gives no sign of having glimpsed – is that Othello, a man of heroic capacity and generosity of soul (Cassio describes him at the end as being 'great of heart'), is able to be traduced into degenerating into a murderous criminal by a man, Iago, who

himself, the play implies, has been turned 'the seamy side out' by his susceptibility to envy and jealousy. Shakespeare, as his imitative practice confirms,
had no illusions as to the sinful propensities of human nature, and his imitation of Italian sources assisted him to convey his perception of that reality
imaginatively to his contemporary audience.

In the later stages of Shakespeare's career as a dramatist, the final great
theme that Italianate imitation enabled him to address was that of the meaning of the human situation itself. Faced with the irreducible corruptibility of
human nature, Shakespeare needed to find a way of accounting for how life
could be approached and conducted without despair. In several of the
tragedies – notably *Hamlet* and *King Lear* – one senses that he came close to
concluding that the unaccountable capriciousness of Fortune and the limit-
less capacity for human degeneration left no scope for optimism on that
score; there was always an ironic twist of fortune that could undo every
human expectation, or a 'worst' that could outdo any 'worst' that one had
thought to have been reached. In *Measure for Measure* and *Cymbeline*, however, one finds Shakespeare using Italianate imitation as a pretext for exploring the possible nature of the kind of 'special providence' identified in
Protestant preaching as the force upon which human beings are ultimately
impelled to depend in a world governed by the consequences of human sinfulness. In both plays Shakespeare exploits his Italian sources to generate an
exemplification of the experiential processes whereby a supernatural governing intelligence may use the vicissitudes wrought by human sinfulness to
work towards an ameliorative good, the encompassing wisdom of which no
human foresight can have the power to predict. In this respect, Shakespeare
was truly a product of his Elizabethan Protestant times – a Calvin or a
Grindal would have been proud of him.

Once the motive for Shakespeare's imitation of Italian sources begins to be
appreciated, one can begin to appreciate why Tudor drama was potentially
such a powerful instrument for determining the direction of social change. In
terms of social mores, Shakespeare was addressing an extremely volatile situation in which primary values, and the regulatory codes – juridical, moral
and religious – that were going to be invoked to enforce them, were being
vigorously contested. Italianate imitation enabled him to actualize the emotional response of the men and women who constituted his audience to the
concerns that lay buried in their subconscious minds relating to the new religious and political order being imposed upon them. The ultimate effect of
Shakespeare's imitative efforts, one conjectures, may have been to deprive his
popular audience of easy acquiescence in falsely based or untested assumptions, and to activate in them a willingness to participate in the search for
positive alternatives that would not falsify the nature of human experience.
The continuing relevance of Shakespeare's plays attests to the historical
success of this endeavour.

Conclusion

If this investigation has proved nothing else, it should have shown that the English Renaissance cannot be separated from the English Protestant Reformation; the aspects in the literature of the former that we most admire – thematic complexity, the cult of aesthetic beauty, and engagement with humane issues of enduring interest – mostly sprang from the efforts of the most imaginative minds of the time to comprehend the deeper psychological, moral, political and sociological implications of the Protestant order that had begun to come into being with Henry VIII's political break with Rome in the 1530s, and which was progressively entrenched during the reign of his daughter, Elizabeth I.

It is not insignificant that the texts produced by writers who chose to imitate Renaissance Italian texts are some of the most admired works that constitute the traditional 'canon' of English literature. This only goes to show how important the efforts remain to us of those imaginative writers who, in the Elizabethan age, tried to come to terms with what the emergent Protestantism of their society meant to them as far as humane values and the conduct of daily life were concerned. The process of creative imitation by which they attempted to wrestle with the issues was dynamic, variable and, for the most part, idiosyncratic as between particular authors. More ominously, it remained incomplete at the end of Elizabeth's regime as – in retrospect – we can see that it was doomed to be, given the profound incongruities residing in the fundamental issues that formed the subjects of imaginative debate: the status of desire in a world dominated by sin; the extent to which appreciation of the beautiful was legitimate given the susceptibility of human nature to the corrupting effects of concupiscence; the degree to which obligations arising from natural bonds of humanity could be reconciled with obligations imposed by an arbitrary divine will, and so on.

Almost predictably, Italianate literary imitation began to die out in England soon after the accession of James I. The main motivating incentive was gone, in that the new Stuart order was not capable of sustaining the impression that Elizabeth and her ministers had been able to maintain, that a considerable latitude existed for the ultimate shape of the order to come still to be determined by the efforts of her subjects to seek acceptable forms of creative compromise. As it turned out, the synthesis of cultural values that Spenser had tried to articulate as the foundation upon which the edifice of English national identity should be erected could not, at that point in history, prevail. The spiritual passions of 'godly' Protestants were simply too intense for them to be reconciled to Spenser's vision of an order in which a sensuous experience of the world could be legitimized by, and harmonized with, a Protestant spiritual probity. Equally, the cautious reserve of the vast majority of 'parish anglicans' regarding the bitterer aspects of Calvinist doctrine ensured that Arminianism would have a fertile seed bed in the reign of Elizabeth's successor.

The outcome, therefore, of the inability of these writers to secure the goal towards which their efforts were directed was, inevitably, the civil war of the next century. Ironically, successive generations have been trying to complete their unfinished work throughout the succeeding four centuries – with no greater success. Matthew Arnold, Walter Pater and T.S. Eliot tried to cut through the problem by variously attributing a religious dimension to the experience of art, and by aestheticizing the experience of religion, but the politicized sentiments of intellectuals and critics of the late twentieth century have precluded the separation of 'high art' from social and political concerns to the extent that Arnold, Pater and others like them would have judged necessary. The issues that Renaissance English authors tackled in engaging in Italianate imitation, therefore, are still with us – unresolved, yet needing to be contemplated as postmodern societies enter the twenty-first century under the awesome influence of the new technological revolution. What the outcome of that necessity may be is a story that remains to be told.

Bibliography

Alpers, Paul, 'Pastoral and the Domain of Lyric in Spenser's *Shepheardes Calender*', *Representations*, 12 (1985): 83–100.

Anon, *Duke Humfrey and English Humanism in the Fifteenth Century: Catalogue of an Exhibition Held in the Bodleian Library Oxford*, Oxford, n.d.

Anon, ed., *Rime di diversi antichi autori Toscani in dieci libri racolte. Di Dante Alighieri; Di M. Cino da Pistoia; Di Guido Caualcanti; Di Dante da Maiano; Di Fra Guitone d'Arezzo; Di diuerse canzoni e sonetti senza nome d'autore*, Venice, 1532.

Ariosto, Ludovico, *Orlando furioso, Translated into English Heroical Verse by Sir John Harington (1591)*, ed. Robert McNulty, Oxford, 1972.

———, *Orlando furioso (The Frenzy of Orlando)*, trans. and ed. Barbara Reynolds, 2 vols, Penguin Classics, London, 1975.

———, *Orlando furioso*, ed. Marcello Turchi, 2 vols, Milan, 1982.

Ascham, Roger, *English Works: Toxophilus, Report of the Affaires and State of Germany, The Scholemaster*, ed. William Aldis Wright, Cambridge, 1904.

Ascoli, Albert Russell, *Ariosto's Bitter Harmony: Crisis and Evasion in the Italian Renaissance*, Princeton, 1987.

Bandello, Matteo, *Tutte le opere di Matteo Bandello*, ed. Francesco Flora, vol. 1, Verona, 1966.

Barbour, Reid, 'Recent Studies of Prose Fiction, 1603–1660, Including Sidney's *Arcadia*', *English Literary Renaissance*, 26, no. 1 (1996): 167–97.

Barclay, Alexander, *The Eclogues of Alexander Barclay*, ed. Beatrice White, vol. 175, Early English Text Society, Original Series, London, 1928.

Barnes, Barnabe, *A Divine Centurie of Spirituall Sonnets*, ed. Alexander B. Grosart, London, 1875.

———, *Parthenophil and Parthenophe*, ed. Victor A. Doyno, Carbondale and Edwardsville; London and Amsterdam, 1971.

Barnfield, Richard, *Richard Barnfield: The Complete Poems*, ed. George Klawitter, Selinsgrove; London and Toronto, 1990.

Bennet, Josephine Waters, *The Evolution of the Faerie Queene*, Chicago, 1942.

Bernard, John D., *Ceremonies of Innocence: Pastoralism in the Poetry of Edmund Spenser*, Cambridge, 1989.

_____, 'Recent Studies in Renaissance Pastoral', *English Literary Renaissance*, 26, no. 2 (1996): 356–84.

Bettenson, Henry, ed., *Documents of the Christian Church*, 2nd edn, Oxford, New York and Toronto, 1963.

Blanchard, H.H., 'Spenser and Boiardo', *PMLA*, 40 (1925): 828–51.

_____, 'Imitations of Tasso in the *Faerie Queene*', *Studies in Philology*, 22 (1925): 208–9.

Boccaccio, Giovanni, *A Pleasaunt Disport of Diuers Noble Personages. Written in Italian by M. Iohn Bocace Florentine and Poet Laureat; in his Boke which is Entituled Philocopo* [i.e. *Filocolo*], trans. H.G., London, 1567.

_____, *Decameron; Filocolo; Ameto; Fiammetta*, ed. Carlo Salinari, Enrico Bianchi and Natalino Sapegno, vol. 8, La Letteratura Italiana: Storia e Testi, Milan and Naples, 1952.

_____, *The Decameron*, trans. and ed. G.H. William, London, 1972.

_____, *L'Ameto*, trans. Judith Serafini-Sauli, vol. 33, Garland Library of Medieval Literature, Series B, New York and London, 1985.

_____, *Eclogues*, trans. Janet Levarie Smarr, vol. 11, Garland Library of Medieval Literature, New York and London, 1987.

Boiardo, Matteo Maria, *Orlando innamorato. The three first Bookes of that famous Noble Gentleman and learned Poet, Mathew Maria Boiardo Earle of Scandiano in Lombardie. Done into English Heroicall Verse by R.T. Gentleman*, trans. R.T., London, 1598.

_____, *Orlando innamorato*, trans. Charles Stanley Ross, Biblioteca Italiana, Berkeley and London, 1989.

_____, *Amorum libri: the Lyric Poems of Matteo Maria Boiardo*, trans. and ed. Andrea di Tommaso, Binghamton and Ottawa: Medieval and Renaissance Texts and Studies, 1993.

Boitano, Piero, *Chaucer and the Italian Trecento*, Cambridge, 1983.

Brand, C.P., *Tasso: A Study of the Poet and His Contribution to English Literature*, Cambridge, 1965.

_____, 'Tasso, Spenser, and the *Orlando furioso*', in *Petrarch to Pirandello: Studies in Italian Literature in Honour of Beatrice Corrigan*, ed. Julius A. Molinaro, Toronto, 1973, pp. 95–110.

_____, *Ludovico Ariosto: Preface to the Orlando furioso*, vol. 1, Writers of Italy Series, Edinburgh, 1974.

Briggs, William Dinsmore, 'Political Ideas in Sidney's *Arcadia*', *Studies in Philology*, 28 (1931): 137–61.

_____, 'Sidney's Political Ideas,' *Studies in Philology*, 29 (1932): 534–42.

Brown, John Russell and Bernard Harris, eds, *Elizabethan Poetry*, vol. 2, Stratford-upon-Avon Studies, London, 1960.

Bullough, Geoffrey, ed., *Narrative and Dramatic Sources of Shakespeare*, 8 vols, London and New York, 1957–75.

Buxton, John, *Sir Philip Sidney and the English Renaissance*, 3rd edn, London, 1987.

Calendar of State Papers, Venetian, ed. R. Brown and others, London, 1864–98.

Calvin, Jean, *Institutes of the Christian Religion*, trans. Henry Beveridge, 3 vols, Edinburgh, 1845.

_____, *Institutes of the Christian Religion*, trans. Ford Lewis Battles, ed. John T. McNeill, 2 vols, vol. 20, The Library of Christian Classics, Philadelphia, 1960.

Camaiora, Luisa Conti, 'The Treachery of Translation: Wyatt and Surrey's Versions of Petrarch's Sonnet CXL', in *Italy and the English Renaissance*, ed. Sergio Rossi, Milan, 1989, pp. 55–88.

Capasso, Aldo, *Commento al 'Rinaldo' del Tasso*, vol. 17, Studi e Ritratti: Collezione di Monografie Letterarie, Genoa, Rome and Naples, 1939.

Carey, John, 'Structure and Rhetoric in Sidney's *Arcadia*', in *Sir Philip Sidney: An Anthology of Modern Criticism*, ed. Dennis Kay, Oxford, 1986, pp. 245–64.

Chaney, Edward and Peter Mack, eds, *England and the Continental Renaissance: Essays in Honour of J.B. Trapp*, Woodbridge, Suffolk, 1990.

Charnes, Linda, *Notorious Identity: Materializing the Subject in Shakespeare*, Cambridge, Massachusetts, 1993.

Chatterjee, Kalyan K., *In Praise of Learning: John Colet and Literary Humanism in Education*, New Delhi, 1974.

Chaucer, Geoffrey, *The Riverside Chaucer*, gen. ed. Larry D. Benson, 3rd edn, Oxford, 1987.

Churchill, Kenneth, *Italy and English Literature 1764–1930*, London, 1980.

Ciccuto, M., *Novelle Italiane: Il Cinquecento*, Milan, 1982.

Clubb, Louise George, 'Shakespeare's Comedy and Late Cinquecento Mixed Genres', in *Shakespearean Comedy*, ed. Maurice Charney, New York, 1980, pp. 129–39.

_____, *Italian Drama in Shakespeare's Time*, New Haven, 1989.

Collinson, Patrick, *The Birthpangs of Protestant England: Religious and Cultural Change in the Sixteenth and Seventeenth Centuries*, London, 1988.

_____, 'Ecclesiastical Vitriol: Religious Satire in the 1590s and the Invention of Puritanism', in *The Reign of Elizabeth I: Court and Culture in the Last Decade*, ed. John Guy, Cambridge, 1995, pp. 150–70.

_____, *The Elizabethan Puritan Movement*, Berkeley and Los Angeles, 1967.

_____, 'England and International Calvinism, 1558–1640', in *International Calvinism 1541–1715*, ed. Menna Prestwich, Oxford, 1985, pp. 197–223.

_____, *The Religion of Protestants*, Oxford, 1982.

Constable, Henry, *The Poems of Henry Constable*, ed. Joan Grundy, Liverpool, 1960.

Cooper, Helen, *Pastoral: Mediaeval into Renaissance*, Ipswich, 1977.

Cox, Virginia, *The Renaissance Dialogue: Literary Dialogue in its Social and Political Contexts, Castiglione to Galileo*, Cambridge, 1992.

Craft, William, *Labyrinth of Desire: Invention and Culture in the Work of Sir Philip Sidney*, Newark, 1994.

Croce, Benedetto, *Ariosto, Shakespeare e Corneille*, vol. 2, *Opere di Benedetto Croce*, Bari, 1968.

Cunliffe, John W., *Early English Classical Tragedies*, Oxford, 1912.

D'Amico, Jack, ed., *Petrarch in England: An Anthology of Parallel Texts from Wyatt to Milton*, Ravenna, 1979.

D'Andrea, Antonio, 'Giraldi Cinthio and the Birth of the Machiavellian Hero on the Elizabethan Stage', in *Il teatro italiano del Rinascimento*, ed. Maristella de Panizza Lorch, Milan, 1980, pp. 605–18.

Dana, Margaret, 'The Providential Plot of the *Old Arcadia*', in *Sir Philip Sidney: An Anthology of Modern Criticism*, ed. Dennis Kay, Oxford, 1987, pp. 83–102.

Daniel, Samuel, *Daniel's Delia and Drayton's Idea*, ed. Arundell Esdaile, London, 1908.

Dasenbrock, Reed Way, *Imitating the Italians: Wyatt, Spenser, Synge, Pound, Joyce*, Baltimore and London, 1991.

Davies, John, *The Poems of Sir John Davies*, ed. Robert Krueger, Oxford, 1975.

Davis, Walter R., *A Map of Arcadia: Sidney's Romance in its Tradition*, in *Sidney's Arcadia*, New Haven and London, 1965.

Della Casa, Giovanni, *Galateo of Maister Iohn Della Casa, Archebishop of Beneuenta. Or rather, a Treatise of the Manners and Behauiours, it Behoueth a Man to Vse and Eschewe, in his Familiar Conuersation*, trans. Robert Peterson, London, 1576.

Desportes, Philippe, *Les amours de Diane*, ed. Victor E. Graham, 2 vols, Textes Littéraires Français, Geneva and Paris, 1959.

Dickens, A.G., *The English Reformation*, London, 1964; revised edn 1972.

Dirks, Nicholas B., Geoff Eley and Sherry B. Ortner, eds, *Culture/Power/History: A Reader in Contemporary Social Theory*, Princeton, 1994.

Dodge, R.E. Neil, 'Spenser's Imitations from Ariosto', *PMLA*, 12 (1897): 151–204.

Dollimore, Jonathan, *Radical Tragedy*, 2nd edn, Hemel Hempstead, 1984.

Donno, Elizabeth Story, ed., *Three Renaissance Pastorals: Tasso–Guarini–Daniel*, Binghamton, New York: Medieval and Renaissance Texts and Studies, 1993.

Doran, Madeleine, *Endeavours of Art*, Madison, 1954.

Dowland, John, *The First Booke of Songes or Ayres of Fowre Partes with Tableture for the Lute ...*, London, 1597.

Dubrow, Heather, *Echoes of Desire: English Petrarchism and its Counterdiscourses*, Ithaca and London, 1995.

Duncan-Jones, Katherine, *Sir Philip Sidney: Courtier Poet*, New Haven and London, 1991.

Durling, Robert M., 'The Bower of Bliss and Armida's Palace', in *Essential Articles for the Study of Edmund Spenser*, ed. A.C. Hamilton, Hamden, Connecticut, 1972, pp. 113–24.

_____, *The Figure of the Poet in the Renaissance*, Cambridge, Massachusetts, 1965.

Einstein, Lewis, *The Italian Renaissance in England*, Burt Franklin Research and Source Works Series No. 26, New York, 1902.

Elton, G.R., *England Under the Tudors*, 3rd edn, London and New York, 1991.

Empson, William, *Some Versions of Pastoral*, London, 1986.

Fenton, Geoffrey, *Bandello: Tragical Tales. The Complete Novels Translated by Geoffrey Fenton (Anno 1567)*, ed. Robert Langton Douglas, London, n.d.

_____, *Tragical Discourses*, ed. Hugh Harris, London, 1967.

Ferguson, Arthur B., *The Articulate Citizen and the English Renaissance*, Durham, North Carolina, 1965.

Fichter, Andrew, *Poets Historical: Dynastic Epic in the Renaissance*, New Haven, 1982.

Fineman, Joel, *Shakespeare's Perjured Eye: The Invention of Poetic Subjectivity in the Sonnets*, Berkeley, 1986.

Fletcher, A.J., 'The Origins of English Protestantism and the Growth of National Identity', in *Religion and National Identity: Papers Read at the Nineteenth Summer Meeting and the Twentieth Winter Meeting of the Ecclesiastical History Society*, ed. Stuart Mews, Oxford, 1982, pp. 309–17.

_____, 'The Protestant Idea of Marriage in Early Modern England', in *Religion, Culture and Society in Early Modern Britain: Essays in Honour of Patrick Collinson*, ed. Anthony Fletcher and Peter Roberts, Cambridge, 1994, pp. 161–81.

Fletcher, John, *The Faithful Shepherdess*, ed. Florence Ada Kirk, New York and London, 1980.

Florio, John, *A Worlde of Wordes, or Most Copious Dictionarie in Italian and English*, London, 1598.

Forster, Leonard, *The Icy Fire: Five Studies in European Petrarchism*, Cambridge, 1969.

Forsythe, R.S., 'A Plautine Source of *The Merry Wives of Windsor*', *Modern Philology*, 18 (1920): 401–21.

Foster, K., *Petrarch: Poet and Humanist*, Edinburgh, 1986.

Fox, Alistair, 'The Complaint of Poetry for the Death of Liberality: the Decline of Literary Patronage in the 1590s', in *The Reign of Elizabeth I: Court and Culture in the Last Decade*, ed. John Guy, Cambridge, 1995, pp. 229–57.

_____, *Politics and Literature in the Reigns of Henry VII and Henry VIII*, Oxford, 1989.

_____ and John Guy, *Reassessing the Henrician Age: Humanism, Politics and Reform 1500–1550*, Oxford, 1986.

Frye, Northrop, *Anatomy of Criticism: Four Essays*, New York, 1966.

Gataker, Thomas, *Marriage Duties Briefly Couched Together out of Colossians 3: 18 & 19*, London, 1620.

Gellner, Ernest, *Nations and Nationalism*, Ithaca, 1983.

The Geneva Bible: A Facsimile of the 1560 Edition, ed. Lloyd E. Berry, Madison, 1969.

Giamatti, A. Bartlett, *The Earthly Paradise and the Renaissance Epic*, Princeton, 1966.

Gilbert, Allen H., *Literary Criticism: Plato to Dryden*, Detroit, 1970.

Gilman, Ernest, *Iconoclasm and Poetry in the English Reformation: 'Down Went Dagon'*, Chicago, 1986.

Giraldi Cinthio, Giambattista, *De gli Hecatommithi di M. Giovanbattista Gyradi Cinthio nobile Ferrarese*, Monte Regale, 1565.

_____, *Giraldi Cinthio on Romances: Being a Translation of the Discorso intorno al comporre dei romanzi with Introduction and Notes by Henry L. Snuggs*, ed. Henry L. Snuggs, Lexington, 1968.

Godshalk, William Leigh, 'Sidney's Revision of the *Arcadia*, Books III–V', in *Essential Articles for the Study of Sir Philip Sidney*, ed. Arthur F. Kinney, Hamden, Connecticut, 1986, pp. 311–26.

Goldberg, Jonathan, *James I and the Politics of Literature: Jonson, Shakespeare, Donne, and Their Contemporaries*, Baltimore, 1983.

Goodman, Anthony and Angus Mackay, eds, *The Impact of Humanism on Western Europe*, London and New York, 1990.

Googe, Barnabe, *Eclogues, Epitaphs, and Sonnets*, ed. Judith M. Kennedy, Toronto, 1989.

Gosson, Stephen, *Plays Confuted in Five Actions* [1582], ed. Arthur Freeman, New York and London, 1972.

_____, *The Schoole of Abuse, and A Short Apologie of The Schoole of Abuse*, ed. Edward Arber, English Reprints, London, 1868.

Grafton, Anthony and Ann Blair, eds, *The Transmission of Culture in Early Modern Europe*, Philadelphia, 1990.

Greek Pastoral Poetry: Theocritus, Bion, Moschus, the Pattern Poems, trans. Anthony Holden, Harmondsworth, 1974.

Greenblatt, Stephen, *Renaissance Self-Fashioning: From More to Shakespeare*, Chicago, 1980.

_____, 'Sidney's *Arcadia* and the Mixed Mode', in *Essential Articles for the Study of Sir Philip Sidney*, ed. Arthur F. Kinney, Hamden, Connecticut, 1986, pp. 347–56.

Greene, Thomas M., *The Light in Troy: Imitation and Discovery in Renaissance Poetry*, New Haven and London, 1982.

Greenlaw, Edwin, 'Sidney's *Arcadia* as an Example of Elizabethan Allegory', in *Kittredge Anniversary Papers*, New York, 1913, pp. 327–37.

Greg, Walter W., *Pastoral Poetry and Pastoral Drama: A Literary Inquiry, with Special Reference to the Pre-Restoration Stage in England*, London, 1906.

Greville, Fulke, *The Prose Works of Fulke Greville, Lord Brooke*, ed. John Gouws, Oxford, 1986.

Guazzo, Stefano, *The Civile Conuersation of M. Steeuen Guazzo Written First in Italian, and Nowe Translated out of French by George Pettie, Deuided into Foure Bookes*, trans. George Pettie, London, 1581.

Guss, Donald, *John Donne, Petrarchist*, Detroit, 1966.

Guy, John, ed., *The Reign of Elizabeth I: Court and Culture in the Last Decade*, Cambridge, 1995.

Hadfield, Andrew, *Literature, Politics, and National Identity: Reformation to Renaissance*, Cambridge, 1994.

Haigh, Christopher, *English Reformations: Religion, Politics, and Society under the Tudors*, Oxford, 1993.

Hale, J.R., *England and the Italian Renaissance*, London, 1954.

Hamilton, A.C., 'The Renaissance of the Study of the English Literary Renaissance', *English Literary Renaissance*, 25, no. 3 (1995): 372–87.

_____, ed., *The Spenser Encyclopedia*, Toronto and Buffalo, 1990.

Hamilton, Donna S., *Shakespeare and the Politics of Protestant England*, Lexington, Kentucky, 1992.

Harrison, T.P. Jr, 'The Relations of Spenser and Sidney', *PMLA*, 45 (1930): 712–31.

Havely, N., *Chaucer's Boccaccio: Sources for Troilus and the Knight's and Franklin's Tales*, Woodbridge, 1992.

Hazlitt, W.C., ed., *Shakespeare's Library: A Collection of the Plays, Romances, Novels, Poems, and Histories Employed by Shakespeare in the Composition of His Works*, 2nd edn, 4 vols, London, 1875.

Heinemann, Margot, *Puritanism and Theatre: Thomas Middleton and Opposition Drama Under the Early Stuarts*, Cambridge, 1980.

Helgerson, Richard, *Forms of Nationhood: The Elizabethan Writing of England*, Chicago, 1992.

Hough, Graham, *A Preface to the Faerie Queene*, London, 1962.

Howard, Henry, Earl of Surrey, *Poems*, ed. Emrys Jones, Oxford, 1964.

Howell, Thomas, *The Arbor of Amitie, Wherin is Comprised Pleasant Poems and Pretie Poesies, Set Foorth by Thomas Howell Gentleman*, London, 1568.

Hume, Anthea, *Edmund Spenser: Protestant Poet*, Cambridge, 1984.

Hunter, G.K., 'Italian Tragicomedy and the English Stage', *Renaissance Drama*, 6 (1973): 123–48.

Jack, R.D.S., *The Italian Influence on Scottish Literature*, Edinburgh, 1972.

James, Mervyn, *Society, Politics and Culture: Studies in Early Modern England*, Cambridge, 1986.

Jardine, M.D., 'New Historicism for Old: New Conservatism for Old? The Politics of Patronage in the Renaissance', in *Patronage, Politics, and Literary Traditions in England 1558–1658*, ed. Cedric C. Brown, Detroit, 1991, pp. 291–309.

Javitch, Daniel, *Proclaiming a Classic: The Canonization of Orlando furioso*, Princeton, 1991.

Johnson, William C., *Spenser's Amoretti: Analogies of Love*, Lewisburg, Pennsylvania, 1990.

Jones, Norman L., *Faith by Statute: Parliament and the Settlement of Religion, 1559*, Royal Historical Society Studies in History Series, no. 32, London and New Jersey, 1982.

K, J., *The Courtiers Academie: Comprehending Seuen Seuerall Dayes Discourses: Wherein be Discussed, Seuen Noble and Important Arguements, Worthy by all Gentlemen to be Perused. 1. Of Beautie. 2. Of Humane Loue. 3. Of Honour. 4. Of Combate and Single Fight. 5. Of Nobilitie. 6. Of Riches. 7. Of Precedence of Letters or Armes. Originally written in Italian by Count Haniball Romei, a Gentleman of Ferrara, and translated into English by I. K.*, London, [1598]).

Kalstone, David, *Sidney's Poetry*, Cambridge, Massachusetts, 1965.

———, 'Sir Philip Sidney and "Poore Petrarchs Long Deceased Woes"', in *Essential Articles for the Study of Sir Philip Sidney*, ed. Arthur F. Kinney, Hamden, Connecticut, 1986, pp. 241–54.

Kay, Dennis, ed., *Sir Philip Sidney; An Anthology of Modern Criticism*, Oxford, 1987.

Kennedy, William J., *Authorizing Petrarch*, Ithaca and London, 1994.

———, *Jacopo Sannazzaro and the Uses of Pastoral*, Hanover and London, 1983.

King, John N., *Spenser's Poetry and the Reformation Tradition*, Princeton, 1990.

Kirkpatrick, Robin, *English and Italian Literature from Dante to Shakespeare: A Study of Sources, Analogy, and Divergence*, London, 1995.

Klein, Lisa, '"Let us love, dear love, lyk as we ought": Protestant Marriage and the Revision of Petrarchan Loving in Spenser's *Amoretti*', *Spenser Studies*, 10 (1992): 109–37.

Kostíc, Veselin, *Spenser's Sources in Italian Poetry: A Study in Comparative Literature*, Belgrade, 1969.

Lake, Peter, *Anglicans and Puritans? Presbyterianism and English Conformist Thought from Whitgift to Hooker*, London, 1988.

———, *Moderate Puritans and the Elizabethan Church*, Cambridge, 1982.

Lanham, Richard, *The Old Arcadia*, in *Sidney's Arcadia*, New Haven, 1965.

Leishman, J.B., *Themes and Variations in Shakespeare's Sonnets*, 2nd edn, London, 1963.

Levenson, Jill, 'Romeo and Juliet before Shakespeare', *Studies in Philology*, 71 (1984): 325–47.

Lever, J.W., *The Elizabethan Love Sonnet*, London, 1956.

Levin, Harry, *The Myth of the Golden World in the Renaissance*, London, 1969.

Lyotard, Jean-François, *The Postmodern Condition: A Report on Knowledge*, trans. Geoff Bennington and Brian Massumi, Minneapolis, 1984.

MacArthur, Janet H., *Critical Contexts of Astrophil and Stella and the Amoretti*, Victoria, British Columbia, 1989.

McCoy, Richard C., *Rebellion in Arcadia*, New Brunswick, 1979.

_____, *The Rites of Knighthood: The Literature and Politics of Elizabethan Chivalry*, Berkeley, 1989.

McLane, P., *Spenser's Shepheardes Calender: A Study in Elizabethan Allegory*, Notre Dame, 1961.

Marenco, Franco, *Arcadia Puritana*, Bari, 1968.

_____, 'Double Plot in Sidney's Old '*Arcadia*', in *Essential Articles for the Study of Sir Philip Sidney*, ed. Arthur F. Kinney, Hamden, Connecticut, 1986, pp. 287–310.

Marlowe, Christopher, *The Complete Plays*, ed. J.B. Steane, Harmondsworth, 1969.

Marot, Clement, *Œuvres lyriques*, ed. C.A. Mayer, London, 1964.

Marotti, Arthur, 'Love is Not Love: Elizabethan Sonnet Sequences and Social Order', *English Literary History*, 49 (1982), pp. 396–428.

Marshall, Roderick, *Italy in English Literature 1755–1815*, New York, 1934.

Marston, John, *The Insatiate Countess*, ed. Giorgio Melchiori, Manchester, 1984.

Mason, H.A., *Sir Thomas Wyatt: A Literary Portrait*, Bristol, 1986.

Mellamphy, Ninian, 'Pantaloons and Zanies: Shakespeare's "Apprenticeship" to Italian Professional Comedy Troupes', in *Shakespearean Comedy*, ed. Maurice Charney, New York, 1980, pp. 141–51.

Minta, Stephen, *Petrarch and Petrarchism*, Manchester and New York, 1980.

Miola, Robert S., *Shakespeare and Classical Comedy: The Influence of Plautus and Terence*, Oxford, 1994.

Montgomery, Robert, *Symmetry and Sense*, Austin, 1961.

Montrose, Louis Adrian, 'Of Gentlemen and Shepherds: The Politics of the Elizabethan Pastoral Form', *English Literary History*, 50 (1983): 415–59.

Morley, Thomas, *Canzonets. Or Little Short Songs to Three Voyces: Newly Published by Thomas Morley, Bachiler of Musicke, and One of the Gent. of Hir Maiesties Royall Chappel*, London, 1593.

Mortimer, Anthony, *Petrarch Canzoniere in the English Renaissance*, Bergamo, 1975.

Muir, Kenneth, 'Sonnets in the Hill Manuscript', *Proceedings of the Leeds Philosophical Society*, 6 (1944–52): 464–71.

_____, *The Sources of Shakespeare's Plays*, London, 1977.

Murray, J. Ross, *The Influence of Italian upon English Literature during the Sixteenth and Seventeenth Centuries*, Cambridge, New York, 1886.

Nelson, William, *Fact or Fiction: The Dilemma of the Renaissance Story-Teller*, Cambridge, Massachusetts, 1973.

Noble, Richmond, *Shakespeare's Biblical Knowledge*, London, 1935.

Norbrook, David, *Poetry and Politics in the English Renaissance*, London, 1984.

Nowell, Alexander, *A Catechisme or First Instruction and Learning of Christian Religion*, trans. Thomas Norton, Delmar, New York, 1975.

Orr, David, *Italian Renaissance Drama in England before 1625: The Influence of Erudita Tragedy, Comedy, and Pastoral on Elizabethan and Jacobean Drama*, Chapel Hill, 1970.

Osborn, James M., *Young Philip Sidney, 1572–1577*, New Haven, 1972.

Painter, William, *The Palace of Pleasure*, ed. Joseph Jacobs (1890), New York, 1966.

Parker, Patricia, *Shakespeare from the Margins: Language, Culture, Context*, Chicago, 1996.

Parnell, Paul E., 'Barnabe Googe: A Puritan in Arcadia', *Journal of English and Germanic Philology*, 60 (1961): 273–81.

Parry, G.J.R., 'The Creation and Recreation of Puritanism', *Parergon*, NS 14 (1996): 31–55.

_____, *A Protestant Vision: William Harrison and the Reformation of Elizabethan England*, Cambridge, 1987.

Patey, Caroline, 'Beyond Aristotle: Giraldi Cinzio and Shakespeare', in *Italy and the English Renaissance*, ed. Sergio Rossi, Milan, 1989, pp. 167–88.

Patterson, Annabel, *Courtship and Interpretation: The Condition of Writing and Reading in Early Modern England*, Madison, 1984.

_____, *Pastoral and Ideology: Virgil to Valéry*, Berkeley, 1988.

_____, *Shakespeare and the Popular Voice*, Oxford, 1989.

_____, 'Under ... Pretty Tales: Intention in Sidney's *Arcadia*', in *Sir Philip Sidney: An Anthology of Modern Criticism*, ed. Dennis Kay, London, 1987, pp. 265–85.

Petrarca, Francesco, *Petrarch's Bucolicum Carmen*, trans. Thomas G. Bergin, New Haven and London, 1974.

_____, *Petrarch's Lyric Poems: the Rime sparse and Other Lyrics*, trans. and ed. Robert M. Durling, Cambridge, Massachusetts, and London, 1976.

_____, *Petrarch's Secret, or the Soul's Conflict with Passion: Three Dialogues between Himself and S. Augustine*, trans. W.H. Draper, London, 1911.

_____, *Secretum*, ed. Enrico Carrara, in Francesco Petrarca, *Prose*, ed. G. Martellotti and others, La Letteratura Italiana: Storia e Testi, vol. 7, Milan and Naples, 1955, pp. 22–215 .

Phillipy, Patricia Berrahou, *Love's Remedies: Recantation and Renaissance Lyric Poetry*, Lewisburg and London, 1995.

The Prayer-Book of Queen Elizabeth, 1559, ed. Edward Benham, Edinburgh, 1909.

Praz, Mario, *The Flaming Heart: Essays on Crashaw, Machiavelli, and Other Studies in the Relations between Italian and English Literature from Chaucer to T.S. Eliot*, New York, 1958.

Prescott, Anne Lake, 'Allegorical Deer and *Amoretti* 67', in *Edmund Spenser's Poetry*, ed. Hugh Maclean and Anne Lake Prescott, New York and London, 1993, pp. 809–13.

_____, *French Poets and the English Renaissance: Studies in Fame and Transformation*, New Haven, 1978.

Prince, F.T., *The Italian Elements in Milton's Verse*, Oxford, 1954.

Prosatori volgari del quattrocento, ed. Claudio Varese, vol. 14, La Letteratura Italiana: Storia e Testi, Milan and Naples, 1955.

Proudfoot, Richard, "It is an Accident that Heaven Provides': Shakespeare's Providence in *Measure for Measure*', in *Italy and the English Renaissance*, ed. Sergio Rossi, Milan, 1989, pp. 155–66.

Pruvost, René, *Matteo Bandello and Elizabethan Fiction*, Paris, 1937.

Puttenham, George, *The Arte of English Poesie*, ed. Gladys Doidge Willcock and Alice Walker, Cambridge, 1936.

Quilligan, Maureen, 'Sidney and His Queen', in *The Historical Renaissance: New Essays on Tudor and Stuart Literature and Culture*, ed. Heather Dubrow and Richard Strier, Chicago, 1988.

Quint, David, *Origin and Originality in Renaissance Literature*, New Haven, 1983.

R.T., *Two Tales, Translated out of Ariosto: The One in Dispraise of Men, the Other in Disgrace of Women. With Certain Other Italian Stanzas and Prouerbs*, London, 1597.

Rees, D.G., 'Italian and Italianate Poetry', in *Elizabethan Poetry*, ed. J.R. Brown and B. Harris, Stratford-upon-Avon Studies 2, London, 1960.

Rich, Barnabe, *Barnabe Riche, His Farewell to Military Profession*, ed. Donald Beecher, Ottawa, 1992.

_____, *Riche His Farewell to Militarie Profession: Conteinyng Verie Pleasaunt Discourses Fit for a Peaceable Tyme …*, London, 1581.

Rich, Townsend, *Harington and Ariosto: A Study in Elizabethan Verse Translation*, New Haven, 1940.

Roche, Thomas P., 'Ending the *New Arcadia*: Virgil and Ariosto', *Sidney Newsletter*, 10 (1989): 3–12.

_____, *Petrarch and the English Sonnet Sequences*, New York, 1989.

Rodax, Yvonne, *The Real and the Ideal in the Novella*, Chapel Hill, 1968.

Rosenberg, Eleanor, *Leicester, Patron of Letters*, New York, 1955.

Rosenmeyer, Thomas G., *The Green Cabinet: Theocritus and the European Pastoral Lyric*, Berkeley and Los Angeles, 1969.

Rossi, Sergio, ed., *Italy and the English Renaissance*, Milan, 1989.

Rostvig, Maren-Sofie, 'Canto Structure in Tasso and Spenser', *Spenser Studies*, 1 (1980): 177–200.

Rotonda, D.P., *Motif Index of the Italian Novella in Prose*, Bloomington, 1942.

Rudenstine, Neil, *Sidney's Poetic Development*, Cambridge, Massachusetts, 1967.

Said, Edward W., *Culture and Imperialism*, New York, 1993.

Sannazzaro, Jacopo, *Arcadia & Piscatorial Eclogues*, trans. and ed. Ralph Nash, Detroit, 1966.

_____, *Opere de Iacopo Sannazzaro*, ed. Enrico Carrara, Turin, 1952.

_____, *Opere volgari*, ed. Alfredo Mauro, Bari, 1961.

Sansovino, Francesco, *The Quintesence of Wit, being a Corrant Comfort of Conceites Maximies, and Poleticke Deuises, Selected and Gathered Together by Francisco Sansouino. Wherein is Set Foorth Sundrye Excellent and Wise Sentences, Worthie to be Regarded and Followed. Translated out of the Itallian Tung, and Put into English for the Benefit of All Those that Please to Read and Vnderstand the Works and Worth of a Worthy Writer*, trans. Robert Hitchcock, London, 1590.

Scarisbrick, J.J., *The Reformation and the English People*, Oxford, 1984.

Scott, Mary Augusta, *Elizabethan Translations from the Italian*, Boston and New York, 1916.

Sells, A. Lytton, *The Italian Influence in English Poetry from Chaucer to Southwell*, Bloomington, Indiana, 1955.

Sercambi, Giovanni, *Novelle di Giovanni Sercambi Lucchese ora per la prima volta pubblicate*, Venice, 1816.

Shakespeare, William, *Complete Pelican Shakespeare*, ed. Alfred Harbage and others, 3 vols, Harmondsworth, 1969.

_____, *Shakespeare's Sonnets*, ed. Stephen Booth, New Haven and London, 1977.

Shapiro, Marianne, *The Poetics of Ariosto*, Detroit, 1988.

Sidney, Philip, *An Apology for Poetry or The Defence of Poesy*, ed. Geoffrey Shepherd, London, 1965.

_____, *The Correspondence of Sir Philip Sidney and Hubert Languet*, ed. Steuart A. Pears, London, 1845.

_____, *The Countess of Pembroke's Arcadia (The Old Arcadia)*, ed. Jean Robertson, Oxford, 1973.

_____, *The Countess of Pembroke's Arcadia*, ed. Maurice Evans, Penguin Classics, London, 1987.

_____, *The Miscellaneous Prose of Sir Philip Sidney*, ed. Katherine Duncan-Jones and Jan Van Dorsten, Oxford, 1973.

_____, *The Poems of Sir Philip Sidney*, ed. William A. Ringler, Jr, Oxford, 1962.

_____, *The Prose Works of Sir Philip Sidney*, ed. Albert Feuillerat, 4 vols, Cambridge, 1963.

Silberman, Lauren, 'Spenser and Ariosto: Funny Peril and Comic Chaos', *Comparative Literature Studies*, 25 (1988): 23–34.

Sinfield, Alan, 'Astrophil's Self-Deception', *Essays in Criticism*, 28 (1978): 1–18.

_____, *Faultlines: Cultural Materialism and the Politics of Dissident Reading*, Berkeley and Los Angeles, 1992.

_____, *Literature in Protestant England 1560–1660*, Totawa, New Jersey, 1983.

_____, 'Power and Ideology: An Outline Theory and Sidney's *Arcadia*', in *Essential Articles for the Study of Sir Philip Sidney*, ed. Arthur F. Kinney, Hamden, Connecticut, 1986, pp. 391–410.

Skelton, John, *John Skelton: The Complete English Poems*, ed. John Scattergood, Harmondsworth and New Haven, 1983.

Smith, Bruce R., *Homosexual Desire in Shakespeare's England: A Cultural Poetics*, Chicago, 1991.

Spagnuolo, Baptista Mantuanus, *The Eclogues of Baptista Mantuanus*, ed. W.P. Mustard, Baltimore, 1911.

Spenser, Edmund, *Edmund Spenser's Poetry: Authoritative Texts and Criticism*, ed. Hugh Maclean and Anne Lake Prescott, New York and London, 1993.

_____, *The Faerie Queene*, ed. Thomas P. Roche, Jr, Harmondsworth, 1978.

_____, *The Works of Edmund Spenser: A Variorum Edition*, ed. Charles Grosvenor Osgood, Edwin Greenlaw, Frederick Morgan Padelford and Ray Heffner, 11 vols, Baltimore, 1932–57.

'The State of Renaissance Studies. A Special Twenty-Fifth Anniversary Symposium in Honour of Dan S. Collins', *English Literary Renaissance*, 25, no. 3 (1995).

Steinmetz, David C., *Calvin in Context*, New York, 1995.

Stevens, John, *Music and Poetry in the Early Tudor Court*, London, 1961.

Strype, John, *Annals of the Reformation and Establishment of Religion and of the Various Occurrences in the Church of England during Queen Elizabeth's Happy Reign*, 4 vols, Burt Franklin Research and Source Works Series, no. 122, New York, 1824.

Stubbes, Phillip, *The Anatomie of Abuses*, ed. Frederick J. Furnivall, London, 1877–79.

Sturm-Madox, Sara, *Petrarch's Laurels*, University Park, Pennsylvania, 1992.

Summers, Claude J. and Ted-Larry Pebworth, eds, *Renaissance Discourses of Desire*, Columbia and London, 1993.

Tasso, Torquato, *Discourses on the Heroic Poem*, trans. Mariella Cavalchini, ed. Irene Samuel, Oxford, 1973.

_____, *Godfrey of Bulloigne, or the Recouerie of Hierusalem*, trans. R.C., London, 1594.

_____, *Godfrey of Bulloigne: A Critical Edition of Edward Fairfax's Translation of Tasso's Gerusalemme Liberata*, ed. Kathleen M. Lea and T.M. Gang, Oxford, 1981.

_____, *Opere di Torquato Tasso*, ed. Bortolo Tommaso Sozzi, 3rd edn, vol. 2, Turin, 1974.

_____, *Torquato Tasso, Poesie*, ed. Francesco Flora, vol. 21, La Letteratura Italiana: Storia e Testi, Milan and Naples, 1952.

Taylor, Charles, *The Sources of the Self: The Making of Modern Identity*, Cambridge, 1989.

Tennenhouse, Leonard, *Power on Display: The Politics of Shakespeare's Genres*, New York, 1986.

Tetel, Marcel, *Présences Italiennes dans les Essais de Montaigne*, Etudes Montaignistes, 10, Paris, 1992.

The Thirty-nine Articles, ed. B.J. Kidd, London, 1900.

Thompson, John, *The Founding of English Metre*, London, 1961.

Tomalin, Margaret, *The Fortunes of the Warrior Heroine in Italian Literature: An Index of Emancipation*, Ravenna, 1982.

Trapp, J.B., 'From Guarino of Verona to John Colet', in *Italy and the English Renaissance*, ed. Sergio Rossi, Milan, 1989, pp. 45–53.

Trinkaus, Charles, *The Poet as Philosopher: Petrarch and the Formation of the Renaissance Consciousness*, New Haven, 1979.

Turbervile, George, *Epitaphes, Epigrams, Songs and Sonets, with a Discourse of the Friendly Affections of Tymetes to Pyndaria His Ladie. Newly corrected with Additions, and Set out by George Turbervile Gentleman*, London, 1567.

_____, *Tragicall Tales Translated by Turbervile in Time of His Troubles out of Sundrie Italians, with the Argument and Lenuoye to Eche Tale*, London, 1587.

Vesser, H. Aram, ed., *The New Historicism*, New York and London, 1989.

Virgil, *The Eclogues: The Latin Text with a Verse Translation and Brief Notes*, ed. Guy Lee, Harmondsworth, 1980.

Wallace, D., *Chaucer and the Early Writings of Boccaccio*, Woodbridge and Dover, New Hampshire, 1985.

Waller, Gary F. and Michael D. Moore, eds, *Sir Philip Sidney and the Interpretation of Renaissance Culture*, London, 1984.

Warkentin, Germaine, 'Sonnets and Sonnet Sequences', in *Spenser Encyclopedia*, ed. A.C. Hamilton and others, Toronto, 1990, pp. 662–5.

Watson, George, *The English Petrarchans: A Critical Bibliography of the Canzoniere*, London, 1967.

Watson, Thomas, *Amintae Gaudia*, London, 1592.

_____, *Poems*, ed. Edward Arber, London, 187.

Wayne, Valerie, ed., *The Matter of Difference: Materialist Feminist Criticism of Shakespeare*, Ithaca, New York, 1991.

Weinberg, Bernard, *A History of Literary Criticism in the Italian Renaissance*, 2 vols, Chicago, 1961.

Weiner, Andrew, *Sir Philip Sidney and the Poetics of Protestantism: A Study of Contexts*, Minneapolis, 1978.

Weiss, Roberto, *Humanism in England During the Fifteenth Century*, 2nd edn, Oxford, 1957.

Wells, Robin H., *Spenser's 'Faerie Queene' and the Cult of Elizabeth*, London, 1983.

Whetstone, George, *An Heptameron of Ciuill Discourses*, London, 1582.

_____, *The Rocke of Regard, Diuided into Foure Parts*, London, 1576.

Whitaker, V.K., 'Shakespeare's Use of His Sources', *Philological Quarterly*, 20 (1941): 377–88.

_____, *Shakespeare's Use of Learning*, San Marino, 1953.

Wiggins, Peter de Sa, *Figures in Ariosto's Tapestry: Character and Design in the Orlando Furioso*, Baltimore and London, 1986.

_____, 'Spenser's Use of Ariosto: Imitation and Allusion in Book I of *The Faerie Queene*', *Renaissance Quarterly*, 44 (1991): 257–79.

Wilkins, Ernest Hatch, *A History of Italian Literature*, revised by Thomas G. Bergin, Cambridge, Massachusetts, 1974.

Wilson, Derek, *Sweet Robin: A Biography of Robert Dudley Earl of Leicester, 1533–1588*, London, 1981.

Wright, H.G., 'How did Shakespeare Come to Know the *Decameron?*', *Modern Language Review*, 49 (1955): 45–8.

Wyatt, Thomas, *Collected Poems of Sir Thomas Wyatt*, ed. Kenneth Muir and Patricia Thomson, Liverpool English Texts and Studies, Liverpool, 1969.

Wynne-Davies, Marion, ed., *A Guide to English Renaissance Literature: 1500–1660*, Bloomsbury Guides to English, London, 1992.

Young, Richard, 'English Petrarcke: A Study of Sidney's "Astrophel and Stella"', in *Three Renaissance Studies*, Yale Studies in English, no. 138, New Haven, 1958.

Zeeveld, W. Gordon, *Foundations of Tudor Policy*, Cambridge, Massachusetts, 1948.

Index